The Spirit of Religion and the Spirit of Liberty

The Spirit of RELIGION *and the Spirit of* LIBERTY

The Tocqueville Thesis Revisited

Edited by

MICHAEL ZUCKERT

Selected articles first appeared in various issues of *American Political Thought*.

The University of Chicago Press, Chicago 60637
The University of Chicago Press, Ltd., London

Printed in the United States of America
ISBN: 978-0-226-49067-0
LCN: 2017003579

The paper used in this publication meets the minimum requirements of American National Standard for Information Sciences—Permanence of Paper for Printed Library Materials, ANSI Z39.48-1984. ♾

Contents

Preface

The Spirit of Religion and the Spirit of Liberty is the first in an occasional series of books associated with the journal *American Political Thought* to be published by the University of Chicago Press. Like all the projected books in the series, this one consists of a set of essays, seven of which (in this case) have appeared in the journal and the other three of which have been commissioned to round out the reprinted essays to make for a comprehensive treatment of the topic under consideration.

In this case our topic, Tocqueville's thesis on the relation between religion and liberty, could hardly be timelier. Every day's newspaper, every college campus, and many recent Supreme Court decisions raise the issue in one form or another. From events in the Middle East and the spread of Islamist violence in the name of religion to mandated health insurance coverage under the Affordable Care Act, the interaction between religion and politics has once again become central to our political life. Tocqueville, facing the coming of a new social and political order within the lingeringly traditional society that was France, addressed this relation between politics and religion with freshness and relevance. He was particularly interested in reporting to his French compatriots on how the Americans had, in his opinion, successfully resolved what, to many Frenchmen, looked to be an insuperable conflict. He thought otherwise, and he believed that the Americans had shown why it was not. His surprising thesis was that the right arrangement of the relation—a certain kind of separation of church and state that was not also at the same time a complete separation of religion and politics—was shown in nineteenth-century America to be beneficial to both liberty and religion. Our volume investigates whether Tocqueville's depiction was valid for the America he investigated in the 1830s, whether it was theoretically plausible, and whether it remains valid (if it ever was) in the twenty-first century.

Several of the essays printed here were originally prepared for a conference held at Notre Dame in 2011 on the topic announced in the volume's title. That conference was conducted under the auspices of Notre Dame's Tocqueville Program for Inquiry into the Role of Religion in American Public Life. It also had the generous support of the Liberty Fund of Indianapolis, Indiana. The conference was in part a celebration of the appearance in print of the Liberty

Fund's four-volume bilingual edition of Tocqueville's *Democracy in America*, a reprinting and translation of the masterful French critical edition of Tocqueville's volume edited by Eduardo Nolla, one of the contributors to this volume. The Liberty Fund edition featured a fresh translation by James Schleifer, also one of the contributors to this volume. One of the features of many of the essays in this volume is the significant usage of materials now available to Tocqueville scholars thanks to the work of Professors Nolla and Schleifer.

As editor of this volume, I wish to acknowledge the great aid and support of the Tocqueville Program; the Liberty Fund; Harriett Baldwin, then director of Notre Dame's Office of Conferences; Jakub Voboril for his aid with the manuscript; the Jack Miller Center for its support of *American Political Thought*; the staff of the journal, especially Zack German; and the Journals Division of the University of Chicago Press, especially Adam Gannaway.

Michael Zuckert

Introduction: The Tocqueville Thesis

MICHAEL ZUCKERT

Russell Baker, the satiric columnist, once quipped that "of all the great unread authors, I believe Tocqueville to be the most quoted."[1] There can hardly be a more decisive sign of an author's importance than being among the elite few who are very widely quoted without having been read. It proves that people think that the unread author's name carries enough weight that it can help float whatever facts and ideas the speakers might wish to invent and attribute to the unread authority. In a political context, perhaps even more striking is the fact that since Dwight Eisenhower every president has quoted Tocqueville. That is to say, it is not only that many quote him without reading him, but many highly placed people do so as well. Part of what is striking about that array of presidents who quote Tocqueville is the thoroughly bipartisan nature of the phenomenon: there have been six Republicans and six Democrats in that period, and all have quoted him approvingly. Obama stayed away from Tocqueville for a long time, but finally in 2014 he broke down and followed presidential precedent.

Tocqueville was not always so much on the tip of commentators' tongues as he is today, however. As Cheryl Welch makes clear in her brief account of the history of Tocqueville's reputation, his public reception has something of the character of a pendulum. At first, according to Welch, Tocqueville's *Democracy in America* made a big splash on both sides of the Atlantic Ocean, but especially in America. He was so well received there largely on the basis of the old principle that one cannot go wrong praising the Athenians in Athens. That explanation of Tocqueville's American reputation applied especially well to volume 1 of *Democracy* (the 1835 *Democracy*), which was perceived as very complimentary to the young democracy, compliments especially welcome because they came from "Old Europe," a quarter from which the Americans were not accustomed to hearing praise (Welch 2001, 222–23). That this gratitude for Tocqueville's appreciation of American institutions lasted well into the 1860s is visible in the congressional debates over the proposal that became

1. See psriblog.wordpress.com/2010/10/24/.

the Fourteenth Amendment after the Civil War. John Bingham, chief draftsman of the amendment, rose in the House of Representatives to defend the constitutional change he was proposing by quoting Tocqueville, whom he described as "the most distinguished man who was ever sent hither from the Old World to make a personal observation of the workings of our institutions."[2]

Interest in Tocqueville faded in France by the later nineteenth century, and we see in his place the rise of Marx, who drove Tocqueville out of the minds of French intellectuals for almost a century. Tocqueville became almost forgotten in his own country (Welch 2001, 225).

His fate was never that desperate in America. His study of democracy, especially the 1835 volume, was long read as a text on American government, although in the late nineteenth century it was superseded by the more up-to-date *American Commonwealth* of James Bryce. More generally, Tocqueville lost his luster as populists, Progressives, and Deweyan pragmatists came to dominate American political and intellectual life. From the late nineteenth century on, Tocqueville was not a major figure in American thinking. Although Marx was much less a force in America than in France, the rise of the economic problems associated with industrial capitalism was perceived as the central issue facing the nation and had much to do with the eclipse of Tocqueville in America. So it is no accident that we do not readily find the presidents of the New Deal era—Roosevelt and Truman—quoting him.

Interest in Tocqueville revived in America in what now appears to be two waves. The first revival was a phenomenon of the post–World War II world. The second, a post–Cold War phase, is one we are still living through today. The first wave had a double meaning and significance, one part of it looking backward, the other very present-oriented.

World War II and then the Cold War looked to contemporaries to be great battles between liberal democracies and totalitarian regimes. Great questions arose: How could a civilized country like Germany succumb to the totalitarian disease? How could a country moved by an allegedly humane doctrine like Marxism succumb to the same disease? The postwar world saw a blossoming of the theory of "unitotalitarianism," that is, of the view that different as Hitler's Germany and Stalin's Soviet Union appeared to be, they actually were both best understood as instances of the species *totalitarianism*. Political thinkers set off on a quest for a single theory that could account for the rise of the ideologically opposed but essentially similar totalitarian regimes. The theory that was most promoted in those years and that brought Tocqueville back on the intellectual scene was the theory of mass society. A whole literature

2. Cong. Globe, 39th Cong., 1st Sess. 1292 (1866).

on mass society arose, initiated by some of the leading philosophic and sociological lights of Europe and America—Martin Heidegger, José Ortega y Gasset, Gabriel Marcel, Hannah Arendt, Robert Nisbet, and William Kornhauser, to name a few. Some of this literature looked back to Tocqueville, who was viewed as an early diagnostician of the phenomenon of massification. He saw early in the career of modern democracy how social and psychological forces accompanying modern social organization could sever the ties of community and at the same time reduce all to a bland uniformity. Tocqueville saw not only that this process of massification was an aesthetic or moral loss but also that it produced anxieties that made human beings vulnerable to centralized state power and led them to yearn for a reconnection with community, a yearning that could be satisfied in the primitive emotional bonding of movements like National Socialism.

This aspect of the first revival was an important moment in Tocqueville studies, for it was then that a side of Tocqueville was discovered that had not been much noticed before. We might call it his dark side, or, perhaps better, his diagnosis of the potentially dark side of democracy. This dark side had, of course, been part of his concern from the beginning, but it had been largely overlooked by the Americans in their pride at what appeared to be his favorable treatment of democracy in America. Moreover, that side of Tocqueville's analysis had also been overshadowed for many by the Marxist analysis of the evils of capitalism, which had seemed a more potent depiction of the problems of the age. But it became apparent that developments in Germany and the Soviet Union were not at all what Marx predicted. So the seesaw seesawed: Tocqueville rose, Marx fell.

Tocqueville's increased stature during the first wave of his post–World War II revival arose first from one of his most strikingly accurate predictions. At the end of volume 1 he spoke of "two great peoples on the earth today who, starting from different points, seem to advance toward the same goal: these are the Russians and the Anglo-Americans. . . . The one has freedom as his principal means of action; the other servitude. Their point of departure is different, their ways are diverse; nonetheless, each of them seems called by a secret design of Providence to hold the destinies of half the world in its hands" (Tocqueville 2010, 655).

Tocqueville's way of describing the two powers that came to be the chief antagonists during the Cold War era points to the great service he provided to Americans at this time. The early 1950s were a time of great felt need for a story America could tell of itself in the Cold War. The Progressives (à la Charles Beard and others) had gone a long way toward undercutting the story Americans had told of themselves previously, a story that lionized the founders and their Constitution. But even before the Progressives, America lacked a story with the ideological comprehensiveness and apparent depth of Marxism. The Soviets had Marx; America needed something comparable to counter. Hence, the early 1950s were a time marked by a quest for an American ideology, or, as some put it, a public philosophy.

Tocqueville was not the only candidate put forward, but once again he appeared at the other end of the seesaw from Marx. Tocqueville told something like a comprehensive story about American society and rhapsodized over the greatness of political liberty more or less as practiced in the Western democracies, but not in the Soviet sphere. So Tocqueville's role in the first revival was as a counterweight to Marx and the Soviet empire.

Given this account of the basis for the postwar Tocqueville revival, one might think that the end of the Cold War, with the collapse of Marxist societies and of Marxism itself, would bring another eclipse of Tocqueville. He was no longer needed as a counterweight on the seesaw of history. Instead, something surprising happened—Tocqueville went from being red hot to being white hot. Evidence for Tocqueville's further ascent in public interest abounds. Until the Lawrence translation of 1968, there had been no new translation of *Democracy in America* since the one Henry Reeve made in Tocqueville's lifetime. Since the Lawrence translation, there have been new translations from Penguin, Library of America, and Mansfield and Winthrop for the University of Chicago Press; a new Liberty Fund edition and translation; and two new abridged editions—all since the year 2000. The secondary literature on Tocqueville has exploded in the same period, both in Europe and in America.

What is behind this second Tocqueville revival? It probably would have taken someone as skilled at political prophecy as Tocqueville himself to predict that he would continue to rise as his evil twin Karl Marx sank beneath the horizon. The second wave began just as liberal democracy appeared to be the only player in the game of world politics that had not folded. At about the same time one saw Francis Fukuyama proclaiming "the end of history," by which he meant the irrevocable triumph of liberal democracy and the future as nothing but the spread of democracy to places where it was not yet established.[3] Fukuyama's thesis, expressing a mood accompanying the end of the Cold War, helps make intelligible Tocqueville's second revival. The end-of-history thesis shares something with Tocqueville himself, who had famously argued that democracy was the inevitable wave of the future. The end of the Cold War thus seemed to make him even more prescient than he had seemed before: not only did he predict the Cold War, but he predicted the winners also.

3. See Fukuyama (1992). The original version of Fukuyama's thesis was published as a journal article in 1989.

There was, however, a very major difference between Tocqueville and Fukuyama. The latter was, shall we say, much more optimistic than Tocqueville. For the Frenchman the triumph of democracy was not automatically a good thing. Democracy contained the seeds of very bad—as well as very good—outcomes.

After September 2001, the Fukuyama vision of the world had decidedly less appeal. Since Tocqueville's thesis always had been more nuanced than Fukuyama's, interest in him did not collapse with the Twin Towers. Indeed, in the second wave of interest in the Frenchman his words have become a resource for those worried about the health, survivability, and even desirability of the democratic form of social and political existence. Tocqueville replaced Marx as a resource for critics, for those who came to worry about American democracy and not only to praise it.

Perhaps we are still too close to it, too immersed in this second wave to have enough perspective on it to see the contours clearly, but it appears that there are three main concerns about American democracy that are filtered through Tocqueville today. The first concern is the health of American politics. Many observers are distressed by the decline in political participation and the replacement of public-spirited involvement in favor of narrow interest–based or identity-based politics. One sees concern of this sort in such publicly visible places as Robert Putnam's now famous *Bowling Alone* or in David Brooks's concern for social capital. Tocqueville had seen this potential for the loss of a common good–oriented politics, for a withdrawal from active concern with the political system, but he thought that Americans of the nineteenth century had largely avoided these outcomes of democracy. So Tocqueville is looked to as a resource, both to help us understand why we are seeing these declines and perhaps to suggest remedies.

A related but distinct concern is the fading of community in America. Tocqueville drew a very compelling picture of how democracy tends to disrupt established patterns of communal life through the great geographic and social mobility it fosters and the very short generational frame of reference it encourages. This tendency away from community, this tendency to withdraw into one's self and immediate family, was what Tocqueville called individualism. He considered that to be an especially potent and dangerous possibility in democratic ages. It was also, he argued, psychically threatening, diminishing the quality of life for all. Modern observers are seeing this privatizing trend in modern American society, a trend greatly aided by various technologies that allow one to conduct nearly all one's business, meet nearly all one's needs, and be thoroughly entertained without leaving home. Tocqueville is a resource for understanding this tendency and is a source, it is again hoped, for remedies.

The third concern, which brings us to the chief topic of this volume, is religion. Religion is, of course, a major theme in *Democracy in America*. One might even say that one of Tocqueville's chief goals in the book is to counter the view dominant in postrevolutionary France that partisans of democracy and partisans of religion are natural and inevitable enemies. He looked to America as a place where (in the 1830s) religion and democracy went hand in hand and were mutually supportive. Thus the "Tocqueville thesis": America owed the success of her democracy to the combination of the "spirit of religion" with the "spirit of liberty."

In order to understand Tocqueville's thesis correctly, one must first recapture his orientation as a social and political analyst. His main categories are democracy and aristocracy, and these are both understood as types of *social state*. In a passage too often ignored by his readers, Tocqueville emphasizes the absolutely central role of social state in his analysis: "The social state is ordinarily the product of a fact, sometimes of laws, most often of these two causes united; but once it exists, one can consider it as the first cause of most of the laws, customs, and ideas that regulate the conduct of nations; what it does not produce, it modifies" (2010, 74). I must reiterate again what Tocqueville says here: social state is "the first cause" of most of the laws, customs, and ideas that regulate the conduct of nations. Social state has many, somewhat miscellaneous causes, but once it exists, it is itself the cause of most of the interesting phenomena of political society.

Democracy in America is in one important sense a strange book, for early in the book Tocqueville ushers onto stage this chief actor and all through the book he supplies it with many lines, attributing to social state the chief responsibility for almost every feature of life in America—from the kinds of books Americans write and how they read them, to the kind of religions they practice, to the kind of politics they favor. But the strangeness lies in the fact that he never gives us a general definition of social state as a concept, and he writes as if it is a familiar idea to all his readers, when it is far from that.

Tocqueville requires us to tease out of his text a notion of what social state in general is, a task that would take a long time, and so I will not engage it here, but let me state some of the conclusions of such an effort. Social state is primarily a social and secondarily a political category. So, when Tocqueville speaks of democracy, he means primarily democratic social state, that is, equality of conditions, and not democratic governance. Democracy in Tocqueville's sense is quite compatible with autocratic, that is, thoroughly undemocratic, governance. Social state is a social category, and therefore Tocqueville needs to be seen in the first instance as a political sociologist. The effort to read him as an updated Aristotle, for whom the political regime is the decisive formative fact, is therefore inappropriate.

Social state is, let us say, a measure of relations of social power. Thus, ownership of land is a relevant part of social state—for ownership of land, quite apart from whether it gives one a call on political power per se (as in provisions for electing rulers based on property qualifications), is a factor in social power, that is, in whether human beings have more or less control over the conditions of their lives. There is a connection between social power, as embodied in social state, and political power, but these are not identical.

Tocqueville sees an important link between social state and history: the history of Europe since the twelfth century is a history of the coming of democratic social state, so there is a definite overlap between democracy and modernity. But the overlap is not perfect. Tocqueville presents himself as taking a nearly unique position with respect to the coming of democracy. Unlike his fellow French aristocrats, he does not see it as an unmitigated disaster, productive of nothing but social disorder and human degradation. Unlike his fellow French liberals, he does not see it as an unmixed blessing.

As opposed to the reactionaries, he sees democracy—as social state—as the inevitable or nearly inevitable result of either Providence (on one reading) or well-ensconced social processes (on another reading). As he says, "The gradual development of equality of conditions"—that is, democratic social state—"is therefore a providential fact, and it has the principal characteristics of one: it is universal, it is enduring, each day it escapes human power; all events, like all men, serve its development" (Tocqueville 2010, 10–12). Unlike many of the reactionaries, Tocqueville thus sees the need to accept the coming of democracy and to seek to make the best of it. This project is all the easier for him because, as he indicates when he traces the democratizing process to God, the coming of the democratic social state is fundamentally just and in some sense good.

But it is not unmitigatedly good. Tocqueville has many misgivings, many fears of what a democratic future may bring. He also is a political scientist who seeks to diagnose the downsides of democracy. Although he has complaints about many aspects of democracy, his chief concerns are two: (1) democratic social state as an enemy or at least as an unfavorable ground for the cultivation of human greatness or human excellence, and (2) democratic social state as potentially inhospitable to liberty.

DEMOCRACY AND HUMAN EXCELLENCE

Inegalitarian societies, by definition, have a much greater gradation of social stations, with very great disparity of resources and opportunities marking the different social extremes. In aristocratic societies education is the preserve of a very few. Leisure marks the lifestyle of those at the top; numbing labor, that of those at the bottom. Given the opportunities, the resources, and the discipline of aristocratic societies, they are capable of producing some very great examples of human excellence, especially in the cultural and intellectual spheres.

Democratic societies, on the other hand, have a lower top and a higher bottom. Leisure is not typically a feature of such societies. Opportunity is widely spread but must be exploited quickly. Petty ambition rather than grand aspiration tends to characterize all members of the society. Education is far more widespread but far shallower. The result is what appears to be a general tendency toward mediocrity: more individuals participate in the culture and in political life, but they achieve generally at a lower level—or so it appears.

DEMOCRACY AND LIBERTY

In one of his most widely quoted passages Tocqueville says, "I think democratic people have a natural taste for liberty; left to themselves they seek it, they love it, and they will see themselves parted from it only with sorrow" (2010, 878). That is, there is no inherent or inevitable incompatibility between democratic social state and liberty—but democracy sets off social, psychological, and political dynamics that lead Tocqueville to fear that unless democratic societies act wisely they may lose that liberty. So what is inevitable for Tocqueville is the coming of a democratic social state; what is not inevitable is a democratic political state. He has a complex understanding of how democracy can fail to be free—there are three quite distinct ways in which democratic social state can fail to produce a free political state. That is to say, he sees three possible kinds of tyrannies or despotisms:

1. Tyranny of government over society, by which he means garden-variety despotic or unfree governance or at least nondemocratic government, such as the July monarchy that ruled France when he came to America.
2. Tyranny of part of society over the rest of society. This is a feature of a formally democratic regime, but one beset with tyranny of the majority. This malady can take the form of either tyranny of governing majorities over minorities or, as Tocqueville saw as especially powerful in America, tyranny of majority opinion over minorities.
3. Tyranny of society over itself. This is the "new despotism" about which Tocqueville was especially concerned in volume 2 of *Democracy*.

All three are threats to, or failures of, liberty in one way or another. The third is the one Tocqueville came to fear most, and he considered its diagnosis to be one of his most important original contributions to political science. This kind of despotism accompanied the movement toward centralized government that Tocqueville saw as a natural tendency of democratic societies. It differed from traditional despotism in that it was not overtly cruel or harsh. It killed with kindness; rather than suppressing humanity, it enervated; it was, ironically, self-imposed and self-sought. In Tocqueville's analysis it brought something very like what Nietzsche diagnosed as the reign of the last man; as Nietzsche's Zarathustra puts it, "I show you the last man. 'What is love? What is creation? What is longing? What is a star?'—so asks the last man—and blinks. . . . 'We have discovered happiness'—say the last men, and they blink" (Nietzsche 1961, 46).

Presenting the causes of these three forms of unfreedom takes up major portions of Tocqueville's analysis—the first two in volume 1, and the last one in volume 2. Unlike some, Tocqueville does not look with despair on the prospects for democracy. Indeed, his point in writing is to provide some remedies for the diseases of democracies, building in part on the American experience. Tocqueville's treatment of remedies is also complex, so let me put forward a thesis rather than a detailed statement: He was a great student of two philosophic predecessors, Montesquieu and Rousseau. He drew on both for his understanding of politics and his prescription of remedies. Montesquieu had called for something like a mixed regime, a liberty-producing solution along the lines of the British constitution, and had also looked to the quasi-feudal arrangements of the French monarchy, where the nobles served as intermediate powers, as devices to secure liberty. Tocqueville was impressed with Montesquieu's analysis but famously said, "We need a new political science for a world quite new" (2010, 16). This was directed most expressly against Montesquieu's solutions, which depended heavily on residues of the *ancien régime* remaining viable. Tocqueville believed that not to be possible. But Tocqueville's search for remedies took the form of looking for equivalent features of a wholly democratic society that could play the role of the predemocratic residues no longer able to play their old role. So in this part of his solution, Tocqueville depends on insights about predemocracy (or premodernity if you will) but not on predemocratic elements themselves.

Tocqueville took much also from Rousseau; one of the most significant adaptations taken from Rousseau was the emphasis on the need for a civil religion to maintain democracy. Tocqueville greatly emphasized how the Americans combined the spirit of religion and the spirit of liberty—and how this combination is necessary for successful free government in democratic times. Here Tocqueville believed that democracies would indeed have to rely on residues from the predemocratic world. As he says, religion is the most precious bequest of aristocratic ages to democratic times. Democracy needs religion, he thought, but democratic times are not favorable to the creation of new religions. So it would be crucial to preserve this inheritance from the past. This preservation would be possible because democratic humanity, like all humanity, contains the seeds of religion in its bosom. But he also believed that democratic habits of mind would modify, if not transform, religions, a modification he counseled religious leaders mostly to accept, as it would be the only means whereby religion could survive.

* * *

We now, like the French in Tocqueville's day, have a conflict between religion and the secular political culture, a conflict we speak of in shorthand as "culture wars." Tocqueville, of course, provides a rich analysis of the religion question and a strong set of claims for the benign and necessary contribution of religion to democratic health. Religion, he argued, had been a prerequisite to the emergence of political liberty in America and a counterweight to some of the most unfortunate tendencies of democracy, which, if given free rein, threaten to make the democratic social state a very undesirable condition for humanity.

The essays that follow thoroughly probe the Tocquevillian case for the combination of religion and liberty that he found so effective in America. But it will not be amiss to mention a few of his chief points. Political democracy is marked by the sovereignty of the people, that is, by the ultimately untrammeled power of the people to enact into law what they please. But the people require some restraints on what they are willing to enact, or they could become more tyrannical than Nero. These restraints cannot be external or institutional, for in democracy the power of public opinion can override all such external restraints. The restraints, therefore, must be internal; they must be moral. But only religion, drawing on human hopes and fears regarding eternal life, is potent enough to undergird the required moral restraint in the long run.

Moreover, democracy is characterized by a tendency to encourage or foster materialism in the populace. This materialism threatens to degrade the human soul and, if unrestrained, diminishes humanity. Religion is important because it can lead humankind to raise their eyes above material things and the mere comfortable preservation of their bodies. Religion thus helps counterbalance the tendency of democracy to vulgarize its citizens.

We are, therefore, now in a better position to understand Tocqueville as he intended to be understood than any earlier generation of Americans, for the simple fact is that he did not write this book for us, but for the French. He saw himself as a maverick, standing between the two main political orientations of the day. On the one side were the conservative forces, still attached to throne and altar, dubious about modern democracy and modern commerce. On the other were men like Flaubert's M. Homais, ready to embrace progress in all its forms—democracy, science, commerce. The former group tended to resist democracy, partly in the name of religion; the latter group, descendants of the French Enlightenment of the eighteenth century, tended to resist religion in the name of liberty and democracy. Tocqueville differed from both in that he supported democracy as more just or at least as inevitable, but he also favored many social practices the conservatives clung to—a somewhat ascetic morality and religion chief among them. Where the others would separate the spirit of religion and the spirit of liberty, Tocqueville praised the Americans for combining them; indeed, he attributed the success of the American experience of democracy to that combination.

America in the early twenty-first century seems to stand somewhere between France and America in the 1830s, when Tocqueville visited. We are and for some time have been living through the aforementioned "culture war," with one side committed to smaller government, to traditional morality (especially sexual morality), and to religion as a support for that morality, and the other side continuing to favor the active and large government of modern liberalism and one or another form of moral change and to be less committed to traditional religion. Americans may feel polarized now, but the polarization is not as great as it was in Tocqueville's France. Our conservatives remain committed to democracy, if to more restrained versions of it; our progressives do not (for the most part) wage open warfare on religion (although we have seen the recent phenomenon of openly atheistic writings, something Tocqueville assured us could never have occurred in nineteenth-century America).

Tocqueville's thesis was a strong one, or so it seemed: America succeeded in building a regime of political democracy (political liberty and democratic politics) on top of a democratic social state only because America also retained the "spirit of religion" in which it had been born. Insofar as America is today much more like Tocqueville's France than it was in the nineteenth century, ought we to be concerned with the apparent coming apart of the commitment to liberty and the commitment to religion that Tocqueville spoke of? How solid is Tocqueville's thesis, in the first instance, as a matter of history? Was America what Tocqueville said it was in the nineteenth century? Did America's democratic success depend on the combination of the spirit of liberty and the spirit of religion? Looking back from the twenty-first century, can we agree with his claims that this combination was a necessary if not sufficient condition for successful democracy? What are we to make of twenty-first-century America, where the strict mores he noted and the religious supports for those mores that he posited no longer hold quite the society-wide sway they did in his day? And what are we to make of the European experience of political democracy combined with a very secular society? Or of Japan's political democracy built on non-Christian religion, if on any religion at all? Might Tocqueville rejoin that America has a problematic future before it and that Europe has already moved far toward the kind of soft despotism he warned against as one of the ways democratic social state could destroy liberty, even while keeping the forms of liberty? Tocqueville wrote almost 200 years ago, and it remains to be seen how correct his predictions and analyses regarding the moral and religious prerequisites of liberty have proved to be. In a word, Tocqueville's analysis poses the following large alternatives to us: On the basis of Tocqueville's analysis, should we be very worried about the track the Western democracies are on? Or should we recognize Tocqueville's analysis as brilliant and stimulating, but unable to account for the actual course of development of democracy in the world? That is the very large issue to which this book is devoted.

The essays are divided into four parts. Standing alone in the first part is Aristide Tessitore's essay "Tocqueville's American Thesis and the New Science of Politics," a lucid explication of Tocqueville's argument for that combination of religion and democratic liberty under investigation in this volume. Tessitore's essay is meant to stand as a point of reference for all the essays that follow it.

Part II, "Tocqueville's Contexts," addresses Tocqueville's argument in the dual contexts most relevant to his thinking. Two of the essays, those by James Schleifer and Mark Noll, look again at the America Tocqueville visited and the relation between religion and politics at the time as historians now can best reconstruct it. The second part is chiefly historical. Schleifer raises the following questions: just what was Tocqueville claiming about the contribution of religion to nineteenth-century American democracy, and what reasons did he have for making those claims? Among other things, Tocqueville emphasized that religion could serve liberty so well in America because in one important respect they were thoroughly compatible: each stayed out of the other's way. Religion was so strong in America (as compared to France) because it stayed out of politics. Paradoxically, Tocqueville maintained, the less religion tried to borrow strength from the state, the stronger it was. The less religion and religious concerns were directly mixed up in politics, the greater could be its indirect role through its influence on manners and morals, or, in his terms, mores. But is it true that American religion was as removed from politics as Tocqueville thought it was? Or was it the case, as Mark Noll argues, that Tocqueville's insights into the relation of religion to politics reflected the very moment when he came to America and did not hold for the rest of the nineteenth century, much less for the entirety of American history? Schleifer and Noll pursue these sorts of questions regarding Tocqueville's nineteenth-century America.

The other two essays in Part II focus on the intellectual context in Tocqueville's France. Both essays help establish the novelty and relative optimism of Tocqueville's thesis. Alexander Jech's essay on Pascal and Tocqueville examines the relation between Tocqueville's thought and one of the intellectual loves on whom he spent part of each day, but in doing so Jech also explains how Tocqueville's thesis both draws on important theses in Pascal's analysis of the human "soul without God" and at the same time develops quite different conclusions about the value and positive possibilities of politics. Without Pascal—as both inspiration and opponent—the Tocqueville thesis could not have been formulated, at least as it was by Tocqueville. Aurelian Craiutu and Matthew Holbreich carry forward the consideration of Tocqueville's argument in the context of French thinking about religion and modern democracy. They draw a contrast between Tocqueville and several contemporary French thinkers who had much less sanguine expectations for the coexistence of religion and democracy.

The third part is more philosophical or theoretical. Alan Kahan and Eduardo Nolla probe in quite different ways what Tessitore calls Tocqueville's "American thesis." Both attempt to bring out the intricacies and philosophic meaning of Tocqueville's concern with religion; they attempt to show what magic Tocqueville sees religion performing. Although Tocqueville's ruminations on religion are not exceedingly lengthy, Kahan and Nolla reveal that Tocqueville's thinking on this issue is complex and perhaps ambiguous, for in their carefully written essays they bring out rather different conceptions of religion's role. In part their differences derive from their differential use of the various supplemental materials to *Democracy in America* that are now available. Scholars can now refer to Tocqueville's drafts, his marginal notes, his notebooks, and his correspondence, all of which can add to our understanding of his *Democracy*. These materials make clear, for example, that Tocqueville pulled some of his punches in the published book. As several of our essayists explain, Tocqueville had private reservations about the compatibility of Catholicism and democracy that he did not commit to public paper. He even falsified, we would have to say, what he learned about Catholic priests in America. As our authors make clear, here is one very evident place where Tocqueville's overall aim of trying to make France safe for democracy and democracy safe for France revealed its centrality for what he decided to put into print.

But the accessory materials, doubtless adding to our understanding of *Democracy*, also complicate the effort. Tocqueville's book is complex enough, but the other materials add yet more complexity, for they contain considerations Tocqueville did not bring into the book and that sometimes seem to contradict not only the book but also other unpublished materials. Some of the differences in the accounts of our more theoretical writers stem from textual difficulties of these sorts, but more derive from the different paths the five theoretical writers (including Tessitore) take to bringing out the nerve of Tocqueville's argument on religion and liberty. Tessitore attempts the most comprehensive account of Tocqueville's position on religion of any of our authors; he also draws heavily on Tocqueville's correspondences with Arthur Gobineau. Kahan's focus is narrower than Tessitore's. His concern is with the idea of religion as supplying both checks (i.e., limitations) and balances (i.e., supplementation) to the natural tendencies and deficiencies of democratic souls. Eduardo Nolla explores the image of the pendulum that appears in some of the accessory writings in order to expose Tocqueville's dialectical understanding of the relation between liberty and religion.

Finally, the last two essays in Part III, by Harvey Mansfield and Dana Villa, probe in different ways the relation between religion and philosophy as they bear on Tocqueville's project. Indeed, these two chapters share much with each other, despite the fact that they stand on quite opposite sides with regard to the Tocqueville thesis itself. Villa challenges the thesis both as a description of the path of American democracy and as a prescription for the health of all democracy. Drawing on more recent historical research, Villa assesses Tocqueville's account of the Puritans to be in many places inaccurate and elsewhere to be exaggerated. He likewise challenges the idea that religion is a necessary support for liberty, claiming instead that on Tocqueville's own telling religion in America is rooted in social pressure and conformity and is thus indeed an enemy of liberty, as understood by someone like J. S. Mill. Mansfield, however, largely accepts, or at least does not challenge, Tocqueville's account of the role of religion in securing American liberty, past and present. His chief emphasis is on attempting to bring out the deeper, less explicit grounds for the emphasis on the import of religion as support for liberty.

So Villa and Mansfield are to that degree on opposite sides. Yet both are interested in locating Tocqueville's thinking in the context of surrounding political philosophy. Both see the Frenchman's emphasis on religion to be related to his perception of the inadequacies of liberal politics and political thought. So Mansfield concludes that "religion is more friendly to human greatness than is philosophy." Both emphasize the theme of individualism and the role of religion in combating it. Finally, both are interested in plumbing Tocqueville's strong commitment in light of his now well-known loss and lack of faith.

In Part IV, Catherine Zuckert approaches Tocqueville's thesis from a twenty-first-century perspective. She first tries to complicate our understanding of Tocqueville's claims by bringing out some of the subtle "second thoughts" he had in the 1840 volume of *Democracy*, an enterprise in which Mansfield also engages in a somewhat different way, but she then goes on to examine the empirical evidence on the status of religion and liberty in contemporary America, thus laying the groundwork for revisiting the theme of religion's relation to liberty today.

REFERENCES

Fukuyama, Francis. 1992. *The End of History and the Last Man*. New York: Free Press.
Nietzsche, Friedrich. 1961. *Thus Spoke Zarathustra*. Trans. R. J. Hollingdale. New York: Penguin.
Tocqueville, Alexis de. 2010. *Democracy in America*. 4 vols. Ed. Eduardo Nolla. Trans. James T. Schleifer. Indianapolis: Liberty Fund.
Welch, Cheryl. 2001. *De Tocqueville*. Oxford: Oxford University Press.

Part I

TOCQUEVILLE'S THESIS

Tocqueville's American Thesis and the New Science of Politics

ARISTIDE TESSITORE

ABSTRACT

The core of Tocqueville's American thesis is the singular combination of the spirit of religion and the spirit of liberty characteristic of the Puritan experiment in America, together with his dual claim that this fact both constitutes the proper starting point for understanding "American civilization" and provides "the key to nearly the whole book." This essay gradually traces Tocqueville's religious "point of departure" to its root cause in Christianity, which, I maintain, provides one of two anchors for his new science of politics. In Tocqueville's analysis, religion (and especially Christianity) offsets limitations in the new philosophic theories of the eighteenth century, the other root cause or anchor that profoundly shaped the distinctive character of American politics. I maintain that the tension between these two causes is at the heart of Tocqueville's new science of politics.

Tocqueville's classic study of America is famous, or perhaps infamous, for its unusual starting point. Rather than begin with "the new theory of politics" that gave rise to America's distinctive and unprecedented form of government in the second half of the eighteenth century, Tocqueville insists on the crucial importance of something old—namely, the Puritan experiment in the wilderness of America more than 150 years earlier. Although Tocqueville eventually provides an astute analysis of the new theory of politics, he insists that the Puritan version of biblical religion, one that exudes an "air and aroma of antiquity," constitutes the proper point of departure for anyone who wishes to understand what is most original about "American civilization." The most revealing fact at the core of the Puritan experiment in America was its singular combination of "the *spirit of religion* and the *spirit of liberty*" (1:69).[1] This is

Aristide Tessitore is professor of political science and director of the Tocqueville Program, Furman University, 3300 Poinsett Highway, Greenville, SC 29613 (ty.tessitore@furman.edu).

1. Unmodified citations are keyed to the four-volume Schleifer-Nolla edition of *Democracy in America* (Tocqueville 2010) and are given by volume and page number. Page numbers are identical in both the two- and four-volume Schleifer-Nolla editions. I have also consulted the translation of Mansfield and Winthrop (Tocqueville 2000). Quotations have been occasionally modified based on the French text printed in the Nolla edition (Tocqueville 1990).

[American Political Thought, vol. 4, issue 1, Winter 2015]

the nub of what is here called Tocqueville's American thesis. Tocqueville invites attentive study of the earliest period of American history, together with an examination of its political and social state, so that his readers may become deeply convinced of the following truth: "There is not an opinion, not a habit, not a law, I could say not an event, that the point of departure does not easily explain. So those who read this book will find in the present chapter the seed of what must follow and the key to nearly the whole book" (1:49).

This famous Tocquevillean thesis about the genesis of American political culture may also be considered infamous by some. Can his account of a religious experiment in the forests of New England really bear the weight he assigns to it, which is nothing less than a true understanding of the national character and distinctive principles of American politics? Some might criticize Tocqueville's emphasis on the New England states and consequent (relative) neglect of the South, or his focus on Puritanism itself, rather than the variety of Christian, non-Christian, and Deistic beliefs that constitute part of the fabric of social influences in America. Others might question whether Tocqueville does justice to the complex variety of conflicting social, economic, and political currents in Europe, many of which contributed to the emergence of what he calls "Anglo-American civilization." From the point of view of political philosophy, Tocqueville's emphasis on America's religious foundation appears to demote the contributions of Enlightenment philosophy that gave expression to America's "fundamental law" 150 years later (*Federalist* 9 and 78, in Rossiter 1961, 72–73, 467). While these are legitimate questions and concerns, I maintain that an exclusive preoccupation with them risks missing both the truth embedded in his thesis about America and the underlying conceptual framework that unifies his study as a whole.

In the essay that follows, I consider Tocqueville's American thesis in detail with a view to uncovering the "first causes" of American democracy as Tocqueville understands it. I argue that Tocqueville's decision to focus on the Puritan beginnings of America calls our attention to an important, novel, and enduring truth about religion and politics in America, although its particular form has and will continue to change—a fact anticipated by Tocqueville himself. More importantly, Tocqueville's emphasis on the unique combination of religion and political liberty in the Puritan experiment underscores a key dimension in his own call for "a new science of politics" (1:16), one capable of providing guidance amid an ongoing revolution that was relentlessly displacing aristocratic European forms with a new and uncertain democratic future. Tocqueville's study of American politics is, as he himself acknowledges, about much more than America. It is, above all, a study of the politics of the human soul at a time of profound political change. Viewed in this light, Tocqueville's American thesis announces a seminal feature of his new science as a whole, one that assigns a preeminent place to religion and to Christianity in particular. This essay brings to light the foundational importance of Christianity (as well as its limitations) for the kind of political science Tocqueville considered most appropriate as he looked to an increasingly democratic future.[2]

I hasten to add that while the focus of this essay is on the religious dimension of Tocqueville's study, I am far from suggesting that religion is the sole factor giving rise to the distinctive character of American or, more generally, modern democracy. Among the several sources that helped to fashion American democracy,[3] this essay presupposes an awareness of the crucial importance of Enlightenment philosophy in particular—something to which I return in the final part of the essay. For now, I simply note that although both the American and French Revolutions drew inspiration from ideas generated by modern political philosophy, according to Tocqueville, it was especially in America that "the boldest political theories of the eighteenth-century philosophers" were most effectively put into practice (Tocqueville 1998, 206). This assessment renders Tocqueville's "point of departure" all the more striking, since he chooses neither the founding events of the eighteenth century nor the "entirely new theory" of politics (1:252) that justifies them as starting points for his analysis. Rather, he grounds his study in the religious-political experience of America's first settlers. In sharp contrast to the abstract philosophic

2. After a long period of neglect, several excellent studies on the religious dimension of Tocqueville's thought have been published over the past 30 years. Four in particular have directly influenced my own work on this issue. Peter Augustine Lawler's (1993) book on the centrality of Pascal's religious psychology in Tocqueville's self-understanding and written work and Joshua Mitchell's (1995) erudite exploration of the Augustinian ground for Tocqueville's analyses of democracy both bring to the fore the profoundly religious (albeit unorthodox) impulse that animates Tocqueville and his written legacy. Sanford Kessler's (1994) analysis of the Puritan legacy in his book-length study of American religion and John C. Koritansky's (1990/2010) incisive study of *Democracy in America* both emphasize the central importance of "civil religion," a term that denotes the decisive importance of political philosophy—specifically Montesquieu and Rousseau rather than the biblically inspired thought of Augustine and Pascal—in Tocqueville's religious-political analyses. At the risk of overgeneralizing, what is distinctive about my approach is that I do not think that the foundation of Tocqueville's thought can be described as either philosophic or religious; rather, it is an unsettled and ultimately irreconcilable combination of both. I consider Tocqueville's inability or unwillingness to resolve this fundamental tension to be the source of both his strength and limitations as a political thinker.

3. James Ceaser lucidly explores the amalgam constituted by rationalist, republican, and traditionalist understandings of politics as constitutive of both the American founding and Tocqueville's political science. Although Ceaser recognizes Tocqueville's "notable" insistence on the importance and utility of a "healthy form" of religiosity, like Kessler and Koritansky, he understands Tocqueville's political-religious analyses to be grounded in modern political philosophy, most notably in the notion of "customary history" inaugurated by Montesquieu (Ceaser 1985; 1990, esp. 166–69; 2011).

theories of the Enlightenment, Tocqueville begins his study with a historical-political fact, and it is a fact that takes its bearings from religious convictions rather than from philosophy.

THE CHRISTIAN ROOTS OF DEMOCRACY

HUMAN DEVELOPMENT AND THE STUDY OF POLITICS

For Tocqueville, the American democratic order is unprecedented in several different respects, the most important of which is that the United States is the only country in the world where one can see and study its origins such that it becomes possible "to clarify the influence that the point of departure exercised on the future of the [United] States" (1:47). It is an opportunity of which Tocqueville takes full advantage. Comparing the development of a nation to that of a human being, Tocqueville suggests what modern science confirms (and many before its advent already knew)—namely, that the circumstances and experiences of early childhood cast a disproportionate influence on the future development of the mature human being.[4] Applying this psychological principle of human development to the realm of politics, Tocqueville observes that, unlike the origins of the mature civilizations of Europe that are now shrouded in the mists of history, it is only in America that one is able to begin at the beginning. This, Tocqueville maintains, makes it possible to study "the first causes of the destiny of nations," at least insofar as these causes come to light and play themselves out in the American experience (1:48).

Perhaps the best way to begin to understand why Tocqueville gives so much weight to the colonial infancy of the American republic and the formative influence of the New England colonies is to examine one of many notes he preserved in the course of writing *Democracy in America*. Among the several factors contributing to the distinctive character of the American experience, Tocqueville writes that the point of departure is "the most important of all in my eyes, because it is the one that has had the most influence on *mores*" (1:49e; emphasis added). He goes on to explain, as he also later notes in his book, that among "the three general causes" invoked in his study—mores, laws, and the accidental or providential circumstances of nature—"I regard mores as by far the most powerful" (1:49e; see also 2:451–52 and 2:494–500). For Tocqueville, the powerful "first cause" of the American nation is in some way rooted in the religious mores of "the first age of the American republic," during which a

4. Among those who understood this principle in advance of Freudian psychology and its aftermath, both Plato and Aristotle stress this point and give it a key place in their study of politics (Plato 1986, 377a–c; Aristotle 1979, 2.1.1103b22–25).

"totally democratic and republican political life" was reigning in the townships of New England (1:65–66).[5]

Tocqueville's concern with mores, what he famously describes as "habits of the heart," may in fact help to clarify the essential truth embedded in his initial analogy between human and political development. Tocqueville uses the word *moeurs* in the expansive sense the ancients attached to the term, to comprehend "the whole moral and intellectual state of a people" (2:466–67). As such, mores describe the complex interaction between more or less conscious movements of the heart and mind that furnish the wellsprings of human action and identity. For Tocqueville, mores are both an expression of and a means of shaping the soul of any given individual or people.[6] The new science of politics exhibited in Tocqueville's own writings takes its bearings from the natural affinity between the human soul and politics—or, to state the point more precisely, from the inescapable and reciprocal influence exerted on each other by politics and the human soul. Paradoxically, what is most distinctive about Tocqueville's "new" science of politics is in some way reminiscent of political science in its original, indeed ancient, Greek form.

TOCQUEVILLE'S AMERICAN THESIS

Tocqueville maintains that the New England states succeeded in combining two or three principal ideas that gradually permeated the Union and eventually gave rise to "the foundations of the social theory of the United States" (1:52). Not only is the genesis of America unique in the history of nations by virtue of the visibility of its origins, but the founding of New England offered the world "a new spectacle" in which everything "was singular and original." Whereas most colonies are populated by those without learning, resources, or prospects in their native country, the Pilgrim emigrants who founded New England were educated members of "the comfortable classes" and composed "a society in which there were neither great lords, nor lower classes" (1:53). Far from being mercenary adventurers who came to the New World "to improve their situation or to increase their wealth," the Puritans, Tocqueville writes, "tore themselves from the comforts of their homeland to obey a purely

5. Tocqueville writes that as early as 1650, the New England township "was completely and definitively constituted" (1:65).

6. As far as I can tell, Tocqueville uses the word "soul" in three ways: first, to describe the distinctive animating spirit or life of a given individual or people, especially as it bears on character; second, to refer to a particular and characteristic mode of human acting, thinking, or feeling; and third, as the locus (or placeholder) for beliefs that sustain distinctively human activities.

intellectual need"; they endured "the inevitable hardships of exile . . . to assure the triumph of *an idea*." The "idea" or ideal in question not only was a religious doctrine but encompassed an entire way of life, one that combined religious commitment with "the most absolute democratic and republican theories" (1:54). Puritan religious belief integrated religious conviction, self-government, and a system of public education into a seamless whole. Tocqueville notes that it was as if "democracy . . . burst forth fully grown and fully armed from the midst of the old feudal society" (1:59).

The novelty of this fact was striking from a European and especially French point of view. In stark contrast to Europe, and above all France, it was religion that both encouraged and disseminated enlightenment in America. Even more paradoxically, it was by means of the strict observance of divine laws that the first inhabitants of American civilization were schooled in the practice of political liberty (1:67). In the famous formulation anticipated at the outset of this essay, Tocqueville writes that the distinctive genesis of Anglo-American civilization "is the product of two perfectly distinct elements that elsewhere are often at war," but which have been successfully and marvelously combined in America—namely, "the *spirit of religion* and the *spirit of liberty*" (1:69; italics in original). Whereas Europe found itself in the midst of a long and ongoing revolution in which political liberty had to be wrested, often violently, from the powers of altar and throne, it was an initial experience of deep (although by no means perfect) compatibility between religion and political liberty—and especially the mores generated by that experience—that Tocqueville puts down as the "first cause" of the American experiment in democratic and republican forms of government. For Tocqueville, the most formative experience of democratic-republican government in America was not the result of Enlightenment philosophy; it arose instead from the Puritan desire to practice their faith, without governmental interference, in a manner they thought most acceptable to God. If democracy burst forth directly from feudal society and was transported to the New World by America's first Puritan settlers, Tocqueville appears to suggest that the remote first cause of democracy itself must somehow be traced back to the putatively unenlightened but emphatically Christian world of the Middle Ages.

This leads to a final point bearing on Tocqueville's new science of politics: its overarching aim should not be identified in any simple way with the preexisting canons of science. Although Tocqueville takes pains to ensure the accuracy of the facts upon which his science rests, the science itself is characterized by a twofold aim: it is an attempt first to reveal the nature of democracy in the modern world and secondly to provide practical guidance for those destined to live under its influence. It is this second point that especially determines the particular choices, priorities, and arguments that furnish the contours of Tocqueville's analysis as a whole. While Tocqueville strives to present an empirically sound account of American democracy, his new science does not provide a disinterested or "value-neutral" analysis of its subject matter. It is instead animated by the desire to warn about unseen dangers and uncover available resources that might in any way contribute to human flourishing in the dawning democratic age.

THE NATURE AND LIMITS OF THE PURITAN EXPERIENCE

Although Tocqueville elevates the importance of the Puritan experience for understanding American democracy, he does not romanticize it. In fact, he provides a critical appreciation of the Puritan effort to integrate religion and politics, one that reveals both the seminal contribution he admires and the narrowness and inconsistency he abjures. Tocqueville is most critical of the illiberal and invasive strictures expressed in the Puritan penal code, many of which were taken verbatim from the "primitive" penal laws recorded in the Pentateuch. He also provides examples of the harsh punishments meted out for infractions ranging from serious crimes such as rape to frivolous improprieties such as indiscrete speech or, for those who were unmarried, socializing with members of the opposite sex. The prescription of death for Christians who sought to worship God in a manner that deviated from current practice, Tocqueville critically observes, bespeaks a complete forgetting of "the great principles of religious liberty" that Puritans had originally claimed for themselves when they were a religious minority in Europe. Even if the harshest penalties were seldom, if ever, enforced, Tocqueville maintains that such lapses "shame the human spirit" and point to the all-too-human tendency to swing from one excess to another (esp. 1:63–64).[7]

If the narrow spirit of sect evident in the Puritan penal code attests to "the infirmity of our nature," Tocqueville writes that it was connected to a body of political laws that, while drafted 200 years earlier, "still seems very far ahead of the spirit of liberty of our age." Tocqueville observes that even the "bizarre and tyrannical laws" of the Puritan penal code were not imposed from the outside but were voluntarily voted upon "by the free participation of all those concerned" (1:63–64). The political laws of the New England township in the mid-seventeenth century already allowed its members to participate in public affairs, vote on taxes, require accountability from those in power, enjoy in-

7. Tocqueville attributes (without excusing) the narrow spirit of sect characteristic of the Puritans in America to the religious passions provoked by the still-recent experience of persecution (1:64).

dividual freedom (however circumscribed by contemporary standards), and adjudicate conflicts by a jury of one's peers. Even though the laws governing the New England colonies were still under the aegis of monarchy, the New England township already provided its citizens with a profoundly democratic experience in self-government.[8]

Although the juxtaposition of a "primitive and half-civilized" penal code (1:62) to political laws more enlightened than anything that existed in Europe appears paradoxical, Tocqueville insists on their underlying connection. The double-edged Puritan experiment required strict, although voluntary, adherence to nonnegotiable moral precepts, while at the same time viewing the political world as a sphere for human innovation. Whereas reverence for a moral order directly established by divine decree was accepted on the authority of faith, this same divine legislator left the development of political principles, laws, and institutions to the noble exercise of human intelligence (esp. 1:69–70). Tocqueville, however, goes beyond this helpful elucidation of the distinctive combination of "political theory" and "religious doctrine" characteristic of the Puritans (1:58) when he locates the deepest reason for the underlying connection between these two spheres of human life—religion and politics—in human nature itself.

THE NATURAL BASIS FOR RELIGION IN THE HUMAN SOUL

It is especially in the 1840 edition of *Democracy in America* that Tocqueville provides the fullest account of what he considers to be the natural limits of human freedom. He begins by explaining that human beings are unable to live without dogmatic beliefs, that is, beliefs accepted on trust without questioning. The limited character of time, ability, and opportunity make it impossible for anyone to verify for oneself all the fundamental beliefs upon which each individual draws on a daily basis (3:711–14). As a result, human beings are reduced "by the inflexible law of [their] condition" to accepting on faith a number of beliefs they have not examined for themselves (3:714). In a democratic age, most will defer to the almost irresistible authority of public opinion (esp. 3:717–25). Although there will always be some exceptions, even philosophers don't appear to fare much better in Tocqueville's analysis. "Almost always surrounded by uncertainties," Tocqueville writes, they have succeeded

8. Tocqueville reaches back even further when he traces "the fertile seed of free institutions" evidenced in the New England townships to the "troubled" history of old England, where the struggle between parties and factions—especially as they concerned divisions within Christianity—compelled each one "to place themselves under the protection of the laws" (1:49–50).

in discovering "only a small number of contradictory notions" and have never been able "to grasp the truth firmly" (3:744).

The pervasive uncertainty surrounding fundamental questions coeval with humanity itself applies especially to religious matters. Tocqueville contends that the different, more or less inchoate answers given by human beings to general questions about God and the human soul furnish the ground for almost all human action (3:743). Although some fixed ideas about God and human nature are indispensable for life, they are also the most difficult to acquire inasmuch as they presuppose opportunities and abilities considerably beyond the reach of most (3:743–44). It is precisely for this reason that Tocqueville refers to religious belief as a "salutary yoke," one that allows human beings to make good use of their freedom in other areas of life, by providing "clear, precise . . . , intelligible . . . , and very lasting" answers to those fundamental questions that agitate the human heart. When, however, religion gives way to doubt, Tocqueville maintains that most become accustomed to confused and changing opinions. Despair of resolving the greatest questions for oneself not only weakens the mind but also enervates the soul and slackens the will. Even if religious faith does not bring human beings to heaven, it proves to be very useful for human happiness and greatness here on earth (3:744–45).

The underlying issue, Tocqueville explains, is that contemplation of an unbounded horizon of inquiry or the possibility of limitless independence inspires fear and agitation in the hearts and minds of human beings. This limitation in human nature leads Tocqueville to doubt that the vast majority of human beings are capable of sustaining at one and the same time both complete religious independence and complete political independence (3:745). For Tocqueville, it was precisely the clearly demarcated and religiously grounded moral horizon of the Puritans that supplied the necessary condition for the possibility of radical innovation in politics. As he reflects more generally on the advancing democratic political order, Tocqueville arrives at the following radical conclusion: whereas despotism can do without faith, freedom cannot. Whether he is ultimately right when he suggests that the absence of belief is likely to result in servitude and that freedom requires faith,[9] Tocqueville insists that the maintenance of religion is more important in a democratic republic than in any other regime (2:478, 3:745). This priority is reflected in the prominence he gives to the theme of religion throughout his study of American democracy as a whole and in particular the Puritan point of departure.

9. Kessler maintains that Tocqueville's radical claim about the dependence of political freedom on faith is "highly misleading" because he already recognized that enlightened self-interest had superseded religious faith as the primary moral guarantor of freedom (1994, 120–33). I believe that this underestimates the depth of the Pascalian religious impulse within Tocqueville's soul and subsequent political analyses.

Indeed, despite the separation between religion and politics both noted and advocated by Tocqueville, he describes religion as the first of the political institutions in America. This designation is the result of the powerful influence that religion exerts on both the mores and mind of Americans (2:474; see also 2:472–78). Although it does not directly interfere with government, religion has a direct influence on the family and especially on the souls of women, who are the primary propagators of mores. It is by regulating the family that religion indirectly regulates the state. For Tocqueville, the power of religion's influence in America is predicated on the fact that it does not mix with politics in a direct way but rather draws from its enduring source of strength in human nature itself. Tocqueville explains that the natural ground for religion arises from the simultaneous and paradoxical experience of dissatisfaction with human life and the fact of mortality—both of which are combined with "an immense desire to exist" (2:482; see also 3:940). The sufferings and incomplete joys of life, together with the fear of (or at least dissatisfaction with) nonexistence, naturally incline human beings to look for a better and more enduring experience of life.

Tocqueville, who views religion from a natural and political perspective in his published works (what he describes as evaluating religion "only from a human viewpoint"),[10] describes religion as "a particular form of hope," one that is "as natural to the human heart as hope itself." The religious form of hope, as it is analyzed by Tocqueville, constitutes a permanent part of the human soul, one that is lodged in the deepest fears and longings of the human heart. Human beings can be diverted or distracted from their deepest fears and longings, but for Tocqueville, like Pascal, the fears and longings themselves can never be fully eradicated. Based on an understanding of human beings as part of a more comprehensive order of nature, Tocqueville asserts that "unbelief is an accident; faith alone is the permanent state of humanity." It is, of course, possible for human beings to live without faith. For Tocqueville, however, this constitutes an exception to the general rule, and in some cases it requires the exercise of "a kind of moral violence" on one's own nature (2:482). Contrary to the presumption of many eighteenth-century philosophers who expected religious faith to wane as freedom and enlightenment increased, Tocque-

10. The dominant scholarly view describes Tocqueville as a Deist (Goldstein 1975; Jardin 1998, 61–64, 528–33; Zunz and Kahan 2002, 5, 29–30). Whereas Antoine Rédier (1925) and John Lukacs (1964) maintain that Tocqueville died a believing Catholic and that his Catholic beliefs are fundamental for understanding his ideas, Koritansky (1990/2010) and Kessler (1994) describe him as a nonbelieving proponent of civil religion in the tradition of Rousseau. Cynthia Hinckley carves out something of a middle position, maintaining that Tocqueville suffered "the anguish of a believer" deprived, however, of "the unwavering certitude that characterizes faith of the highest order" (1990, esp. 42–43).

ville comments with understated irony, "It is unfortunate that facts do not agree with this theory" (2:479). As long as religion draws its force from the natural "sentiments, instincts, and passions" of the human soul, it remains among the most dominant and enduring attributes of human life; it is only by attaching itself to political authority that religion "becomes almost as fragile as all the powers of the earth" (2:483).

THE CHRISTIAN ORIGIN OF DEMOCRACY

It is certainly clear to all—including Tocqueville—that the Puritan experiment in Christian living did not endure; however, the initial and unique coupling of religion and political freedom in America continues to persist into the first decades of the twenty-first century. By every empirical measure, America in the twenty-first century remains the most religious nation in the developed world. As Tocqueville continues his thematic development of the relationship between religion and politics in America, it is not only the reformed versions of Christianity that he describes as "democratic and republican"; he also advances the far more surprising claim that recent Catholic emigrants to America "form the most republican and most democratic class there is in the United States" (2:468). The paradoxical character of Tocqueville's claim is sharpened by the fact that his private correspondence reveals serious misgivings about the capacity of Catholicism to adapt to the new democratic dispensation (see Schleifer 2014, esp. 266–67). The underlying problem derives from the often antidemocratic attitude of priests and the corrupting effect of political power (or the memory of that power) exercised by clergy prior to the influence of Enlightenment ideas on the political world. Although Tocqueville candidly describes Catholicism as a kind of absolute monarchy or aristocracy when writing to trusted correspondents,[11] such misgivings are barely alluded to in his published work, which portrays clergy and laity alike as both devout and democratic (e.g., 2:468 and 2:471–72). In *Democracy in America*, Tocqueville insists that "it is wrong to regard the Catholic religion as a natural enemy of democracy." He does, however, at least hint at his privately expressed concerns when he goes on to write, "Catholicism is like an absolute monarchy. Remove the prince, and conditions there are more equal than in republics" (2:469–70).

The discrepancy between Tocqueville's public and private remarks about the ability of Catholicism to overcome attitudes and beliefs incubated during its long and powerful political hegemony in the West suggests a genuine and perhaps unresolved ambivalence about the future of Catholicism within the

11. See his letter to Chabrol, October 26, 1831 (Zunz 2010, 157–60), and his letter to Francisque de Corcelle, 1843 (3:755e).

emerging democratic order. However, Tocqueville's clear decision to withhold his personal misgivings and to insist on both the compatibility and likely progress of Catholicism in a democratic age (3:754–56) reveals two important and related points that I will develop in the rest of this section. First, although Tocqueville believes that Catholicism's embrace of the new democratic age will prove difficult, he does not think that it is impossible. To state this in a slightly different way, he sees no essential incompatibility between Catholicism and political democracy (although the exact meaning of "essential" would undoubtedly be a matter for dispute among Catholics). Secondly, the practical character of Tocqueville's new science of politics leads him not only to emphasize those aspects of Christianity that presage a successful transition to the emerging democratic order but also to offer advice about the practices, beliefs, forms, and obligations imposed by the Christian tradition (especially Catholicism) that might be played down without compromising its essential character (3:746–53).

Tocqueville develops his initially paradoxical claim about the latent democratic propensities concealed within Catholicism in the following way. In America priests stay out of politics (whether by choice, necessity, or some combination of the two), with the result that their authority is confined to those matters that bear directly on religious belief. This American practice provides Tocqueville's cardinal principle, one that is indispensable for the full development and elevation of Catholicism's deeply egalitarian propensities. It also allows Tocqueville to describe the religious and political views of American Catholics in a way that is strangely and surprisingly reminiscent of his presentation of America's first founders: American priests, he writes, have divided the intellectual world into two parts. In the first, the revealed dogmas of faith are believed without question or discussion; in the second, "they put political truth," which they believe "God abandoned . . . to the free search of men." As a result, Tocqueville concludes that American Catholics "are simultaneously the most submissive faithful and the most independent citizens" (2:471). Like the Puritans 100 years earlier, Catholic emigrants to America were characterized by the same combination of religious and moral certainty on the one hand and a great deal of freedom to fashion their political opinions on the other. It was this combination of religious authority and political freedom that made it possible for newly arrived Catholics to adapt their political views to the democratic mores already in effect in America. Tocqueville's unlikely, even jarring, parallel between Puritans and Catholics reflects an underlying truth about human nature to which he has given especial importance—namely, the need for a fixed and certain moral horizon at a time of sweeping political change.

Although I believe that this parallel is important (in a way that will soon become evident), I do not want to overstate it. Tocqueville also points to the contrasting emphases characteristic of Catholic and Protestant Christianity in America. Whereas Protestants of various kinds are more inclined to lead their adherents to independence than equality, exactly the opposite is true of Catholicism. In fact, Tocqueville writes that as long as priests stay out of politics, there are none "who, by their beliefs, are more disposed than Catholics to carry the idea of equality of conditions into the political world" (2:470). Only part of the explanation, Tocqueville suggests, comes from the fact that the poor Catholic minority in America was influenced by their far more dominant Protestant coreligionists (2:470–71). The larger point of this comparative analysis might be expressed in the following way. It is both Protestant and Catholic traditions of Christianity taken together that transmit and sustain the freedom and equality that constitute the hallmark of democracy in America in the mid-nineteenth century. For Tocqueville there is something about Christianity itself—notwithstanding its often undemocratic historical and political manifestations—that favors the emergence of democratic politics.

Although history shows that both Catholic and reformed versions of Christianity can be made compatible with a wide variety of different forms of government, Tocqueville attributes this more to accidental than essential causes (esp. 2:486–87). If, however, we want to understand the fundamental reason for Tocqueville's insistence on the compatibility between Christianity and democracy in American politics, we need to grasp the broader intellectual horizon within which Tocqueville understands the relationship between religion and politics as it developed in the Western world. If democracy first arose in America because of its Puritan point of departure, to what does Western civilization owe the initial emergence of democracy? With respect to this question, Tocqueville is unexpectedly unequivocal. Surprisingly, he does not trace the origin of democracy back to the West's earliest experiments with democratic-republican forms of government in ancient Greece or Rome,[12] although he does acknowledge that gathering "a great part of the human species . . . under the scepter of the Ceasers" disposed humanity to receive "the general truths of Christianity" (3:748 and n. f). The fundamental reason for his refusal to do so lies in the fact that neither of these cultures, nor even their "most profound and far-reaching geniuses," was able to arrive at the simple and general idea "of the *similarity of men* and of the *equal right to liberty* that each one of them bears by birth" (3:432–33; emphasis added). Rather, he continues, "Jesus

12. Tocqueville describes both ancient Athens and Rome as "aristocratic republic[s]" (3:815–16; cf. 2:432–33). Although it is true that all Athenian citizens took part in public affairs, citizens constituted only a fraction of the total population in comparison to the vast majority who were slaves. Tocqueville views the struggle between the patricians and plebeians in ancient Rome through the same political lens, describing it "as an internal quarrel between the junior members and elders of the same family" (3:816).

Christ had to come to earth in order to make it understood that all members of the human species are naturally alike and equal" (3:433).

The initially paradoxical character of this statement is augmented by the fact that Tocqueville considers biblical religion in general, and Christianity in particular, to be "the most precious heritage of aristocratic centuries" (3:958). Notwithstanding the hierarchical character of medieval Christianity or the religiously based "divine right of kings" in prerevolutionary France, for Tocqueville it is Christianity itself that is the deepest source—or, in Tocqueville's language, "the first cause"—of the rise of equality and liberty in the West.[13] Indeed, the initial indication that Christianity is in some sense the original source of the vast and seemingly irresistible democratic revolution is suggested at the very outset of his book on America. When Tocqueville indicates the reach and limits of the ongoing revolution that furnishes the framework for the entirety of his published works, he describes a revolution that is "continuing *in all the Christian universe*" (1:10; emphasis added).

Although Tocqueville rather emphatically states his view of the origin of the idea of democratic equality in the West, he does not fully supply the understanding that supports it in *Democracy in America*. That understanding, however, comes to light three years after the publication of the second volume of *Democracy in America*, most especially in an epistolary exchange (in 1843) with a former student and lifelong friend, Arthur de Gobineau.[14] Like many intellectuals of the eighteenth century before him, the young Gobineau was convinced that Enlightenment philosophers had ushered in an entirely new foundation for politics and morality. Although Gobineau recognizes that it was not yet fully visible for all to see, he insists that both morality and politics had been cut free from their formerly religious, and specifically Christian, foundation. What is more, Gobineau maintains that this development marks something genuinely new in human history. The emergence of the modern world represented nothing less than a fundamental break with everything that preceded it. For Gobineau, the religious foundations for ethical thinking and political practice characteristic of all previous political cultures had been decisively overthrown—at least in principle—by the philosophically driven project of modern politics (Tocqueville 1959b, esp. 195–204).

13. Additional indications of the centrality of Christianity for the development of equality and liberty in the West can be found in Schleifer (2014, 265–67, and n. 9).

14. Tocqueville's correspondence with Gobineau has been translated into English by John Lukacs (Tocqueville 1959b), and I have referred to this edition here. Unfortunately, Lukacs's book inexplicably excludes some key passages from Tocqueville's letters and an important letter from Gobineau. In such cases, I refer to volume 9 of the French edition of Tocqueville's collected works (Tocqueville 1959a). Translations from the French are my own.

In sharp contrast, for Tocqueville the decisive shift in the West did not occur with the onset of the Enlightenment, but with the advent of Christianity. According to Tocqueville, the political triumph of Christianity in the fourth century generated a new culture that profoundly displaced, without altogether extinguishing, the political culture of antiquity. This dislocation amounted to nothing less than a "*revolution* . . . in all the ideas that concern duties and rights" (Tocqueville 1959b, 191; emphasis added; see also Tocqueville 1998, 100). Tocqueville's summary of the far-reaching results of Christian faith even alludes to the revolutionary slogan of 1789: he writes that, for the first time in human history, "Christianity put in grand evidence the equality, the unity, the fraternity of all men" (Tocqueville 1959b, 191). Even if some of these elements were to some degree already present in the world, Tocqueville points out that it was only Christianity that bound them together into a single religion, one that managed to "inundate every human intelligence" (*inonda toutes les intelligences*) (Tocqueville 1959b, 191; see also 211). To invoke a subsequent nineteenth-century author, the Christian revolution had effected, in Friedrich Nietzsche's famous phrase, a "transvaluation of values" (Nietzsche 1967, esp. 33–35).[15]

For Tocqueville, Christianity constitutes the deepest wellspring of modern democratic ideas, notwithstanding the fact that Christianity itself emerged in an aristocratic age. It is not the overcoming of Christianity but precisely the profoundly Christian ideas of equality and universal love that provided the underlying impetus for modern democratic politics. The principle of equality proclaimed by the French Revolution is, at root, a remote product of biblical culture, and the transformation of the Christian virtue of "charity" into a public activity is part of a modern attempt to rekindle something akin to the flourishing political life of antiquity.[16] Although it may be true that the modern world finds itself alienated from Christianity's core theological beliefs, it nevertheless remains profoundly indebted to Christianity for its most perva-

15. Like Tocqueville, Nietzsche attributes the decisive dislocation in the West to the advent of biblical morality, which he also regards as the remote cause of the French Revolution. Nietzsche writes, "With the French Revolution, Judea once again triumphed over the classical ideal, and this time in an even more profound and decisive sense: the last political *noblesse* in Europe . . . collapsed beneath the popular instincts of *ressentiment*" (1967, 54). Although Tocqueville evaluates Christian morality far more positively than Nietzsche, both recognize a profound continuity between Christian morality and the ethical impulse of the Enlightenment, particularly as it found expression in the French Revolution.

16. The early modern political philosopher Francis Bacon sought to refashion the Christian virtue of charity into a political project directed to the "relief of man's estate," one jointly taken over by a new and distinctively modern collaboration between science and politics (see *Advancement of Learning* 1.5.11 in Bacon 2001, 33–34).

sive ethical and political convictions (consider Tocqueville 1959b, 192).[17] As Tocqueville explains, it is not that there is nothing new in the modern world, but that "almost all that we call modern principles should be considered as new consequences drawn from the old Christian principles" (Tocqueville 1959b, 211; see also 193–94, 207).

THE POLITICAL IMPORTANCE OF RELIGION IN A DEMOCRATIC AGE

Notwithstanding Tocqueville's own apparent unbelief, we are now in a position to understand more fully the attention he gives to religion, not only in his American thesis but in his study as a whole. First, as a constitutive element of human nature, religion is in principle a renewable resource for human beings. The political importance of religion stems from the limited nature of the human capacity for freedom, limitations that become most apparent in the psychologically debilitating uncertainty that is the necessary concomitant of complete or radical freedom. Religion, by offering clear and lasting answers to fundamental moral questions (questions that, according to Tocqueville, philosophers debate endlessly and without resolution), provides most human beings with the solace of a bounded horizon—one that makes it possible to withstand and even embrace the challenges and uncertainties that necessarily accompany political freedom.

Secondly, in sharp contrast to the experience of revolutionary France, Tocqueville argues that there is no essential incompatibility between religion and democratic politics. As long as religion draws from its natural source of strength in the human soul and resists the shortsighted temptation to rely on the artificial support of politics as a way of bolstering its strength, there is no necessary or principled reason for thinking that human religiosity will ineluctably wane in the democratic centuries ahead—notwithstanding the expectation of Enlightenment philosophers. Stated in a more positive way, Tocqueville argues that there is in fact a deep affinity between the Christian religion and democracy. By insisting on the spiritual equality and God-given dignity of all human beings before the one and only God (whether acknowledged or not), Christianity effectively nurtured the seeds of political equality and individual freedom in the souls of those who inhabited the Christian world. For Tocqueville, those seeds had been pushing their way into politics with all but irresistible force for the past 700 years. Far from being opposed to the dawning age of

17. The sustainability of this split is a much-debated question. For Strauss's view of the matter, consider his 1952 essay "Progress or Return?" (Strauss 1989, 227–70; cf. Kessler 1994, 180–88; Manent 1996, 91).

democracy, Christianity is not only its remote first cause but also—at least in principle—an important and renewable resource capable of providing much-needed guidance as the democratic revolution continues to propel itself toward a democratic but uncertain future.

ENLIGHTENMENT PHILOSOPHY AND CHRISTIAN MORES

Whereas the biblical principles that inspired America's first Puritan founders in the seventeenth century bequeathed to America the dominant and bounded horizon within which American mores would develop, the Enlightenment principles given expression in America's foundational documents in the eighteenth century produced the laws that frame in a direct way the American experience of politics. Although this essay focuses especially on America's first religious founding, it is important to recognize that Tocqueville simultaneously admires and criticizes both America's biblical and Enlightenment foundings. While he elevates the importance of the Puritan experience and its consequences in his study of America, he does not, as we have seen, fully sanction it. Nor is he able to identify in a personal way with Christianity's core religious beliefs. Something similar must be said regarding Tocqueville's account of America's Enlightenment founding. Although Tocqueville does qualify his more pervasive appreciation for the new political science relied on by the architects of the Declaration of Independence and the Constitution, his sharpest criticism of Enlightenment philosophy is directed against the French.[18] Notwithstanding some specific criticisms, what most attracts Tocqueville to the American political experience is the result of a fragile but comparatively healthy interplay between the two competing sources or "causes" of the American experiment in democracy.

In this final section of the essay, I sketch something of the effect that America's competing principles have had on the souls of Americans—the more positive consequences characteristic of America at the time in which Tocqueville was writing, as well as Tocqueville's warnings about less apparent and

18. Whereas America drew especially from the earlier Enlightenment tradition of Locke and Montesquieu, the French attempted to fashion an "abstract and literary politics" based on the writings of Voltaire and the "physiocrats" without any understanding of the kind of obstacles that "existing facts might place before even the most desirable reforms," or even the serious "dangers which always accompany even the most necessary revolutions" (Tocqueville 1998, 195–202). Particularly egregious was the French failure to understand the innately religious character of human beings. As a consequence, the attempt to eradicate religion in France merely redirected religious passions with the result that the revolutionary cause itself became a new and truncated "kind of religion . . . without God, without ritual, and without life after death, but one which nevertheless . . . flooded the earth with its soldiers, apostles, and martyrs" (101).

more insidious imbalances that could jeopardize the American experiment in the future.

RELIGION AND ENLIGHTENMENT IN MID-NINETEENTH-CENTURY AMERICA

An important positive example of the mixture of America's biblical and Enlightenment principles is found in Tocqueville's analysis of the way in which the Enlightenment principle of self-interest was circumscribed by religious mores in mid-nineteenth-century America. Tocqueville remarks that legislators in America have little confidence in the honesty of citizens, preferring instead to appeal to personal interest, "the great principle one constantly finds when studying the laws of the United States" (1:128–29). Although the doctrine of self-interest well understood is itself the product of modern political thought (Tocqueville specifically cites the early modern thinker and essayist Montaigne), what is distinctive about America is its universal acceptance of this principle (3:920). Tocqueville's own study leads him to conclude that "of all philosophical theories," self-interest well understood "is the most appropriate to the needs of the men of our time," and he expects "individual interest to become more than ever the principal, if not the sole motivating force of men's actions" (3:922–23).

The framers of the Constitution had learned from Enlightenment philosophy to abandon the quixotic attempt to reform human beings; they sought instead to build government on a sober, even harsh, understanding of human nature.[19] Although the architects of the Constitution would prefer, of course, to have enlightened and virtuous leaders at the helm (such as Washington), both Hamilton and Madison argue that the chances of success for the American enterprise would be increased by institutional measures directing, and even employing, the darker and more self-interested motives of the human heart.[20] Justice, public-spiritedness, and political prudence are difficult virtues to nurture in citizens. It is distinctive of modern political thought to teach that a sufficient and reliable simulacrum for these virtues could be grounded in the

19. Hamilton maintains that human beings are "ambitious, vindictive, and rapacious" and that, as a consequence, the causes of war arise from the unalterable ground of human nature itself (*Federalist* 6 in Rossiter 1961, 54). Madison famously echoes these sentiments when he explains that the causes of faction cannot be removed because they are sown into the nature of man. He adds that it is vain to rely on enlightened statesmen and that moral or religious motives are insufficient to curb the base tendencies of the human heart (*Federalist* 10 in Rossiter 1961, 79–81).

20. Again echoing Hamilton, who summons his reader to wake from the dangerous dream of "a happy empire of perfect wisdom and perfect virtue" (*Federalist* 6 in Rossiter

appeal to self-interest and greed.[21] Indeed, as Tocqueville contemplated the mixture of vice and virtue in America, he was inspired to pen a new beatitude: "How happy the country of the New World, where the vices of man are nearly as useful to society as his virtues!" (2:462). If this was in some part due to the fortuitous circumstances of history and geography, it was more deeply indebted to law, or, more precisely, the wisdom of those who made the laws.

Although Tocqueville marvels at the astuteness of the work of the founding generation and appreciates as well the novelty of their accomplishments, he was at the same time keenly sensitive to the kind of dangers to which their handiwork could give rise. His deepest concern was that a framework for law that, however indirectly, effectively sanctions self-interest, greed, envy, and ambition could inadvertently facilitate the gradual erosion of any solid foundation for the distinction between virtue and vice as a standard for political practice. Tocqueville writes, "*Up to now* no one has been encountered in the United States who dared to advance the maxim that everything is permitted in the interest of society" (2:475; emphasis added). America in the 1830s had so far managed to resist this "impious" conclusion, and Tocqueville is unambiguous about the reason. The salutary restraint practiced by Americans did not arise from the profound insight or clever institutional design of the Constitution, but from the indirect influence of religious belief on mores in America (2:474–75). Whereas "the law allows the American people to do everything, religion prevents them from conceiving of everything and forbids them to dare everything."[22] It was precisely because of its powerful and salutary effect on the mind and imagination of the American people that Tocqueville describes religion as "the first of their political institutions" (2:475). By itself, the political deployment of the philosophic doctrine of self-interest is both dangerous and politically unsustainable. It is only when the tendencies inherent in this principle are bounded or leavened by the mores of America's first founding

---

1961, 59), Madison explains that opposite and rival interests will supply the dearth of lofty motives because the Constitution is arranged so as to use ambition to counteract ambition (*Federalist* 51 in Rossiter 1961, 320–22).

21. Rather than depend on lofty notions of justice, Americans are motivated by the perception that it is in their own best interest to abide by the law (2:393–95; 3:918–25). In place of heroic examples of public-spiritedness, a less generous but more rational patriotism engendered by enlightenment and mingled with self-interest is widespread in America (2:384–89). The insatiable passion for well-being gives rise to commercial habits that foster characteristically American expressions of prudence: appreciation for order, regularity in mores, and sober good sense arise from a pervasive and frenetic American concern to accumulate wealth (2:384–89; 3:930–38).

22. The law permits Americans "to do everything" because law is subordinate to majority opinion. The omnipotence of the majority is the greatest danger to which Tocqueville directs the attention of readers in the 1835 edition of *Democracy in America* (esp. 2:410–15).

that Tocqueville is able to marvel at the uniquely American mixture of virtue and vice and even deem it a source of happiness.

If religion has been able to moderate some of the potentially destructive effects of Enlightenment philosophy on American politics, it is also the case that Enlightenment philosophy has been able to return the favor, especially with regard to the incendiary passions periodically ignited by religion. In his most sustained analysis of religion in the 1835 volume, Tocqueville distinguishes between "ages of fervor" and ages of "indifference" (2:485–86; see also 3:965–66). The European wars of religion that led to the Puritan settlement of the New World constitute Tocqueville's most relevant example of an age of fervor. Whereas religious persecution had deepened the understanding and zeal of the Puritans, it also gave rise to the narrow and intolerant character of their faith. For Tocqueville, "some degree of intolerance" is inseparable from the moral goods that religion brings with it (Tocqueville 1959a, 58).[23] American Puritanism, however, was initially spared the more extreme expressions of intolerance that ravaged Europe, in part because of its geographic remoteness and the territorial bounty of the New World. This external constraint was, however, powerfully supported by an internal one. As the philosophic principles of the Enlightenment founding gradually suffused the American Union, religious and political practice was increasingly shaped by the unprecedented and far-reaching Enlightenment principle that separated church and state.[24]

Toward the end of his life Tocqueville wrote that he had "always thought that there was danger even in the best of passions when they become ardent and exclusive." He goes on to explain that this is especially true of religious passion "because, pushed to a certain point, it, more than anything else, makes everything disappear that is not religion, and creates the most useless or the most dangerous citizen in the name of morality and duty" (Tocqueville 1985, 357). It was especially the influence of Enlightenment philosophy that made it possible not only for Puritanism but for a great variety of religious traditions to live together in America without the deleterious effects of the wars of religion that had wreaked havoc on European politics in the seventeenth century. While respect for this principle of Enlightenment philosophy lies behind Tocqueville's critique of the illiberal penal laws and practices of American Puritanism, he is also aware of the dangers that accompany Enlightenment

23. This is one of two sentences inexplicably left out of this letter in Lukacs's English translation of the Tocqueville-Gobineau Correspondence.

24. If John Locke (together with others) effectively pioneered a successful philosophic argument for disestablishing religion, Kessler points to elements within Puritan theology (ultimately traceable to Luther) that eventually led to the subordination of religious to secular tendencies within Puritanism (Kessler 1992).

philosophy, particularly its tendency to sow seeds of doubt that subtly incline religious believers toward religious indifference. Whereas Tocqueville is consistently critical of the deep-seated and shortsighted antipathy toward religion characteristic of the democratic revolution in France, America presented him with a different and more complicated spectacle, one that intimated the uncertain future of his American thesis.

In each of these examples, Tocqueville illustrates something of the constructive influence that biblical religion and Enlightenment philosophy have exerted on each other in the American past and could in principle continue to exert in the future. At the same time, however, these illustrations also begin to suggest something of the enormous challenge involved in maintaining the always volatile and politically messy balance between America's ancient religious and modern philosophic foundations. This challenge, it seems to me, continues to agitate contemporary American politics, under the rubric of the so-called culture wars. Is it really possible to maintain the tension inherent in Tocqueville's American thesis without succumbing to the allure of a simpler and more logically consistent—although politically disastrous—position, one that would reduce the principled basis of American politics to a single foundation by politically banishing the other? However we might be inclined to answer this question, Tocqueville's own view of this matter is clear. Toward the end of his life (1853), he wrote to his lifelong friend Louis de Kergolay, "[My] sole political passion for thirty years has been to bring about . . . the harmony of the liberal sentiment and the religious sentiment" (Tocqueville 1985, 295).

THE UNCERTAIN FUTURE OF TOCQUEVILLE'S AMERICAN THESIS

It is especially in the 1840 volume of *Democracy in America* that Tocqueville brings to light and offers guidance about the uncertain future of the American soul in both its individual and collective dimensions. He begins with an analysis of the consequences of modern rationalism on the American soul: Without ever having read Descartes, the pervasive influence of an ever-increasing equality of conditions on the minds and sentiments of Americans has effectively led them to adopt Descartes's philosophic method as their own (3:698–710). In almost all the operations of the mind, Americans unknowingly follow Descartes, both by doubting external sources of authority and by making their own individual reason the final arbiter of truth. Paradoxically, this seemingly democratic philosophic method both strengthens and weakens each individual's sense of self-worth. On the one hand, the belief that any given citizen is the equal of any and every other in some sense fortifies and elevates the intrinsic importance of each and every individual. On the other hand, the social condition of equality simultaneously erodes self-confidence and individual pride insofar as it places before each individual an inescapable psychological image of his or her own insignificance, one conjured up by the vast spectacle of innumerable others equal and similar to oneself (*semblables*).

The accompanying political danger is likely to be withdrawal from public affairs (What possible difference can I make, given the size, scale, and complexity of government?) and immersion within the smaller and more isolated sphere composed of family and friends. This novel and characteristically democratic phenomenon, which Tocqueville refers to as "individualism" (3:881–84), inclines citizens to submit to a mild and rational form of administrative bureaucracy, one quite happy to shoulder the burdens of providing peace, security, and prosperity (4:1250–51). For Tocqueville, this kind of soul-deadening administrative despotism appears to constitute the most likely path to a future of democratic servitude. Indeed, he concludes his book as a whole by painting a powerful and chilling image of precisely this prospect—one calculated to awaken any lover of liberty to the dangers inherent in an apparently benign form of government, even one compatible with the external forms of democratic election (4:1250–61).

Human servitude in any form is only possible if individuals or peoples are willing to relinquish the sense of individual dignity or pride that had originally become pervasive through the influence of Christianity and was emphatically reasserted as an article of faith in Enlightenment philosophy.[25] In Tocqueville's view, some such understanding of human dignity or pride constitutes the indispensable ground for self-respect and provides the necessary condition for the full development of human beings (4:1126). The underlying problem lies in the prospect that Americans—and, more generally, members of increasingly democratic societies—might be tempted to surrender their belief in the existence of the human soul altogether. Whereas Tocqueville considered the desire for well-being to be both natural and legitimate, he is also cognizant of the dangerous excesses to which it is prone in democratic societies. He explains that the democratic social state, unlike the aristocratic one, naturally inclines democratic peoples to perfect the useful arts, and in so doing it renders life easier, milder, and more comfortable (3:698–99). While Tocqueville admires the energy, creativity, and dynamism with which Americans characteristically seek to improve the material conditions of life (3:956–57), he also regrets

25. The second paragraph of America's most famous Enlightenment document begins not with an argument but with a ringing confession of faith: "We hold these truths to be self-evident. . . ." For Jefferson's view of the Declaration of Independence as an expression of Enlightenment thinking, see his final and most considered evaluation of its importance (letter to Roger C. Weightman, June 24, 1826, in Peterson 1984, 1517).

and expresses concern about the mediocre character of their ambition and absence of pride (4:1116–28). While ambition is far more pervasive in dynamic democratic societies than it is in relatively static aristocratic ones, the objects of ambition tend to be less lofty and far more uniform. They are almost entirely directed to economic success (pursuing what we now call the American Dream), rather than, say, the Socratic admonition to develop a healthy soul (see *Apology* 29d–e in Plato 1985).

Tocqueville explains that the tendency to become absorbed in the pursuit of material enjoyments renders democratic peoples especially susceptible to the doctrine of materialism. A philosophic teaching that reduces everything to matter and motion comports very well with the already-existing American preoccupation with material goods (3:957–60). The time, energy, and intensity with which Americans devote themselves to the pursuit of those goods, together with the simplicity of an abstract, secular, and universal doctrine that reduces everything to that which already most engages their attention, are, according to Tocqueville, likely to increase the appeal of materialism over time. Although philosophic materialism is as old as philosophy itself, Tocqueville considers it to be particularly pernicious in modern democratic nations because "it combines marvelously" with its most characteristic vice. Not only does materialism augment "with an insane fervor" the rush toward material enjoyments, but it also weakens and in some cases jeopardizes an appreciation for spiritual realities (3:957–60). Although Tocqueville speaks of the utility of religion as an antidote in this context, the most radical problem with materialism is articulated and developed in the critical notes he preserved for this chapter: a gradual and ever more pervasive belief in materialism necessarily entails the erosion or loss of belief in the existence of the human soul as the locus of individual dignity (3:958–61, esp. nn. h and k).

The growing authority of science in the modern world is in large part due to vast improvements in the quality of human life, including substantially extended life span, greater material comfort, and the generation of unprecedented prosperity for unprecedented numbers of human beings. Without in any way diminishing the magnitude of these accomplishments (for which the proper response must be one of gratitude), it is nevertheless the case that modern science also contributes to the erosion of belief in the human soul. Although it is not difficult to find scientists who believe in the existence of God or the human soul, this is not a belief that is or could be scientifically established. The strict canons of scientific progress are based on empirically verifiable research and mathematical precision, neither of which is capable of demonstrating the existence of incorporeal substances. To be clear, the problem is not science itself but rather an increasingly widespread belief accompanying its growing authority in the modern world—namely, the tendency to discredit any approach to reality that does not adhere to the remarkably fruitful, albeit reductionist, canons that guide scientific research.

The reductionist tendencies inherent in modern science are especially evident in evolutionary biology, which was beginning to get a hearing at the time in which Tocqueville was writing and currently provides the reigning paradigm for science. Although one might welcome the thick bonds it reestablishes between the human species and the rest of the animate world, taking one's bearings in a consistent way from the random character of natural selection also undermines any scientific basis for affirming the intrinsic dignity of individual members of the human species. Bigger brains and more complex neurological systems may be sufficient to differentiate human beings as a distinct species and explain such higher-order skills as language, but these quantitative differences cannot confer upon any—much less every—member of the human species a qualitatively different status, usually expressed by the inescapably ambiguous but highly useful word "dignity." Interestingly, Tocqueville's quip about the discoveries of evolutionary science does not dispute the findings but takes issue with the pride with which they are presented: "When they believe that they have sufficiently established that men are only brutes, they appear as proud as if they had demonstrated that men were gods" (3:957 and n. e). What draws Tocqueville's ire is not science but a growing belief that modern science constitutes the only mode of rational inquiry—a view that, were it to be held in a consistent way, would require knowledge of the whole of which human beings are a part. Not only are human beings far from possessing that knowledge, but for Tocqueville (like Pascal) awareness of this limitation is constitutive of what it means to be human.

Although he did not think it inevitable, Tocqueville considered philosophic materialism a grave threat to both individual and political health in the newly emerging democratic order. About those destined to live in the enlightened and free democratic societies of the future, Tocqueville writes, "It is to be feared that in the end [they] may lose the use of [their] most sublime faculties, and that by wanting to improve everything around [them], [they] may in the end degrade [themselves]" (3:957). The loss of belief in the soul, and thereby any credible or consistent religious or philosophic basis for affirming the transcendent dignity of each individual, not only diminishes the intrinsic worth of any given person but also raises a serious question about the sustainability of democratic freedom itself.

CONCLUSION

The primary aim of this essay has been to bring to light the relationship between Tocqueville's point of departure and the overarching perspective governing his study as a whole. Otherwise stated, I have attempted to understand Tocqueville's American thesis in light of the new science of politics he offers for the new and increasingly democratic world that will be inhabited by successive generations of readers. Tocqueville's new science calls attention to the Puritan combination of biblical religion and democratic-republican politics, which he presents as a seminal first cause of democratic politics in America. This claim is complemented by Tocqueville's analysis of what is usually taken to be the starting point of the American experiment, particularly the attention given by him to the "wholly new discoveries" in political science utilized by the architects of the Constitution (*Federalist* 9 in Rossiter 1961, 72; cf. Tocqueville 2010, 1:252). The attempt to trace each of these unprecedented "founding" events back to their respective first causes in religion and philosophy leads to the recognition that, for Tocqueville, Anglo-American civilization draws its inspiration from not one but two distinct sources, each of which stands in some tension with the other.[26] America is the product of both an ancient biblical faith that insists on the equal dignity of every human being, each of whom has been made in the image and likeness of God, and a modern philosophic teaching on individual rights, grounded in the natural equality and freedom characteristic of human beings in their original natural state. Tocqueville's critical appreciation for each of these rival sources of American democracy renders clear in a precise way what he admired most in the American experience—namely, the dynamic, albeit volatile, political equilibrium that had resulted from the competition between ancient biblical faith and modern philosophy for the soul of America.

The uncertain future of the American soul and democratic politics arises from the inherent instability of the dual founding brought to light in Tocqueville's analysis. Although Tocqueville was confident that the future of America and other formerly Christian nations would be democratic, he repeatedly warns his readers that democracy is compatible with either freedom or servitude. In the American case, the danger resides in the possibility that America's philosophic Enlightenment inheritance could completely overwhelm its biblical one, with dangerous consequences for both individual and political freedom. It is precisely this virulently antireligious scenario that played itself out in violent fashion in France in the eighteenth century and on a global scale during

26. Tocqueville notes not only that "philosophy and religion are two distinct things" but that they are also "natural antagonists." Philosophy pertains to what can be discovered by "the individual effort of reason" and tends toward "intellectual individualism without limits." Religion refers to what is "accepted without discussion" on the basis of authority and tends toward the acceptance of dominant opinion and "intellectual slavery." While each of these extremes is bad, Tocqueville insists that both philosophy and religion are needed and that each is in some way dependent on the other (3:705–13, esp. nn. b, e, and r).

most of the twentieth century under the influence of Marxist-inspired principles. It is the "interested" character of Tocqueville's new science, that is, his desire to provide guidance for future generations of democratic citizens, that leads him to choose a religious point of departure for his study of America, and more generally to encourage attentiveness to the salutary effects of religion—both individual and political—on the human soul throughout his study as a whole. Should adherents of biblical religion become increasingly intolerant not only of modern rationalism but of reason itself, they would inadvertently hasten the complete victory of the Enlightenment alternative by further discrediting religion among thoughtful citizens. It was to offset the emergence of intelligent (or at least clever) but soulless politics that Tocqueville, notwithstanding his own problematic relationship with Christianity, was at pains to present it as a resource capable of enlarging the soul and thereby stabilizing and ennobling politics. Rather than the spectacle of an Enlightenment philosophy tolerant of everything except serious religious conviction, clashing with a variety of "almost fierce" or "bizarre" religious sects ungrounded in nature and skeptical of reason (2:477–78, 3:939–41), Tocqueville encourages readers to consider, on the one hand, the enduring value and benefit of religious faith that is open to reason and grounded in a comprehensive view of nature (one that includes human beings) and, on the other, a generally enlightened and philosophically informed public capable of appreciating the salutary influences of religious belief on the souls and politics of citizens.

As Tocqueville indicates toward the end of his study, if he had considered the path to democratic servitude inevitable, he would have limited himself "to groaning in secret" rather than giving over 10 years of his life to writing a book on the nature and possible futures of democracy (4:1277). He explains that he has attempted to bring to light "the most formidable" and "least foreseen" challenges to the future of democracy, precisely because he does "*not* believe them insurmountable" (4:1277; emphasis added). Although he did not think it possible for the human race to be "entirely independent or perfectly slave," Tocqueville affirms that "within these vast limits" both human beings and peoples are "powerful and free." Whereas neither nations nor peoples will be able to turn back the rising tide of democracy for the foreseeable future, Tocqueville concludes that it does depend on them to determine whether the uncertain democratic future will lead "to servitude or liberty, to enlightenment or barbarity, to prosperity or misery" (4:1285).

REFERENCES

Aristotle. 1979. "Ethica Nichomachea." Ed. J. Bywater. Oxford: Oxford University Press.

Bacon, Francis. 2001. *The Advancement of Learning*. Ed. G. W. Kitchen. Philadelphia: Dry.

Ceaser, James. 1985. "Alexis de Tocqueville on Political Science, Political Culture, and the Role of the Intellectual." *American Political Science Review* 79:656–72.

———. 1990. *Liberal Democracy and Political Science*. Baltimore: Johns Hopkins University Press.

———. 2011. "Alexis de Tocqueville and the Two-Founding Thesis." *Review of Politics* 73:219–43.

Goldstein, Doris S. 1975. *Trial of Faith: Religion and Politics in Tocqueville's Thought*. New York: Elsevier.

Hinckley, Cynthia J. 1990. "Tocqueville on Religious Truth and Political Necessity." *Polity* 23 (1): 39–52.

Jardin, André. 1998. *Tocqueville: A Biography*. Trans. Lydia Davis with Robert Hemenway. Baltimore: Johns Hopkins University Press.

Kessler, Sanford. 1992. "Tocqueville's Puritans: Christianity and the American Founding." *Journal of Politics* 54 (3): 776–92.

———. 1994. *Tocqueville's Civil Religion: American Christianity and the Prospects for Freedom*. Albany, NY: SUNY Press.

Koritansky, John C. 1990/2010. *Alexis de Tocqueville and the New Science of Politics*. Durham, NC: Carolina Academic Press.

Lawler, Peter. 1993. *The Restless Mind: Alexis de Tocqueville on the Origin and Perpetuation of Human Liberty*. Lanham, MD: Rowman & Littlefield.

Lukacs, John. 1964. "The Last Days of A. de Tocqueville." *Catholic Historical Review* 50 (July): 155–70.

Manent, Pierre. 1996. *Tocqueville and the Nature of Democracy*. Trans. John Waggoner. Lanham, MD: Rowman & Littlefield.

Mitchell, Joshua. 1995. *The Fragility of Freedom: Tocqueville on Religion, Democracy, and the American Future*. Chicago: University of Chicago Press.

Nietzsche, Friedrich. 1967. *On the Genealogy of Morals*. Trans. Walter Kaufmann and R. J. Hollingdale. New York: Random House.

Peterson, Merrill D., ed. 1984. *Thomas Jefferson: Writings*. New York: Library of America.

Plato. 1985. "Apologia Socratis." In *Platonis Opera*, vol. 1, ed. John Burnet. Oxford: Oxford University Press.

———. 1986. "Poleiteia." In *Platonis Opera*, vol. 4, ed. John Burnet. Oxford: Oxford University Press.

Rédier, Antione. 1925. *Comme Disait M. de Tocqueville*. Paris: Librairie Académique Perrin et Cie.

Rossiter, Clinton, ed. 1961. *The Federalist Papers*. New York: Penguin.

Schleifer, James. 2014. "Tocqueville, Religion, and *Democracy in America*: Some Essential Questions." *American Political Thought* 3 (2): 254–72.

Strauss, Leo. 1989. *The Rebirth of Classical Political Rationalism: An Introduction to the Thought of Leo Strauss*. Ed. Thomas Pangle. Chicago: University of Chicago Press.

Tocqueville, Alexis de. 1959a. *Correspondance D'Alexis de Tocqueville et d'Arthur de Gobineau*. Ed. M. Degros. In *Tocqueville: Oeuvres Complète*, vol. 9, ed. J.-P. Mayer. Paris: Librairie Gallimard.

———. 1959b. *The European Revolution and Correspondence with Gobineau*. Ed. and trans. John Lukacs. Garden City, NY: Doubleday.

———. 1985. *Selected Letters on Politics and Society*. Ed. Roger Boesche. Trans. Roger Boesche and James Taupin. Berkeley: University of California Press.

———. 1990. *De La Démocratie en Amérique: Première edition historico-critique*. Ed. Eduardo Nolla. Paris: Librairie Philosophique J. Vrin.

———. 1998. *The Old Regime and the French Revolution*. Ed. François Furet and Françoise Mélonio. Trans. Alan S. Kahan. Chicago: University of Chicago Press.

———. 2000. *Democracy in America*. Ed. and trans. Harvey C. Mansfield and Delba Winthrop. Chicago: University of Chicago Press.

———. 2010. *Democracy in America: Bilingual French-English Edition*. 4 vols. Ed. Eduardo Nolla. Trans. James T. Schleifer. Indianapolis: Liberty Fund Press.

Zunz, Oliver, ed. 2010. *Alexis de Tocqueville and Gustave de Beaumont in America: Their Friendship and Their Travels*. Trans. Arthur Goldhammer. Charlottesville: University of Virginia Press.

Zunz, Oliver, and Alan S. Kahan. 2002. *The Tocqueville Reader: A Life in Letters and Politics*. Oxford: Blackwell.

Part II

TOCQUEVILLE'S CONTEXTS

Tocqueville, Religion, and *Democracy in America*: Some Essential Questions

JAMES T. SCHLEIFER

ABSTRACT

Religion played a central role in Tocqueville's thinking and writing, and it was one of the major features of American society and culture as described by Tocqueville. This paper draws upon the working papers and text of his *Democracy in America* to revisit some of the key questions he asked about religion and to raise a few further questions that emerge from his responses. This paper also demonstrates how Tocqueville sometimes trimmed his opinions and arguments in order to appeal more effectively to his intended audience, the French reader.

Religion is not often the central theme of books or articles about Tocqueville.[1] And gatherings on Tocqueville usually examine a broad range of topics, or focus on such familiar ground as Tocqueville's views on centralization, or despotism, or liberty, or examine some of Tocqueville's key sources, such as Montesquieu or the *doctrinaires*. Religion plays, nonetheless, a central role in his thinking and writing. The following remarks draw upon the working papers and text of Tocqueville's *Democracy in America* to revisit some of the questions he asked about religion and to raise a few further questions that emerge from his responses.

The 1835 portion of Tocqueville's *Democracy* originally appeared in two volumes. The first primarily surveys American political institutions; the second examines selected civil institutions, especially in terms of their political roles. In an initial sketch, however, Tocqueville planned not two but three major divisions for his 1835 work: "*political society*—relations between federal and state governments and [between] the citizens of the Union and of each state; *civil*

James T. Schleifer is professor emeritus of history and former dean of Gill Library, College of New Rochelle (jschleifer@cnr.edu).

1. Although religion is not the most common topic in Tocqueville scholarship, a number of books and articles on the theme have been written; see Eduardo Nolla's extensive bibliography in Tocqueville (2010, 4:1397–1430).

[American Political Thought, vol. 3, issue 2, Fall 2014]

society—relations of the citizens among themselves; [and] *religious society*—relations between God and the members of society, and of the religious sects among themselves" (Schleifer 2000, 9). In another early outline, he elaborated: "Religious society. Nomenclature of the various sects—from Catholicism to the sect that is furthest from it. Quakers, Methodists—point out what is antisocial in the doctrine of Quakers, Unitarians. Relations among the sects. Freedom of worship—toleration: in the legal respect; with respect to mores. Catholicism. Place of religion in the political order and its degree of influence on American society" (Tocqueville 2010, 2:478 n. P).

For reasons that remain uncertain, this third segment—religious society—faded as the writing of *Democracy in America* began. In the end, Tocqueville followed a more scattered approach to the topic, which appeared as the focus of several chapters or subchapters in both the 1835 and 1840 portions of his book. But religion remained an essential theme in his description of American society and in his consideration of democracy more generally.

Tocqueville began *Democracy in America* with the premise that the advance of democracy, or equality of condition, was long-term, inevitable and providential. He admitted that when he contemplated this cosmic drama, he felt a sort of religious terror (Tocqueville 2010, 1:14). From the first, Tocqueville understood the course of history as divinely ordained and confessed his own religious sensibilities. Democracy, he told his readers, brought its own potential benefits and dangers. The moral responsibility for promoting the first and avoiding the second rested with human beings. A profoundly moral and religious vision of human nature marked his assumptions; echoing Pascal, he believed that human beings possess an innate religious impulse and bear a God-given moral responsibility for their choices and actions in the world. He concluded his book by observing that God favored democracy because it was more just; this stood as Tocqueville's ultimate endorsement of the democratic revolution. So even the broad shape of his argument reveals how closely religion fits into his thinking.

During the American journey from May 1831 to February 1832, Tocqueville made several other fundamental discoveries about religion that remained remarkably fixed points in his mind. "The religious state of the American people," he observed in an early letter home, "may be the most interesting thing to study here" (Zunz 2010, 49–53).[2] The topic quickly became one of the most familiar subjects of his reflections while in the New World, appearing repeatedly in his letters home to family and friends and in conversations and

2. See esp. letter to Louis de Kergorlay, June 29, 1831 (Zunz 2010, 50), and see Tocqueville (2010, 2:479).

comments recorded in his travel diaries. To learn more and to test his first impressions, Tocqueville sought out a considerable number of clergy, including Catholic and Anglican priests and Presbyterian and Unitarian ministers, for discussion of the role, current state and likely future in America of certain religious groups and of religion in general. He also attended Roman Catholic, Unitarian, Quaker, Methodist, Shaker, and possibly Anglican religious services.[3]

The working papers for *Democracy in America*, including his journey notebooks and letters, contain detailed accounts of these and other American religious denominations, and lengthy reflections about how both Protestantism and Catholicism relate to democratic values. As he drafted the first part of his book in 1833 and 1834, he also conducted impressive research in the historical sources of colonial America, reading in particular about the role of Puritanism during the founding and early years of New England.[4] The breadth of his experience and knowledge is impressive and should be acknowledged. What did he learn from such research?

Within a few days of his arrival in the New World, Tocqueville recorded some first impressions, including a few queries about religion. "By and large [the Americans] seem to be a religious people. It is clear that no one thinks of ridiculing religious practices, and that the goodness and even the truth of religion are universally admitted in theory. How far is their life regulated by their doctrine? What is the real power of religious principle over their soul? How can the variety of sects not breed indifference? . . . That is what remains to be known" (Tocqueville 1960, 274). Over the next 9 months he would never let go of these questions.

THE POWER OF RELIGION IN AMERICA

Tocqueville treated one feature of religion in America not as a question, but as a fact. In his book he admitted: "When I arrived in the United States, it was the religious aspect of the country that first struck my eyes" (Tocqueville 2010, 2:479; also see 2:468–78). "Religion," he wrote in a travel diary, "still has great sway over people's souls here" (Zunz 2010, 337). It enjoyed enormous influence, both direct and indirect. The extent of Sabbath observance, the closing down of American cities on Sundays, astonished him (Tocqueville 2010, 2:662–65 n. E). And he soon discovered another special feature of religion in America. In his journey notes, Tocqueville began to describe an "intimate mixture of re-

3. See, e.g., app. 3, "Sects in America," in Tocqueville (2010, 4:1360–64).

4. See Tocqueville's own n. F (2010, 2:666–74), and Nolla's bibliography, "Works Used by Tocqueville" (4:1377–95).

ligion and the spirit of liberty." In the United States, he realized, religion strongly supported liberty. It exercised a direct influence on politics by restraining political passions, by setting limits to social and political innovations, and especially by supporting democratic principles and institutions. The prevailing religious opinion was resolutely republican and democratic (Tocqueville 2010, 1:69, 2:479; Zunz 2010, 314).

This union of religion and liberty became one of Tocqueville's favorite themes. After describing the Puritan founding of New England, he wrote: "I have already said enough to reveal Anglo-American civilization in its true light. It is the product (and this point of departure must always be kept in mind) of two perfectly distinct elements that elsewhere are often at odds. But in America, these two have been successfully blended, in a way, and marvelously combined. I mean the *spirit of religion* and the *spirit of liberty*" (Tocqueville 2010, 1:69; see also 2:479).

HOW WERE RELIGION, LIBERTY AND DEMOCRACY RELATED?

The indirect influence of religion was even more significant. It inculcated morality and enforced a strict code of (at least outward) religious belief and moral behavior (see Tocqueville 2010, 2:468–78; esp. 474–75). His hosts repeatedly told him that democratic liberty required healthy private and public mores, and that good mores required religion. By shaping mores, religion in America upheld liberty. Mr. Richard, a prominent Presbyterian, declared: "I do not believe that a republic can exist without morals, and I do not believe that a people can have morals when it has no religion. I judge then that the maintenance of the religious spirit is one of our greatest political interests" (Tocqueville 1960, 207).

Tocqueville carried these ideas directly into the opening pages of his 1835 book. "You cannot establish," he asserted, "the reign of liberty without that of mores, nor found mores without beliefs" (Tocqueville 2010, 1:25). In a draft he elaborated: "When democracy comes with mores and beliefs, it leads to liberty. When it comes with moral and religious anarchy, it leads to despotism" (117 n. D).

But how did religion shape mores? What was the mechanism? In a draft for the 1835 portion, Tocqueville announced his thesis. He cited the action of religion on women, and remarked: "It is the women who make mores" (Tocqueville 2010, 2:484 n. U). And the 1835 text declared: "In the United States religion . . . directs mores, and it is by regulating the family that it works to regulate the State. I do not doubt for an instant that the great severity of mores that is noticed in the United States has its primary source in beliefs. . . . [Religion] rules with sovereign power over the soul of the woman, and it is the woman who shapes the mores" (2:473). In 1840, he would devote several chapters on the family and on women in America to this premise (4:1031–67).

HOW DID RELIGION IN AMERICA MAINTAIN ITS POWER?

In the working papers and text of his *Democracy*, Tocqueville repeatedly wondered how to account for the success of the American republic, despite its flaws. His list of essential explanations always included the religious heritage and spirit of the Americans. The influence—both direct and indirect—of religion in the United States could not be overlooked.

So religion in America remained strikingly powerful, but what preserved its strength? The cause, Tocqueville heard repeatedly during his journey, was the careful separation of church and state in the United States. For a Frenchman coming from a society where religious power and political power had long been closely intertwined and where the forces of religion and liberty were then at war, this was an unexpected lesson.

In one of his travel notebooks, Tocqueville recorded conversations with John Spencer of Canandaigua, New York, one of his most influential sources, and with Father Mullon, a Catholic priest then serving as a missionary to Native Americans in Michigan. What, he asked, explained the influence of religion in America? Tocqueville's two informants spoke, first, of removing clergy from any temporal power and, second, of providing no special protection for any particular religious group. Declaring that governmental support was harmful to religion, Father Mullon summed up the argument: "[The] less religion and its ministers are mixed up with government, the less they are involved in political debate, the more influential religious ideas will become" (Zunz 2010, 221–22).[5] From Richard Stewart of Baltimore, Tocqueville learned that although clergy could technically be elected to public office, this rarely happened. "People," Stewart declared, "generally prefer to keep the clergy in their churches and separate from the state" (257).[6]

As Tocqueville realized, this refusal to provide official support for any particular religious group was intended to strengthen religion. The goal of a policy of separating church and state was not more civil tranquility, but greater religious influence within the larger society. Tocqueville also knew that most Americans, including many of the clergy, upheld freedom of worship and free-

5. For Spencer, see Zunz (2010, 220) and see conversation with Mr. Guilleman (279).

6. Compare conversations with Joel Poinsett (Zunz 2010, 286) and with Wainwright and Smith (Zunz 2010, 330–31).

dom of conscience, values that went beyond simple rejection of a religious establishment.

In the 1835 *Democracy*, Tocqueville eloquently condemned "the intimate union of politics and religion," which was, he argued, the main cause for the weakness of Christianity in Europe. "[There] Christianity allowed itself to be intimately united with the powers of the earth. Today these powers are falling and Christianity is as though buried beneath their debris. It is a living thing that someone wanted to bind to the dead; cut the ties that hold it and it will rise again" (Tocqueville 2010, 2:487–88). In the 1840 *Democracy* Tocqueville argued even more emphatically in favor of separation of church and state. "[As] for State religions, I have always thought that if sometimes they could temporarily serve the interests of political power, they always sooner or later become fatal to the Church. . . . I feel so convinced of the nearly inevitable dangers that beliefs run when their interpreters mingle in public affairs, and I am so persuaded that Christianity must at all cost be maintained within the new democracies, that I would prefer to chain priests within the sanctuary than to allow them out of it" (3:961–62).

In a letter to Paul Clamorgan dated January 1, 1839, when Tocqueville was making the final revisions of the 1840 portion of his book, he was equally direct: "I respect religion, but . . . I have never been nor will I ever be a man of the clergy. I honor the priest in the church, but I will always put him outside of government, if I have any influence whatsoever in affairs. That is a maxim that I preached quite loudly in my book" (Tocqueville 1985, 132).

Democracy in America cites and criticizes two different examples of the religious power moving beyond its sphere and intruding in the political and social realm: Puritanism and Islam. In the 1835 half, despite his admiration for the religious fervor and democratic ideas of the Puritans, Tocqueville found many of their efforts to legislate behavior offensive; such things, he wrote, "shame the human spirit" (Tocqueville 2010, 1:62–64). In 1840, he was even more severe, condemning Islam for setting forth not only religious doctrine but also specific social and political arrangements and even scientific theories. That intrusive nature, he stated bluntly, disqualified Islam from any role in modern democratic society (3:746–47).

So perhaps we are able to summarize what Tocqueville had in mind when he advocated separation of church and state: no established or state religion; no privileged position for any religious group; and no political office or temporal power for the clergy. More broadly, he meant that the religious powers must not be tied in any way to the political powers; that the clergy and interpreters of religion should not get directly involved in public affairs or political matters; that religion should not try to legislate particular social behavior or claim to determine scientific truth; and that all believers should enjoy freedom of worship and freedom of conscience. In all of this, his purpose remained clear; he wanted to preserve, strengthen and even revive the influence of religion in democratic society.

Nonetheless, he leaves his readers, and perhaps his contemporary American readers in particular, with a puzzle. Religion, he argued, plays an essential political role and is a major political institution. Yet the religious world must not get entangled in the political world; the interpreters of religion must stay out of public affairs. How so? Tocqueville seemed to argue that an indirect influence was sufficient and acceptable. Religious faith could attempt to sway public attitudes and opinions, but only indirectly by addressing moral concerns and upholding moral standards. But even this argument does not end the difficulty. Moral positions on such matters as when human life begins or what marriage means differ markedly, depending on religious identity. When establishing public policy, how can such profound differences of moral judgment among diverse religious groups be reconciled? The church and state dilemma was not so easily solved.

Tocqueville's consistent advocacy of separation of church and state and his concurrent desire to blend the spirit of religion and the spirit of liberty set him and his political program apart. As he explained in his 1835 introduction, he wanted to bring together open-minded men of good will, including both those believers who were skeptical about democracy and those lovers of liberty who were skeptical about religion. This effort to end the division between democracy and faith that prevailed in France counted among the primary purposes of Tocqueville's *Democracy*.

WERE AMERICANS TRUE BELIEVERS?

Religious toleration in the United States quickly caught Tocqueville's attention as well. As he searched for explanations, he wondered about "the real power of religious principle" over the American soul and asked himself whether the constant proliferation of religious groups ultimately led to a sort of bland neutrality. He never came to definitive conclusions; his book would present nuanced judgments about both the depth of faith and the reasons for toleration in America.

During his voyage, he heard from John Spencer that in the United States religious tolerance was a matter more of necessity than of principle. It was due "primarily [to] the fact that there are so many denominations (the number is virtually unlimited). If two religions were to square off, we'd cut each other's throats. But since no denomination has a majority, tolerance is essential for all"

(Zunz 2010, 220; also see Tocqueville 2010, 4:1351–52). Tocqueville also knew about fierce anti-Catholic prejudices in America (Zunz 2010, 157–60). So perhaps Spencer's grim comments were not far off the mark.

Or did toleration in the United States reflect instead a lack of belief? Very early in his journey Tocqueville recognized "the strictness of religious practice" in America, but suspected a shallow religious faith. "This so-called tolerance, which in my opinion is nothing but crass indifference, is carried so far," he declared to Kergorlay in a letter dated June 29, 1831, "that in public institutions such as prisons and reform schools for young delinquents, ministers of seven or eight different sects preach one after another to the same congregation. I asked how the men and boys who belong to one sect receive the minister of another. Inevitably, the answer was that since the various preachers deal only in moral commonplaces, they do one another no harm. Furthermore, it is clear that, generally speaking, religion here has no profound effect on the soul" (Zunz 2010, 50–53; cf. 157–60). Whether the cause of religious toleration was commitment to freedom of worship, or necessity, or indifference, it did exist in America, at least outwardly. And Tocqueville faithfully described it to his readers in the 1835 *Democracy* (Tocqueville 2010, 2:472–73).

But the question of faith remained. Did Americans truly believe or did they practice religion out of social expectation and the pressure of opinion? In October 1831, Tocqueville asked James Brown, a lawyer and wealthy planter from Louisiana, for his opinion. "Does [the religious principle in this country] exist only on the surface? Or is it deeply rooted in people's hearts? Is it a belief or a political doctrine?" Brown replied: "I believe that for the majority religion is a respectable and useful thing rather than a demonstrated truth. Deep in people's souls I think there is a good deal of indifference to dogma. In church it is never discussed; morality is the issue" (Zunz 2010, 251). Tocqueville remained undecided. In the margin of his working manuscript, he admitted: "I am not sure that the Americans are convinced of the truth of religion, but I am sure that they are convinced of its utility" (Tocqueville 2010, 2:472 n. G).

In his text he carefully distinguished what could be observed from what would always remain unknown. "You are free to think that a certain number of Americans, in the worship they give to God, follow their habits more than their convictions. In the United States, moreover, the sovereign is religious, and consequently hypocrisy must be common; but America is still the place in the world where the Christian religion has most retained true power over souls" (Tocqueville 2010, 2:473). And: "Among the Anglo-Americans, some profess Christian dogma because they believe them; others, because they fear not appearing to believe them" (2:474). He concluded: "I do not know if all Americans have faith in their religion, for who can read the recesses of the heart?

But I am sure that they believe it necessary for maintaining republican institutions" (2:475).

WHAT DANGERS DID RELIGION IN AMERICA POSE?

Despite Tocqueville's praise for the power of religion in the United States, his impressions were not entirely favorable. Buried in letters written while in America is a fleeting acknowledgment that remnants of an established church still existed in Massachusetts (Zunz 2010, 182–83). A bit incredulous and resistant to a fact so contrary to one of his core arguments, Tocqueville refrained from any hint at such a religious arrangement in the pages of his *Democracy*. Perhaps what he feared most was the abuse of the power of religious opinion over thought and behavior. Antireligious books, he observed, were rare in the United States. The young who were unbelievers soon learned to keep quiet. And the court testimony of witnesses who refused to swear an oath on the Bible was dismissed as untrustworthy. In his 1835 text he pointedly criticized religion for opening the door to tyranny of the majority (Tocqueville 2010, 2:418–20). If in his book Tocqueville praised the power of religion to shape mores, he also warned against the potential abuses of control by the believing majority over free thought and expression.

As we have seen, Tocqueville suspected that much of American religious faith was lukewarm. But he had another, quite opposite concern as well. After witnessing the Shakers, hearing the fire and brimstone preaching of a Methodist minister, and learning about camp meetings in the West, Tocqueville began to wonder about religious excesses in America.

In January 1832, in his travel diaries, he noted that in the South religious feeling was more intense than in the North. "In the North," he was told, "you have religion; [in the South] you have fanaticism. The Methodists are the dominant sect" (Zunz 2010, 282). Much of American Protestantism, Tocqueville charged, tended to spawn increasingly bizarre sects and produce strange rituals and behaviors; it threatened to descend into absurdity. He took this message directly into his 1840 text where he warned against the dangers of excessive spiritualism and religious madness among the Americans (Tocqueville 2010, 3:939–41). The religious anarchy and extremism, he observed, was enough to drive many thoughtful Americans into the arms of Catholicism. In contemporary America, Tocqueville leaves readers with still another puzzle. He described religion as a restraint on excessive political passions, but worried about religious fanaticism. What would he say about religious faith that sometimes today acts as a spur to political extremism?

Tocqueville had yet another sharp criticism of American Protestantism. In August 1831, while visiting Quebec and observing the care provided by the

Catholic clergy, he reflected on what he had seen in the United States. "Here [in Quebec], the priest is truly the pastor of his flock and not an entrepreneur in the religious industry, like most American ministers" (Zunz 2010, 317).[7] With this remark, Tocqueville implied that among American Protestants, religion had largely become simply another business within a wider commercial society.

Nor did he spare American Catholicism. Although the portrait presented in his published text is very positive, his travel notebooks and letters home offer two serious rebukes to the Catholic clergy in America. First, he detected a deeply antidemocratic attitude. "I have spoken with a good many priests; their democracy is purely skin-deep. One senses in the depths of their souls a great contempt for the rule of the multitude and a great desire to rule and direct society" (Zunz 2010, 158). And, second, he found considerable intolerance. "I have a feeling that their dogma on freedom of conscience is almost the same as in Europe, and I am not sure that they would not persecute the others [the Protestant denominations] if they became the more powerful group" (51).

Tocqueville had even broader concerns about the influence of religion. He did not always praise religion as the handmaiden of liberty. In the 1835 *Democracy*, he explicitly disagreed with Montesquieu's idea that fear was the principle of despotism. Tocqueville asserted instead that religion, not fear, sustained despotic nations (Tocqueville 2010, 1:158–59). He worried, as we have just noted, about religious excesses in America, but he cautioned more generally against extreme religious passions of any sort. "I have always thought that there was danger even in the best of passions when they become ardent and exclusive. I do not make an exception of the passion for religion; I would even put it in front, because, pushed to a certain point, it . . . creates the most useless or the most dangerous citizens in the name of morality and duty" (Tocqueville 1985, 357).

As this later letter makes clear, Tocqueville harbored yet another telling complaint against religion, especially as preached and practiced in his own country. He believed religion had the responsibility to teach men and women morality. And for him, moral behavior involved both private and public virtues. Too exclusively attuned to private morality, religion often failed, according to Tocqueville, to uphold and honor individual duties toward public life, toward others, and toward society as a whole (Tocqueville 1985, 338–39).[8]

7. Also see letter to Kergorlay, June 29, 1831 (Zunz 2010, 51).

8. See letter to Kergorlay, August 4, 1857 (Tocqueville 1985, 356–57); also see Tocqueville (2010, 2:472).

So religion could pose serious threats to democratic societies. It could be oppressive; extreme; secretly opposed to democratic values; and unable or unwilling to teach the public virtues that made citizens.

WHAT ARE THE FUNCTIONS OF RELIGION?

Tocqueville's *Democracy in America* sets forth a catalog of the essential roles or functions of religion in democratic society. We have already touched on some of them. First, religion fosters healthy mores. But what did Tocqueville mean by good mores? Within a few weeks of his arrival in the United States, he wrote to Kergorlay: "To my knowledge, clearly, this country still has a deeper reservoir of Christian religion than any other country in the world, and I have no doubt that this mentality continues to influence the political regime. It gives a moral and disciplined coloration to ideas. It prevents the spirit of innovation from getting too far out of line" (Zunz 2010, 53). This concept of discipline and morality, both inspired by religion, was echoed by Joel Poinsett in January 1832, when he described the direct influence of religion in America on politics as the softening of political passions and its indirect influence as the teaching of morality (286). In the working papers and text of the 1835 *Democracy*, Tocqueville repeated this emphasis, usually mentioning "habits of restraint" (Tocqueville 2010, 2:474–75; also see 1:69–70, 3:744–45, 3:954–62, 3:965–68) and high standards of moral behavior, both private and public.

In 1840, he reiterated these points, but broadened his argument (see esp. Tocqueville 2010, 3:742–53). Religion, he stated, provided an intellectual framework for answering the most difficult spiritual questions facing each human being, thus freeing individuals to pursue the ordinary matters in their lives. For Tocqueville, authority in religious matters seemed desirable, even necessary. "I doubt that man can ever bear complete religious independence and full political liberty at the same time" (3:744–45). Religion, in his view, also had an essential teaching function; as we saw, he expected it to teach not only private morality, but also the public virtues that made good citizens: social conscience, shared responsibility, and a willingness to participate in civil life. And by promoting nonmaterial goals, a sense of duty toward others and toward the wider society, and an awareness of the future, religious faith helped to counterbalance several of the worst democratic dangers: materialism, individualism, and a shortsighted focus on the present and on immediate satisfactions. In all of these ways, religion fostered the healthy mores most essential to liberty. Even more broadly, religion, in Tocqueville's view, served as a necessary social bond; religion provided the shared values, beliefs, attitudes and behavior that defined a true community.

By inculcating healthy mores, religion supported liberty. But Tocqueville asserted as well that religion functioned as a spur to liberty. Thinking of early New England, Tocqueville pointed out that religious convictions often fed the drive for freedom. "Nearly all the efforts that the moderns have made toward liberty they have made because of the need for manifesting or defending their religious opinions. It is religious passion that pushed the Puritans to America and led them to want to govern themselves there" (Tocqueville 1985, 192).

An emphasis on the functions of religion should not be interpreted as an assertion that Tocqueville's treatment of religion was essentially utilitarian. He clearly recognized that religious faith was useful, but his argument went beyond that observation. Tocqueville wrote as a moralist deeply influenced by Pascal. Religion, he declared, "is as natural to the human heart as hope itself. It is by a type of mental aberration and with the help of a kind of moral violence exercised over their own nature, that men remove themselves from religious beliefs; an irresistible inclination brings them back to beliefs. Unbelief is an accident; faith alone is the permanent state of humanity" (Tocqueville 2010, 2:482; also see 3:940, 3:959–61).

For Tocqueville, the moralist, religious faith arose out of innate human needs; it addressed the human condition and met the restlessness and yearnings of the human soul. The role of religion was not simply utilitarian, but profoundly spiritual.

HOW DO CHRISTIANITY, CATHOLICISM AND PROTESTANTISM RELATE TO DEMOCRACY?

Tocqueville began with the premise that every religion is paired with a particular political opinion or stance; each one has a natural affinity with a given political condition (Tocqueville 2010, 2:467). *Democracy in America* contains a strong defense of Christianity as the religion most compatible with democracy. In his working papers and book, he repeatedly presented Christianity as the source for both liberty and equality, ascribing to Christianity the first insistence on the fundamental spiritual equality of all human beings and praising it for the universal scope of its message.[9]

His opinion about Protestantism was more mixed. While in the United States, he consistently described American Protestantism as an eminently republican and democratic religion; the affinity between Protestantism and de-

9. See Tocqueville (2010, 2:467–73, 3:742–53; esp. 2:468–69, 2:482 n. U); also see letter to Arthur de Gobineau, January 24, 1857 (Tocqueville 1985, 343–44).

mocracy seemed clear (Tocqueville 2010, 1:75 n. D).[10] In the pages of the 1835 *Democracy*, however, he presented a somewhat divided judgment. On the one hand, he asserted: "Most of English America . . . brought to the New World a Christianity that I cannot portray better than by calling it democratic and republican: this will singularly favor the establishment of the republic and of democracy in public affairs. From the outset, politics and religion found themselves in accord, and they have not ceased to be so since" (Tocqueville 2010, 2:467; also see 1:69, 3:699 n. E, 3:702 nn. K and M). But elsewhere in his text he identified Protestantism as the religious orientation that carried "men much less toward equality than toward independence" (Tocqueville 2010, 2: 469). Tocqueville's father, reading the working manuscript, noticed the contradiction and urged his son to drop the offending statement; the advice was rejected however, and the sentence remained.

A different sort of debate took place as Tocqueville weighed the compatibility of Catholicism with democracy. Was Catholicism democratic by nature, and could it effectively adapt to democratic times and values? In his travel notes, letters home and other working papers, Tocqueville's answers were far more uncertain than the position he would present to his readers in his published text. As we noted, Tocqueville, while in America, found many Catholic priests deeply antidemocratic. And in letters home he described Catholicism as a kind of absolute monarchy or aristocratic republic, emphatically not the natural religious partner of a democratic republic or even of a representative or constitutional monarchy (see, e.g., Zunz 2010, 157–60). In a letter written to his friend Francisque de Corcelle after the publication of the 1840 *Democracy*, he was even more critical. "Catholicism, I am afraid, will never adopt the new society. It will never forget the position that it had in the old one and every time that [it] is given some powers, it will hasten to abuse them. I will say it only to you. But I say it to you, because I want to have you enter into my most secret thought" (Tocqueville 2010, 3:755 n. E).

Little of this private opinion would appear in the pages of his book, where he observed that, in America, Catholics and their priests were at once fervently devout and firmly democratic. "I think that it is wrong," he declared, "to regard the Catholic religion as a natural enemy of democracy. Among the different Christian doctrines, Catholicism seems to me on the contrary one of the most favorable to equality of conditions. Among Catholics, . . . the priest alone rises above the faithful; everything is equal below him. . . . Catholicism is like an absolute monarchy. Remove the prince, and conditions there are more

10. See conversation with John Spencer (Zunz 2010, 220).

equal than in republics" (Tocqueville 2010, 2:469–70; also see 2:467–71). But even in the margin of his working manuscript, his message remained ambiguous: "Catholicism favors the spirit of equality in the manner of absolute power. It places one man beyond all rank and leaves all the others mingled together in the crowd" (2:469 n. B; also see 3:755 n. E). A resemblance to absolute power was hardly a ringing endorsement of the democratic nature of Catholicism.

WHAT IS THE FUTURE OF RELIGION IN AMERICA AND IN OTHER DEMOCRATIC SOCIETIES?

During his American journey, Tocqueville quickly arrived at a prediction of the future of religion in the United States. In an early letter to Kergorlay he wrote that American Protestantism would move toward the cold, pure reason of Unitarianism (or as Tocqueville also called it, deism or natural religion; Zunz 2010, 50–53, 244, 245–46, 256–57, 258–60, 292). Those Americans who needed faith and spiritual sustenance would convert to Catholicism. He repeatedly told family and friends about the remarkable growth of Catholicism in the United States, due to both conversion and immigration. He foresaw a religious landscape in America divided between Unitarianism (or deism) and Roman Catholicism. In the 1840 *Democracy*, if Tocqueville dropped any mention of his expectations about Unitarianism and predicted instead the rise of unbelief and pantheism as the alternatives to Christianity, he did not fail to write about the progress of Catholicism (Tocqueville 2010, 2:468, 3:754–56, 3:757–58).

But he had broader hopes and expectations about the future of religion in the age of democracy. Although religion, by shaping mores, profoundly influenced democratic nations, Tocqueville did not abandon one of his fundamental convictions: the social state modifies all areas of a society, including the realm of religion and faith. Democracy would, therefore, inevitably transform religion; and religion, he argued, must in turn adapt to democratic values. The influence between religion and democracy moved in both directions. In the working papers and text of his book, Tocqueville carefully described how religion would have to change in democratic times (Tocqueville 2010, 3:750–53).

In a short chapter, entitled "Religious Eloquence or Preaching," drafted but never included in the final text, Tocqueville specifically examined how democracy would reshape religious expression. "Not able to change the substance of Christianity, which is eternal, [democracy] at least modifies the language and the form" (Tocqueville 2010, 3:859–60 n. M). In the piece he mentioned an oratorical style marked by greater informality; a move away from traditional ecclesiastical authorities; an appeal to contemporary ideas, events and voices;

and an effort to engage listeners on their own everyday terms. His essay in fact described the democratic transformation not only of the language of the pulpit, but also of religious approaches, forms, and practices.

What did Tocqueville hope for religion in democratic times? He wanted religion to remain strong and urged men of religious faith to rally to the side of democracy as a divinely ordained fact. But beyond those key desires, he hoped for a religious renewal in France. How to achieve such a rebirth of religion? Tocqueville provided at least three answers. First, religious powers and political powers had to be kept strictly apart; separation of church and state had to be respected. Second, religion had to learn to adapt appropriately to democratic ideas, attitudes, assumptions, preferences and behavior; the days of an unchanging church, rigidly refusing to bend to the contemporary world, were over. And third, he urged those who govern democratic nations to set an example; by looking toward the future and acting with a long-term perspective, they would subtly encourage the governed to return to an essentially religious viewpoint (Tocqueville 2010, 2:485–88; esp. 487–88). Of course, the last of these prescriptions was almost embarrassingly weak, and Tocqueville recognized that only God could truly bring about a religious revival. Nonetheless, his longing for a renewal of religious faith, perhaps on a personal as well as on a social level, needs to be acknowledged.

DID TOCQUEVILLE GRASP AMERICAN PROTESTANTISM?

We have already observed that, for Tocqueville, American Protestantism was headed toward Unitarianism, which he described as deism or natural religion, grounded in reason and devoid of any warmth or nourishment for the human soul. He described the proliferation of Protestant denominations, but found many of them strange. He realized that major Protestant religious bodies often worked together, and that those in the East were organizing to spread the faith and duplicate their churches in the newly settled frontier areas of the West. And he knew about the camp meeting phenomenon, with its itinerant preachers, crowds of believers, and intense spirituality. Yet it can be argued that he missed the essential dynamism of American Protestantism. He arrived in the United States at the cusp of the Second Great Awakening in the 1830s and of the powerful reform movements that would emerge, in large part, from that religious renewal. Revivalism was about to sweep once again across America; the frontier camp meeting was only a small part of a much larger and enduring story that Tocqueville missed (Noll 2014).

When considering his understanding of American Protestantism, two other matters also deserve our attention. In the opening chapter of the 1840 *Democracy*, Tocqueville examined the philosophical method of the Americans and argued that, despite a complete lack of interest in formal philosophy, the American intellectual approach is Cartesian. The attitude of the American, he wrote, is to "escape from the spirit of system," to "take tradition only as information," and to "seek by yourself and in yourself alone the reason for things." Each person claims to judge the world on his own; each relies on his own witness (Tocqueville 2010, 3:698–710; esp. 699, 701). The Americans, according to Tocqueville, are good disciples of Descartes, despite never having read him.

Did Tocqueville miss the point? Perhaps what he was describing arose not from Cartesian principles or any other philosophical method, but from the fundamental approach and beliefs of the dissenting Protestant tradition that had arrived in America with the colonial founding. To explain what he was seeing, he could have simply called upon the attitudes of dissenting Protestants. Here perhaps he did not quite grasp the essential Protestantism of the Americans.

A second occasion when Tocqueville possibly failed to understand the full effect of dissenting Protestantism in America occurs in his discussion of the concept of self-interest well understood or interest well understood, which he called "a social and philosophical theory" developed by the Americans (Tocqueville 2010, 3:918–25, 926–29). For him, this doctrine explained the remarkable American ability to blend private and public interests, to grasp the larger public interest, and to understand how private interest fit into the broader public good. Americans seemed to realize that no radical break could exist between the private and public realms. But what was he really seeing?

At least two Tocqueville scholars have recently suggested that this unique American understanding of the intimate link between private and public interest was grounded in the covenant tradition of dissenting Protestantism.[11] Among the Puritans, for example, the individual, the religious congregation, and the community as a whole existed within a closely interconnected web of religious and social covenants. Tocqueville touched on this concept when, in the 1835 *Democracy*, he singled out and praised John Winthrop's definition of civil liberty as freedom hedged in by moral constraints and by the community good, liberty grounded in religious belief and social and political covenants (Tocqueville 2010, 1:68–69). This Puritan understanding of liberty perhaps captured the essence of what Tocqueville meant and admired when he described the blending of religion and liberty. But Winthrop's definition also acknowledged the mutual private and public understandings and agreements that marked what Tocqueville later called the doctrine of interest well understood.

11. Consult Kloppenberg (1998) and Allen (2005) on this point.

The contemporary interpretation just mentioned asserts that, although the specific language of covenant had faded by the early nineteenth century, the long-standing tradition still shaped American attitudes and behavior (mores). So perhaps the doctrine of interest well understood was not philosophical, but religious; not a social innovation, but the remnants of a religious legacy. If this is true, then Tocqueville once again overlooked an important part of the American Protestant heritage.

CONCLUDING COMMENTS

What can we conclude from this brief discussion of Tocqueville's ideas about religion? Our survey demonstrates the persistent importance of religion in his thinking and his conviction that any democratic society, to remain free, needs religious faith. And our review illustrates how Tocqueville worked as a researcher and how he frequently left aside valuable information gathered and lessons learned while in the New World. For a variety of reasons, he sometimes simply dropped observations and opinions that had first appeared in his working papers. His *Democracy* presents, for example, only part of what he had discovered and knew about religion in the United States.

We have seen that several questions quickly surfaced in Tocqueville's mind. For some, he reached firm and remarkably consistent conclusions. For others, his answers remained unresolved; he could offer his readers only vacillating or divided responses. For still others, he presented answers in private papers that were strikingly different from his published pronouncements. His complex opinions about religion, in turn, leave attentive readers with questions of their own about the meaning, accuracy, frankness or continuing relevance of his message.

Tocqueville's double insistence on the unusual blending of liberty and religion and on the democratic nature of the religious heritage in the United States raises the question of how religion intersects with the American political identity. In his travel diaries Tocqueville recorded conversations that touched on the way in which patriotism and religion were mutually reinforced in the United States. The same idea recurred in the working manuscript of his *Democracy* where, in an aside, he noted the "patriotic affection of the Americans for religion" (Tocqueville 2010, 2:472 n. G). And in his text, he observed that "Americans mix Christianity and liberty so completely in their mind that it is nearly impossible to make them conceive the one without the other" (2:476; also see 2:479). As many commentators have pointed out, Tocqueville was describing an American civil religion in which patriotic feeling and religious zeal were mingled in such a way that love of country became inseparable from religious faith.

Tocqueville always wrote with his audience in mind. His ideas about religion serve as one of the best examples of how he trimmed his message to suit his expected readers. The quite critical comments about American Catholicism that appear in his travel notes and letters were either dropped entirely or considerably softened in his final text. He wanted, above all, to rally devout Catholics in France to the cause of democracy. For this purpose, he needed to portray Catholics in America as faithful, yet democratic, and to persuade his countrymen that Catholicism suited democracy by nature. If the argument in his *Democracy* seemed a bit labored and differed from his secret opinions, it was made with a specific goal in mind and with a finely tuned awareness of his own intended audience.

Tocqueville called himself a liberal of a new kind. Perhaps the best way to understand this self-identification is to recall his effort to combine the spirit of liberty and the spirit of religion. As already noted, he wanted to join together all men of good will, those who valued liberty and those who valued faith. He aimed at nothing less than a novel political coalition with a new set of values. His political program was distinctive; and, in the end, he did not succeed either as author or politician. But his goal helped to define his particular brand of liberalism, as well as his originality as a political theorist.

At this time of expanding interest in Tocqueville's thought in other societies and cultures, his insistence on the role of religion, in general, and of Christianity, in particular, raises yet other questions. What would he say about contemporary democratic societies in which religion now plays a minimal role? What would he say about societies, democratic, but non-Christian, which possess profoundly different religious traditions?[12] Does his analysis of religion and democracy still apply? Or is Tocqueville's attachment to religion—and more particularly to Christianity—outmoded? Recent work on Tocqueville and his *Democracy* by scholars from other countries around the world compels us to face these issues. The consideration of Tocqueville's ideas about religion and democracy is far from over.

REFERENCES

Allen, Barbara. 2005. *Tocqueville, Covenant, and the Democratic Revolution: Harmonizing Earth with Heaven.* Lanham, MD: Rowman & Littlefield.

Craiutu, Aurelian, and Sheldon Gellar, eds. 2009. *Conversations with Tocqueville: The Global Democratic Revolution in the Twenty-First Century.* Lanham, MD: Rowman & Littlefield.

Kloppenberg, James T. 1998. *The Virtues of Liberalism.* New York: Oxford University Press.

12. See, e.g., the volume of essays by Craiutu and Gellar (2009).

Noll, Mark A. 2014. "Tocqueville's *America*, Beaumont's *Slavery*, and the United States in 1831–32." *American Political Thought* 3 (2): 273–302.

Schleifer, James T. 2000. *The Making of Tocqueville's "Democracy in America."* 2nd ed. Indianapolis: Liberty Fund.

Tocqueville, Alexis de. 1960. *Journey to America*. Ed. J. P. Mayer. Trans. George Lawrence. New Haven, CT: Yale University Press.

———. 1985. *Alexis de Tocqueville: Selected Letters on Politics and Society*. Ed. Roger Boesche. Trans. James Toupin and Roger Boesche. Berkeley: University of California Press.

———. 2010. *Democracy in America*. Ed. Eduardo Nolla. Trans. James Schleifer. 4 vols. Indianapolis: Liberty Fund.

Zunz, Olivier, ed. 2010. *Alexis de Tocqueville and Gustave de Beaumont in America: Their Friendship and Their Travels*. Trans. Arthur Goldhammer. Charlottesville: University of Virginia Press.

Tocqueville's *America*, Beaumont's *Slavery*, and the United States in 1831–32

MARK A. NOLL

ABSTRACT
This essay first outlines Alexis de Tocqueville's well-known argument from *Democracy in America* that religion shapes the mores that keep American "equality of conditions" from deteriorating into the "tyranny of the majority." The paper then turns to the superb research of scholars who have published the notes, letters, and journals that Tocqueville and his traveling companion, Gustave de Beaumont, produced during their 1831–32 US journey. That material allows a clearer picture of where Tocqueville was perceptive, where he failed to record important aspects of American religion as it actually existed, and where what he observed accurately in 1831–32 changed significantly shortly thereafter. More attention to the neglected book that Beaumont published after their trip, *Marie; or, Slavery in the United States,* shows that his detailed assessment of United States' deeply ingrained racist attitudes would have helped make Tocqueville's insightful analysis of American democracy even more compelling.

Alexis de Tocqueville wrote *Democracy in America* in order to provide what he called "a new political science" for a world that was being made "entirely new" (Tocqueville 2010, 1:16). Tocqueville believed that the primary reality recasting the world was "the equality of conditions" (1:4) that he found far advanced in the new United States and that he suspected would soon sweep over the rest of Christendom. The best evaluations of Tocqueville's *Democracy* have always kept in view the theoretical purpose that was conspicuous in the first two parts of the work published in 1835 and that became even more dominant in the last two parts from 1840. *Democracy in America* was never intended to be merely informative about the United States in the way of other well-known travel accounts by Europeans such as Achille Murat (1832), Mrs. Frances

Mark A. Noll is Francis A. McAnaney Professor of History, University of Notre Dame, 219 O'Shaughnessy Hall, Notre Dame, IN 46556 (Mark.Noll.8@nd.edu).

I would like to thank the two anonymous reviewers for their most helpful critiques, and Notre Dame's Michael Zuckert and Vincent Phillip Muñoz for expert management of many things Tocquevillian.

[American Political Thought, vol. 3, issue 2, Fall 2014]

Trollope (1832), Charles Dickens (1842), or Frederica Bremer (1849–51/1976) that were published at roughly the same time as Tocqueville's work. Tocqueville's clear statement of his purpose should be a warning against the tendency of historians to treat the immediate contexts surrounding the formulation of theoretical statements as more important than the statements themselves.[1] Nonetheless, historians now have at hand an extraordinary wealth of detailed contextual scholarship for the 10 months that Tocqueville and Gustave de Beaumont spent in the United States and Canada as well as for the following decade during which Tocqueville went through the painstaking process of "making known what I saw in America" by subjecting the "ideas" of his systematizing intelligence to the "facts" he had observed during his journey (Tocqueville 2010,1:30).

Thus, historians could now be tempted to think that since so much evidence has been made available concerning who the French travelers visited, what they saw, and, most important, when they saw it, *Democracy in America* might actually be more significant for understanding the United States circa 1830 than for illuminating perennial American circumstances. Yet historians should acknowledge Tocqueville's original intent and resist this temptation. Instead, if historians do their work well, a sharpened political theory might result. More light on the immediate contexts in which Tocqueville saw America should bring the abstractions of his theorizing closer to the realities with which they were first engaged and, therefore, allow political scientists to determine with greater precision how well the grand Tocquevillian principles have explained the variegated realities of American political life.

That prospect of reaping more theoretical precision from more detailed historical investigation is supremely the case when the subject is Tocqueville's treatment of religion in American democracy. This article first outlines Tocqueville's argument about how religion acts as the most important check keeping American "equality of conditions" from spiraling out of control into the "tyranny of the majority" (Tocqueville 2010, 2:427) before turning to the magnificent labors of Tocqueville scholars who have traced the occasions, people, and events that either gave Tocqueville the raw materials for his conclusions about religion and American democracy or verified the premonitions with which he came to the new world.[2] Thanks to their work, it is possible as never before to travel with

1. For a particularly forceful articulation of reasons for this tendency, see Skinner (2002).

2. The first full study to exploit the extensive archive of notes, journals, and letters from 1831ff. that the travelers used to draft their books was Pierson (1938/1996). That work has been succeeded by a substantial line of scholarship reaching a brilliant summit in the landmark edition of Tocqueville's text by Nolla and Schleifer (Tocqueville 2010) and in the meticulously edited documents in Zunz (2010). I have also benefited from Kammen (1996), Schleifer (2000), Brown (2010), and Damrosch (2010).

Tocqueville and Beaumont and to peer over their shoulders as they wrote about the nation they visited.[3]

Understanding better how Tocqueville's experiences contributed to his argument about religion and American democracy leads to at least three conclusions concerning what Tocqueville saw in America and what he wrote in *Democracy*. First, Tocqueville's depiction in *Democracy* represented an unusually perceptive understanding of the actual state of religion and politics that existed in the United States from about 1820 to shortly after Tocqueville and Beaumont returned to France in early 1832. Second, in their travels, Tocqueville and Beaumont were frequently in close proximity to people and events that would drive significant changes in religion and politics from the early 1830s onward. Yet because Tocqueville was not aware of those people and events, his conclusions about religion and American democracy require at least some adjustment in order to remain valid for what came after the early 1830s. Third, and most generally, the timing of Tocqueville's visit was crucial. The changes that accelerated from the early 1830s altered substantially the landscape from which Tocqueville drew his conclusions about religion and politics. That shift of landscape does not mean that Tocqueville's conclusions have been invalidated; it does mean that more care is required to differentiate between where *Democracy* was perceptive about only the American situation of the 1820s and early 1830s and where it remains compelling even after the landscape began to shift.

Significantly, if that differentiation results in a clearer sense of where Tocqueville's *Democracy* possesses perennial value, it may also lead to a greater appreciation for the other book that came out of the Frenchmen's journey, Gustave de Beaumont's *Marie; or, Slavery in the United States: Portrait of American Mores*.[4] In contrast to Tocqueville, who took as his ambitious theme the whole gamut of American institutions and the entire range of American mores, Beaumont chose to write primarily about the effects of race and slavery. Closer attention to what the French travelers saw in 1831–32 and then to what happened in America after they departed shows why Beaumont's hybrid novel-sociological study deserves at least some of the attention that has been concentrated on Tocqueville's justly famous tome.

3. All students of Tocqueville in America now also benefit from the unusually perceptive insights for the period in Howe (2007).

4. This book appeared in five French editions between 1835 and 1842 as *Marie ou l'esclavage aux États-Unis. Tableau de moeurs américains*. The first English translation, by Barbara Chapman, appeared only in 1958; it was later reprinted with a new introduction by Gerard Fergerson (see Beaumont 1958/1999). This translation includes almost all of the romantic tale that made up slightly more than half of the original book. It also includes some of the many notes and appendices with which Beaumont festooned his novel, but not his extensive "*Note sur le mouvement religieux aux États-Unis*," which I have used in the recent critical edition by Marie-Claude Schapira (see Beaumont 2009).

THE ARGUMENT

In early October 1831, when Tocqueville and Beaumont had been in the United States for about 5 months—after, that is, they had visited New York City, upstate New York, the Great Lakes, French Canada, and New England—Tocqueville drew up a short list of "causes" for "the social state and current government of America" with which he was obviously very impressed. Heading the list was an "excellent point of departure" for later American history, including "the intimate mix of religion and spirit of liberty." The fifth point in its entirety read "*the prevailing religious spirit:* republican and democratic religion." The seventh of 10 points read "Very pure morals."(Zunz 2010, 314).[5] The prominence of religion in this preliminary list from October 1831 grew into the prominence of religion in Tocqueville's book.

Tocqueville's hope that American democracy could avoid fatal majoritarian debilities arose from his understanding of the United States' geography, its British legal traditions, and the religious character of its mores (Tocqueville 2010, 2:451ff.). Underlying his account of the United States that he observed in 1831 and 1832 was an assumption that American civilization rested on a New England foundation and that this foundation bequeathed an ideal relationship between religion and politics: "Restrained by the tightest bonds of certain religious beliefs, they were free of all political prejudices. [Religion led them to enlightenment; the observance of divine laws brought them to liberty]" (1:69). American religion, according to Tocqueville, was free of political prejudices because it exerted its sway without the "obstacles" (2:474) that encumbered religion in Europe.[6] Tocqueville paused to suggest that with religious profession as widespread as he found it in the United States, there was bound to be much nominal, hypocritical religion. Nonetheless, the practice of religion without obstacles meant that "America is . . . the place in the world where the Christian religion has most retained true power over souls" (2:473). Tocqueville clarified what he meant by the United States' being free of "obstacles" when he highlighted" the complete separation of Church and State." Crucially, Tocqueville reported that his informants uniformly told him that this separation was the principal reason for "the peaceful dominion that religion exercises in their country" (2:480).

Tocqueville then posed the question that all Europeans steeped in the traditions of Christendom had to ask: If religion was pervasive in America, yet

5. For the dating of Tocqueville's list, see Schleifer (2000, 68 n. 19).

6. As observed below, it is important to remember that Tocqueville evaluated American religion and politics by comparison with what he had experienced of religion and politics in France.

without connections between church and state, how did it exert its influence? The key, according to Tocqueville, was indirection, which he explained in his well-known account of religion in relation to mores and mores in relation to political life. Tocqueville admitted that there might be rare moments of organized public religion, like the occasion he witnessed when "in one of the largest cities of the Union" at "a political meeting" the audience was led in prayer for the liberation of Poland by "a priest, dressed in his ecclesiastical robes" (Tocqueville 2010, 2:471). But "indirect action" was much more common and seemed much "more powerful. In fact, "it is when religion is not speaking about liberty that it best teaches the Americans the art of being free" (2:472).

The ground for these assertions from near the middle of tome two had been prepared early in tome one. Considered in the abstract, Tocqueville held that "Christianity, which has made all men equal before God," was the strongest possible promoter of equality of conditions. With his mind no doubt on hierarchical French Catholicism, he did go on to say that in Europe "by a combination of strange events" some highly placed Christians "reject . . . the equality that [religion] loves and curses liberty as an adversary." These Europeans took such a position in opposition to liberty because they were "involved amid the powers that democracy is overturning." But in America, the proper view prevailed: "by taking liberty by the hand, religion could be able to sanctify its efforts" (Tocqueville 2010, 1:24). Tocqueville fleshed out these preliminary statements with his full-scale argument in tome two: the spiritual egalitarianism of Christianity actually supported the equality of conditions that democracy sought, but at the same time it restrained the democratic excesses that many European Christians combated and mistakenly assumed were evils inherent in all forms of democracy.

Also in tome one, Tocqueville succinctly explained the linkage that connected religion, mores, and politically beneficial freedom: "Liberty considers religion as the safeguard of mores, mores as the guarantee of laws and the pledge of its own duration" (Tocqueville 2010, 1:70). Then in tome two he explained at length why "mores" were critical for "maintaining the Democratic Republic in the United States." His attempt to define "mores" in that second tome sounded a great deal like efforts today to define "culture": "I understand the expression *mores* here in the sense that the ancients attached to the word *mores*; I apply it not only to mores strictly speaking, which could be called habits of the heart, but to the different notions that men possess, to the diverse opinions that are current among them, and to the ensemble of ideas from which the habits of the mind are formed" (2:466).

Tocqueville regarded the "innumerable multitude of sects in the United States" as an advantage for the protection of democracy. "All agree on the duties of men toward one another . . . all sects preach the same morality in the name of God" (Tocqueville 2010, 2:472–73).[7] As if to underscore the broad sway exerted by religion, Tocqueville even complicated his use of terms: "In the United States, religion regulates not only mores; it extends its dominion even to the mind" (2:474).

In Tocqueville's understanding, the pervasiveness of religion protected Americans from the excesses of democracy that Europe's traditional Christians feared: even "the revolutionaries of America are obliged to profess publicly a certain respect for Christian morality and equality that does not allow them to violate laws easily when the laws are opposed to the execution of their designs" (Tocqueville 2010, 2:475). As he tried to communicate what that protection meant, Tocqueville sometimes lapsed into thinking dictated by his French background. Thus, he asserted that "In America, religion is perhaps less powerful than it has been in certain times and among certain peoples, but its influence is more durable" (2:485). But what he meant by American religion as "less powerful" referred almost entirely to the absence of political influence exerted directly by church representatives.

The absence of overt clerical influence was so important to Tocqueville's argument about the indirect political effect of mores that he repeated it several times: "American priests . . . fill no public position. . . . Most of [the clergy] seemed to remove themselves voluntarily from power, and to take a kind of professional pride in remaining apart from it. . . . I saw them separate themselves with care from all parties, and flee contact with all the ardor of personal interest" (Tocqueville 2010, 2:480–81).

Tocqueville drew his observations together into broad concluding statements that have been often cited, if perhaps too little analyzed:

> So religion, which among the Americans never directly takes part in the government of society, must be considered as the first of their political institutions; for if it does not give them the taste for liberty, it singularly facilitates their use of it. (Tocqueville 2010, 2:475)

> When I arrived in the United States, it was the religious aspect of the country that first struck my eyes. As I prolonged my journey, I noticed the great political consequences that flowed from these facts. I had seen among us the spirit of religion and the spirit of liberty march almost always in opposite directions. Here, I found them intimately joined the one to the other: they reigned together over the same soil. (Tocqueville 2010, 2:479)

7. Beaumont mostly agreed, but singled out the Quakers' nonresistant principles as a significant exception to the common Protestant morality; see Beaumont (2009, 98, 102).

Finally, along with another reference to hypocrisy where religious is so conventionally embraced, Tocqueville asserted that Americans themselves perceived the connections he was laboring to spell out. While admitting that he did not know "if all Americans have faith in their religion, for who can read the recesses of the heart" he nonetheless want on to claim, "I am sure that they believe it necessary for maintaining republican institutions. This opinion does not belong to one class of citizens or to one party, but to the whole nation; you find it among all ranks" (Tocqueville 2010, 2:475).

But what exactly had Tocqueville "found" in his travels? Who were the "all ranks" whose opinions he synthesized into his "new political science?" And what difference did it make for the enduring value of his argument who he interviewed and when and where? These are historians' questions that can be at least partially answered by attending to the wealth of detailed scholarship that now exists on the manuscripts that the travelers wrote during and after the course of their journey.

Before examining that scholarship, however, it is important to have a general picture of Beaumont's *Marie* in order to understand how well the novel complemented Tocqueville's *Democracy,* but also went beyond it in several important particulars. This romantic tale and its attending social commentary mostly echoed Tocqueville's observations. The story tells of a young Frenchman, Ludovic, who immigrated to the United States in the mid-1820s and was befriended by a Baltimore family, father Daniel Nelson, son George, and daughter Marie. Ludovic falls in love with Marie, but she tries to put him off because her mother, a Creole from Louisiana, was a mulatto descended from one Negro great grandmother. Therefore, Marie "has been soiled by a drop of black blood" even though she "surpasses all the women of Baltimore in intelligence, talent, and goodness" (Beaumont 1958/1999, 55, 57). Daniel Nelson agrees to let Ludovic wed Marie if he would first travel throughout the United States to explore the extent of race prejudice in the country. Ludovic does so, and although he is appalled by the slave system and even more by the general racial prejudice in both North and South, he maintains his resolve to marry Marie. Visceral antagonism against their "amalgamation" fuels a race riot in New York City on the day of their wedding.[8] Meanwhile, George is first denied the right to vote because of his mulatto status before he is killed trying to help an Indian tribe that has rebelled against removal to the trans-Mississippi West. Ludovic and Marie try to find a refuge from prejudice in the Michigan wilderness west of Detroit, but Marie dies of grief soon after they reach the hoped-for sanctuary.

8. Beaumont used an actual riot in July 1834, which was sparked by offense against clergy who married whites and blacks, as the basis for this part of his novel.

The novel and the book's extensive apparatus echoed much of what Tocqueville wrote in *Democracy:* for example, on the lack of social distinction in the United States, the American passion for moneymaking, and the potential for democracy in "the land of liberty" to slide toward "tyranny" (Beaumont 1958/1999, 20, 36, 13). Likewise on religion and society, Beaumont stressed the importance of the separation of church and state, described the powerful but indirect influence of religion on mores, and called Christianity the surest guarantor of liberty (Beaumont 2009, 99, 101–2). It was almost the same on the status of African Americans where much of Beaumont's long "Note on the Social and Political Condition of the Negro Slaves and of Free People of Color" (Beaumont 1958/1999, 189–216) made many of the same cutting observations found in tome two of *Democracy in America* (Tocqueville 2010, 2:548–82).[9] The major difference is that in the form of a novel Beaumont spoke more emotionally about a forward-looking nation that could tolerate slavery: "what an accursed country, oh God! What depravity! What cynical immorality! And what scorn of the word of God in a Christian society!" (Beaumont 1958/1999, 54). Beaumont also encapsulated succinctly what Tocqueville mostly intimated: "in America the very race of the slave is a more serious problem than their slavery" (214). And he dramatized more starkly the contradiction between, on the one side, habits of equality and principles of liberty, and, on the other, the effects of race prejudice: "Obsessed with liberty, while human bondage abounds! Discoursing on equality, among three million slaves; forbidding distinctions among men, and proud to be white, as of a mark of nobility; with strong and philosophical mind condemning the privilege of birth, and with stupidity maintaining the privilege of color!" (120). To read *Marie* alongside *Democracy in America* is to find one of the general arguments in the treatise drawn to a sharpened point in the novel.

THE SITUATION IN 1831–32

Tocqueville's account of religion and American politics becomes more impressive as the details of his American travels come more sharply into focus. Throughout the duration of the trip, he heard from all sides that religion was critical for the success of the United States' democratic order, and indeed in exactly the way *Democracy in America* would later explain: religion shaped the

9. A footnote at the beginning of Tocqueville's section on slavery commends Beaumont's forthcoming *Marie* to "those who want to understand to what excesses of tyranny men are pushed little by little once they have begun to go beyond nature and humanity" (Tocqueville 2010, 2:548).

peoples' mores, the peoples' mores transformed mere democracy into true liberty. Furthermore, from many corners came the message that a secret to the flourishing of both religion and liberty was the clergy's self-imposed avoidance of overt politics.

So it was that in the fall of 1831 and into the new year, the French travelers received repeated confirmation of what they had already concluded from their very first impressions of the spring and summer. In Boston, after a lengthy conversation with former president John Quincy Adams on October 1, Tocqueville wrote that Adams "apparently regards [religion] as one of the most [important] safeguards of American society" (Zunz 2010, 244). In the same city, "a very ardent Presbyterian" told Tocqueville the same thing: "I believe that Protestantism is indispensable to a republican people. Religion is our best security for liberty. It enhances our freedom and sanctifies its principles" (246). The next month in Baltimore he heard that although the clergy were never elected to public office, they nonetheless "exert considerable indirect influence" (257). He received a similar message early in 1832 in New Orleans where "there's no political or other animosity toward Catholic priests, who, for their part, never mingle in politics" (259). In the long overland trip that came next, from New Orleans to Norfolk, he enjoyed extended conversation with Joel Poinsett, who had recently returned from Mexico as the United States' initial minister and who would later serve in the cabinet of President Van Buren. Poinsett told Tocqueville that "that the state of religion in America is among the most important reasons why we are able to support republican institutions here. The religious spirit exerts a direct influence on political passions as well as an indirect influence by inculcating morality" (286).

The themes that the travelers heard from scattered American locations only reinforced their settled convictions. Documentation from earlier in 1831 points to Tocqueville and Beaumont's visit to Auburn, New York, as the moment when the main points of what *Democracy in America* would claim about religion fell into place. The visit to Auburn and its prison in upstate New York, just a little south of Lake Ontario's eastern shore, provided their second extensive examination of an American penal institution. They arrived in Auburn on July 9, 2 months after first setting foot on American soil. There they learned about an even more direct and purposeful use of religious instruction to promote reform than they had been surprised to find in their first prison visit at Sing Sing north of New York City. At Sing Sing, Beaumont was especially intrigued by the fact that ministers from different denominations took turns preaching Sunday sermons for the inmates, an instance of "perfect tolerance" that he found hard to square with the competition among denominational belief systems outside the prison (Zunz 2010, 33).[10] Now at Auburn they heard from the warden that "the prison chaplain visits the prisoners' cells every night in an effort to awaken their sense of honor and virtue" (452). The ability of the denominations to cooperate and the common moralism the different denominations taught to prisoners impressed the visitors. They also observed in both prisons a movement from religion to mores to public responsibility. Later Tocqueville would develop into grand principles what these early prison visits showed him as a concrete instance.

Even more important at Auburn was what Tocqueville heard from several clergymen. On July 12 he interviewed Jonathan Mayhew Wainwright, an Episcopal minister whom he described as "rare" for being "intelligent" and presiding over a "fashionable church." When Tocqueville asked whether there "was any point of contact here between religious ideas and politics doctrines," the answer was "No. These are two entirely different worlds, and each of them lives in peace." When Tocqueville pressed for more, Wainwright ascribed this peace to "The fact that ministers of the various sects have never become involved in politics and never claimed to wield political power." In fact, Wainwright said "Many of us even abstain from voting in elections" (Zunz 2010, 330–31).[11] The same day, Tocqueville asked the same questions of the young Presbyterian chaplain at the prison, who gave the same answer: "I am convinced that if one proposed a political role to members of the Presbyterian clergy, they would refuse without a moment's hesitation" (331). The next day the travelers interviewed the Reverend James Richards, head of the Presbyterian theological seminary in Auburn, who in Tocqueville's summary of their conversation stressed the link between religion and mores: "I don't believe that a Republic can exist without *morals* and I do not believe that a people can have morals when it isn't religious. I therefore judge the maintenance of the religious spirit one of our greatest political interests" (Pierson 1938/1996, 214).[12]

Immediately after leaving Auburn and this harmonious chorus of opinion, the travelers proceeded 30 miles westward where at Canandaigua they stopped on July 17 and 18 at the home of John Canfield Spencer, an active lawyer, local political leader, and later member of President Tyler's cabinet, whom Tocqueville described as the first important informant of their trip (Zunz 2010, 83n). To the visitors, Spencer expanded on what they had heard at Auburn. Why is there

10. Later, Beaumont would conclude that intra-Protestant theological differences were much less important than the common front Protestants exhibited in promoting "*la pureté de la morale*" and offering themselves "*au service de la liberté*" (Beaumont 2009, 98, 102).

11. This interview, which Tocqueville dates in July at Auburn (Zunz 2010, 330), is recorded by Pierson as taking place earlier in New York City (Pierson 1938/1996, 137–38).

12. This interview is not included in Zunz (2010).

religious tolerance in the United States? "Primarily the fact that there are so many denominations (the number is virtually unlimited)." What does religion do for the republic? "Many people, including myself, are of the opinion that some kind of religion is essential if man is to live in society, and the freer men are, the more necessary religion becomes." Spencer also agreed that the clergy exercised the greatest good when they "were completely deprived of all temporal influence" (Zunz 2010, 220–22). At least on these matters, if not on others, Tocqueville heard from this thoughtful New York lawyer only strong reinforcement for themes he would later develop in *Democracy*.

Very soon after leaving Canandaigua, Tocqueville received particularly important confirmation of what he had been told in upstate New York from a source of great personal interest. Five days after their conversation with John Canfield Spencer, Tocqueville and Beaumont were in Detroit where they heard Father Gabriel Richard describe the general religious tolerance that prevailed there, even as waves of Protestant settlers poured into once predominately Catholic Michigan. In a comment with some irony, since Father Gabriel had only shortly before served a 2-year term in the US House of Representatives as the delegate from Michigan Territory, the priest told Tocqueville that "the greatest favor that can be done for religion is to separate it entirely from the temporal power" (Zunz 2010, 295).[13]

Then, less than 2 weeks later, the travelers heard the same message from another priest, James Ignatius Mullon, who ministered to Native Americans in the upper Great Lakes. As a European, Tocqueville may have expected a different answer when he quizzed his fellow Catholic, "Do you think that government support is helpful to religion?" Father Mullon replied, "I am deeply convinced that it is harmful. I know that most Catholic priests in Europe think the opposite. . . . If they lived here, they would soon change their minds." Then the priest made a statement that, with some editorial expansion, appeared in Tocqueville's book almost as he phrased it: "All religious beliefs here are on the same footing. The government doesn't support or persecute any of them. Yet surely there is no other country in the world where Catholicism has more fervent supporters or more numerous converts. I will say it again, the less religion and its ministers are mixed up with government, the less they are involved in political debate, the more influential religious ideas become" (Zunz 2010, 221–22).[14]

13. In Beaumont's novel, Father Richard appears as the priest who saves Ludovic from grief-inspired suicide after Marie has died (Beaumont 1958/1999, 174–75).

14. Compare on Catholic possibilities in America, Tocqueville (2010, 2:469–70 and 3:754–56).

In the era of Pope Gregory XVI (1831–46), whose strong assertion of Catholic prerogative and equally strong attacks against non-Catholics were widely known, it was striking that the American Catholics who spoke to Tocqueville told him virtually the same things he heard from the Protestants.[15] For the French reading public that Tocqueville always had in mind, as well as for his own inherited Catholic instincts, these priests must have been unusually important.

It is also noteworthy that what Tocqueville heard in Auburn and shortly thereafter was almost exactly what he would write in his book—about religion being critical for democratic liberty and the complete separation of church and state critical for religion to function at its best in a democracy. It may have been even more important that what Tocqueville heard accurately reflected the actual state of religion and society as it existed in the United States during the period of his visit, and especially in upstate New York.

The ministers and Esquire Spencer, in other words, practiced what they preached. The Presbyterian James Richards was respected as a moderate in his denomination's New School, or more activistic, faction. Although he did engage in some theological polemics, his interests seem to have been exclusively theological and not in the least political (see Marsden 1970, 137–39). The Episcopalian Wainwright carried his political self-denial not only to the extent of not voting but, only a few years before meeting Tocqueville, also showed what it meant for representatives of different denominations to shape mores indirectly by helping to found the nonsectarian New York University (Zunz 2010, 330n). For his part, the lawyer and politician Spencer was a sincere friend of religion, but also a firm believer in removing overt clerical influences from public life.

Historically considered, there is every reason to think that what Tocqueville heard in the course of 1831 and then published in 1835 and 1840 mostly reflected the actual state of religion in American politics before and during the time of his visit. As it happens, some of the best evidence for that conclusion comes precisely from the region he visited in upstate New York. The people there knew what they were talking about when they depicted American religion as widespread, moral, and nonpolitical.

Only weeks before Beaumont and Tocqueville arrived in Auburn, the well-known evangelist Charles Grandison Finney had completed a successful revival campaign in that town.[16] His 6-week preaching series, which extended

15. Gregory issued *Mirari vos*, his strenuous encyclical opposing principles of civil liberty, rebellion against monarchs, and the separation of church and state in August 1832, some months after Tocqueville and Beaumont left America.

16. For detailed treatment, see the account with superb annotations in Finney (1989, 330–36).

through much of March and April, had been written up in a local newspaper, *The Western Recorder*, in its July 12 issue, which the travelers may have seen during their Auburn sojourn (Finney 1989, 332 n. 24). Moreover, just before arriving in Auburn, Finney had conducted one of the most successful, and also one of the most often studied, revivals in US history.[17] This event took place in Rochester, the western terminus on Lake Ontario of the Erie Canal and only 20 miles or so northwest of Canandaigua. Although some historians have suggested that Finney proclaimed a faith tailored to meet the requirements of bourgeois industrial society, observers at the time were more impressed with it for other reasons.[18] The revival touched all classes of society. It drew large numbers to conversion and then to membership in local churches. Cooperation among the Methodists, Baptists, Presbyterians, and smaller Protestant groups was prominent. Finney's message of salvation, with its emphasis on the initiatives that sinners must themselves take to find God, drew opposition from orthodox Calvinists, but the opposition remained strictly theological. Contemporaries stressed its effects in strengthening personal discipline, stabilizing families, caring for the unfortunate, and curtailing alcohol abuse. Finney's strenuous gospel message, in other words, enlisted a spectrum of denominations in promoting religion, and with obvious effects on the mores of the community. And he did so with no, or virtually no, attention to anything political.

During his Rochester campaign, Finney also preached in outlying towns, including Canandaigua (Finney 1989, 324), where Tocqueville would only weeks later hear from John Canfield Spencer that "some kind of religion is essential if man is to live in society, and the freer men are, the more necessary religion becomes" (Zunz 2010, 220). When Finney came to preach in Auburn, he resided with "an earnest Christian man, and a very dear friend of mine," who happened to be Theodore Spencer, a brother of John Canfield (Finney 1989, 330). During his Auburn revival, Finney patched up an earlier dispute with the Rev. Richards so that the theologically conservative Richards and the theologically innovative Finney enjoyed full cooperation in the revival preaching and in furthering the social effects of the revival on Auburn (334 n. 37).

In other words, what the Auburn, New York, area was actually experiencing in 1831, what Auburn area residents told Tocqueville, and what Tocqueville later wrote in *Democracy* were in very close alignment.

17. A full account is provided in Johnson (1978).

18. Criticism of Johnson (1978), which provides a largely economic explanation for the revival, is found in Johnson (1989, 77–80) and Lazerow (1995, 5–6). Outstanding local history on Finney's early revivalism is provided by Perciaccante (2003).

Tocqueville's book was just as informative in grasping what was actually transpiring in the United States during his visit when he turned his attention to the importance of voluntary societies. In both the 1835 (e.g., Tocqueville 2010, 2:302–3) and 1840 (e.g., 3:895–902) parts of *Democracy,* Tocqueville expatiated at length on the importance of voluntary associations for shaping American society. In describing what is now styled American "civil society," he offered a memorable comparison: "Wherever at the head of a new undertaking, you see in France the government, and in England, a great lord, count on seeing in the United States, an association" (3:896).

To be sure, Tocqueville did slight the potential for sectarian division created by the rise of American voluntarism. Oliver Zunz has correctly observed that voluntary associations "were a more contentious issue than Tocqueville realized." The fear of influential founders about the potential of well-organized minorities to illegitimately constrain the majority had been memorably expressed in George Washington's farewell warning against "all combinations and associations of whatever plausible character" (Zunz 2010, xxix). On the religious front, large sectarian groups like the Baptists and the Disciples/Churches of Christ, which received little attention from either Tocqueville or Beaumont, combined theological arguments for congregational government and republican fear of concentrated power to attack the era's most influential religious voluntary societies.[19]

Yet even with this one reservation in view, Tocqueville seems not to have realized how strongly American voluntarism supported his overarching analysis of religion and politics. In the United States, during the 1820s and early 1830s, it was not only that religion shaped mores in general ways, but that voluntary societies inspired by religion had become the driving force behind an extraordinary range of both narrowly spiritual and broadly social endeavors. It is possible that Beaumont and Tocqueville may even had had firsthand knowledge of at least one of the era's great societies, since they arrived in New York City on May 11, 1831, only a single day before the annual public meeting of the American Bible Society. As reported in the press, "an immense concourse of people" gathered to receive reports from the 756 Bible Society auxiliaries "scattered through every State and Territory in the Union." In the chair was Colonel Richard Varick, who during the American Revolution had served as George Washington's private secretary and had later filled several public offices, including mayor of New York City. This 1831 meeting heard that the Society's resolution from 2 years earlier to provide "every destitute family in the United States with a Bible" had been completed

19. The logic behind that position is thoroughly explained in Porter (forthcoming).

in 13 states and territories (including Michigan) and was advancing speedily in the rest.[20] Other somewhat smaller societies also convened their annual meetings in New York while Tocqueville and Beaumont were in the city, including the American Home Missionary Society, the New York Sunday School Union (representing 1735 lay teachers), and the American Seamen's Friend Society.[21]

A few small-scale voluntary societies had been formed in America before the turn of the nineteenth century, but as self-generated vehicles for preaching the Christian message, distributing Christian literature, and advancing Christian social causes, the voluntary society came into its own only after 1810.[22] The most important were founded by interdenominational teams of evangelical Protestants for distinctly Protestant purposes. Congregationalists and Presbyterians, though falling behind Baptists, Methodists, and Disciples in total adherents, took the lead in the societies and so retained considerable cultural leadership among the churches.[23] The best funded and most dynamic societies—the American Board of Commissioners for Foreign Missions (1810), the American Bible Society (1816), and the American Education Society (1816), which aimed especially at education for ministerial candidates—were rivaled only by the rapidly growing Methodists as the nation's most comprehensive organizations of any kind.[24]

To the intimidating challenges posed by disestablishment and the vigorous competition of a rapidly expanding market economy, voluntary societies in league with revivalists like Finney and expanding denominations such as the Methodists, responded boldly. Their energetic labors first reversed the downward slide of Protestant numbers from the Revolutionary era and then began to exert palpable influence on national mores and social activities. From its beginnings to 1828, the US government spent nearly $3.6 million on internal

20. *Daily National Intelligencer* (Washington, DC), May 18, 1831, col. B.

21. *Observer and Telegraph* (Hudson, OH), May 26, 1831, col. C.

22. The following two paragraphs are abridged from Noll (2002, 182–83, 197–98), which drew heavily on Foster (1960) and Mathews (1969). A superb extension of arguments underscoring the importance of voluntary societies and their movement toward politics circa 1830 is Young (2006).

23. A repeated indication that neither Tocqueville nor Beaumont fully grasped the inner workings of Protestantism was their inability to distinguish Congregationalists from Presbyterians; they used the latter name indiscriminately for both groups. The difference between the two, which was not insignificant in 1831–32, became more pronounced by the mid-1830s when questions about the effect of New England Congregational theology contributed strongly to a major schism among American Presbyterians. The full story is told in Marsden (1970).

24. Two excellent studies of how the societies actually did their work have been provided by Nord (1996, 2001).

improvements (roads, canals, communications). In that same span of years the thirteen leading benevolent societies, overwhelmingly Protestant in constituency and purpose, had spent over $2.8 million to further their goals (Foster 1960, 21). No broad-based movement, not even the political parties, brought together so many people committed to so much social construction as did the national meetings of the benevolent societies. From the midteens, the societies were sponsoring major local and regional gatherings. By the late 1820s many of the societies were staging their annual conventions as impressive public spectacles. The high point of this visible demonstration of evangelical social construction may have occurred only a few years after the Frenchmen visited during the first week of May, 1834. In that week, at least 16 different societies gathered in New York City for reports and exhortation relating to their work (Foster 1960, 48–53). The activities pursued by these societies represented the fabric of the nation: three were missionary societies, three others distributed the Bible or religious literature, four provided scholarships for advanced study, and six were organized for social benevolence. The last group is especially important in the historical context of *Democracy in America*. Societies for specific religious purposes (Bible, tract, missionary, religious education) were being joined by an increasing number aimed at social reform. The American Temperance Society was somewhat unusual when it was established in 1826 because its goals were as much social and public as private and religious. By 1833, when the American Anti-Slavery Society was formed, the number of social service societies was growing rapidly. Tocqueville and Beaumont journeyed through the United States exactly when the spiritually driven societies were at their peak and just as voluntarism was beginning to expand from narrow religious purposes to broader goals of social—and therefore also political—reform.

The conclusion from considering the scope and social reach of religion in the United States during the years immediately before and during Tocqueville's trip must be that he got it right. Religion was practiced with greater freedom than in any other part of the world. The many denominations of American Protestants may have bewildered the French visitors, but they soon concluded that whatever their theological or ecclesiastical differences, most Protestants worked commonly to exert a moral influence on society. And not only the Protestants, for Catholics in America, unlike many of their coreligionists in Europe, also embraced the separation of church and state and looked only for indirect public influence. Through the ever-expanding denominations and even more the voluntary societies, American believers (whether with heartfelt sincerity or only out of social conformism) were exerting a decisive influence on public mores. And they did so with little overt politicking. Tocqueville, in other words, wrote perceptively in *Democracy* about what was going on in America during his visit.

WHAT THE VISITORS FAILED TO NOTICE

The qualifications that historians must offer to the Tocquevillian picture concern what he did not notice in 1831–32 and then with what happened in the years immediately after the travelers returned to France. A prime instance is the understandable concentration of both Tocqueville and Beaumont on Catholicism. To be sure, the Catholic presence, which was growing rapidly in the United States by the early 1830s, had reached a new level of visibility in 1829 when the American bishops held their first Provincial Council. Yet religion in America at the time was much more obviously represented by the Methodists, who had come from almost nowhere in the Revolutionary era to become half a century later the nation's largest denomination. In both authors' books, as well as in the notes that Beaumont and Tocqueville made during their journey, however, there are many references to Catholics and very few to Methodists.[25] In both notes and publications, Tocqueville was also much more concerned about the Unitarians, who were already entering a long decline, than about the Methodists, who would continue to grow in numbers and influence for many decades to come. The disproportion of the travelers' interest amounted to a blind spot. Had they paid more attention to the Methodists, who were in fact all around them, they could have observed a transition under way that would have necessitated at least some adjustment to Tocqueville's conclusions about religion and politics. To 1830, the history of American Methodists confirmed the pattern described in *Democracy*; thereafter it was a different story.

Tocqueville and Beaumont arrived in Hartford, Connecticut, on October 3, 1831, the same day that one of Hartford's newspapers reported on what it called "the first commencement" at a new university in nearby Middletown that had taken place 2 weeks earlier.[26] The event was the inauguration of Wesleyan University's first president, Wilbur Fiske, himself a college graduate as well as an experienced Methodist minister and educator (see Potts 1992). When Wesleyan opened its doors in the fall of 1831, there were only three other Methodist institutions of higher learning in the country. All were struggling, and all would fold within the next decade. Wesleyan, by contrast, with solid support from prominent Methodists and reasonable backing from the residents of Middletown, marked the start of a vigorous age of Methodist educational expansion. By 1840, there were a dozen flourishing Methodist colleges, by 1860 three dozen.

25. For their awareness of the Methodists, see Tocqueville (2010, 4:1362–63) and Zunz (2010, 271–72), along with one paragraph in Beaumont (2009, 98–99). My thanks to Alan Kahan for help on this point.

26. *New England Weekly Review*, "Wesleyan University," October 3, 1831, col. A.

The rapid expansion of Methodist higher education spoke to a new phase in the denomination's history. Francis Asbury, the driving force in the early history of American Methodism, had exerted heroic efforts in building up the main overseas branch of the Wesleys' English movement (see Wigger 2009). When Asbury arrived in America in 1771, there were four Methodist preachers caring for about 300 people. By 1813, 3 years before Asbury's death, the official Methodist minutes listed 171,448 white and 42,850 African American members "in full society" served by 678 preachers. (Methodist Episcopal Church 1813, 598–99). By that time these itinerants were visiting about 7,000 local Methodist class meetings, each presided over by a local layperson. As many as one million people (or about one out of eight Americans) were attending a Methodist camp meeting each year (Wigger 1998, 81, 97).

Asbury's constant travel, his straightforward preaching, his genius for organizing circuit riders, his commitment to the small-group class meeting as the engine of Methodist spirituality, and his publishing of plain religious materials for plain folk (hymnals, pamphlets, the *Methodist Discipline*) imparted terrific energy to the movement. Asbury, moreover, could have been considered a perfect exemplum of Tocqueville's conclusions about religion in a democracy. As effective as he was in promoting Methodist religion and through that religion affecting mores, Asbury was just as preemptory in warning Methodists, especially Methodist ministers, away from overt political authority.

Asbury's resolution to live above partisanship—"He never meddled in politicks" was the word at his funeral (Cooper 1819, 83)—was decisive for the whole movement, at least to about 1810. Asbury for some time even shied away from using political designations for the scenes of his labors, preferring instead to speak of his ministry in a simple geographical context: "I want the continent, the world, to flame with the spiritual glory of God," he wrote in a September 22, 1794, letter (Asbury 1958, 3:130). So long as Asbury exercised the controlling voice, American Methodism as a whole followed his kind of apolitical pietism.

But when Asbury died, things began to change. Methodism's success led to growing desires within the movement for institutions of higher learning (which Asbury had discouraged as a potential threat to experiential piety). Bright young ministers contracted a serious case of what can only be called Congregationalism envy as they entered into theological conflict with their better educated peer denominations. Gradually Methodist disdain for politics began to gave way to broader notions of public service. At Wesleyan's first public event on September 21, 1831, the inaugural president, Wilbur Fiske, spoke for the new Methodist era. He proclaimed that "the spirit of reform is abroad" and, as he had written privately only shortly before, he was no longer content to educate Methodist youth "for *themselves*"; now he wanted to "educate all [the young men] I can get *for the world*" (Potts 1992, 17, 19).

Efforts by educators like Fiske could be enlisted to support Tocqueville's claim about the indirect influence of religion in American society. But for the Methodists, the building of stable educational institutions coincided also with ever-increasing engagement in political aspects of public life. In not too many years, Methodists would be hotly debating slavery amongst themselves, with ministers taking various public positions on what the denomination—but also the nation—should do about the peculiar institution. Soon thereafter in 1844 the denomination fell into schism on this question. Then at least a few Methodist ministers completely set aside Asbury's strictures against political involvement. William Brownlow of Tennessee was an extreme case, but one that indicated a general movement from indirect to direct politics.[27] Brownlow, a notoriously aggressive polemicist, began his adult life as a Methodist circuit rider but then, while continuing to exercise pastoral duties, entered public debates by becoming the editor of a Whig newspaper. From the mid-1850s he advocated strongly for the Union; eventually he served as the Republican governor of Union-occupied Tennessee. The level of Brownlow's political involvement was unusual, but it nonetheless represented only an extreme example of the Methodist turn to much more direct political action. From Asbury's intense focus on nonpolitical religion, American Methodists moved to create institutions like Wesleyan aimed at more direct public influence and to the mobilization of at least some of their ministers for direct partisan politics. Tocqueville was in the United States precisely when this transition was gaining momentum, but due to his preoccupation with Catholics and Unitarians, he did not observe it or realize how politicization of the Methodists complicated his general argument.

The situation was the same for other significant developments that took place when the Frenchmen were in the country. In upstate New York, Tocqueville and Beaumont only just missed Charles G. Finney and his largely apolitical revivals. Yet in missing Finney, they also missed learning about Timothy Dwight Weld, Finney's most dynamic convert. Weld, while a student at Hamilton College, had been converted during a Finney revival at Utica, New York, in 1826. Almost immediately he joined Finney as an active evangelist, but then soon also leant his passionate energy to the cause of temperance reform.[28] During the French visitors' time in America, Weld was campaigning hard for both Christian conversions and the temperance pledge. Soon after they left, Weld

27. Brownlow's extensive political involvements are treated thoroughly in Porter (forthcoming).

28. On Finney and Weld, see Finney (1989, 184–88nn.). A fine general study is Abzug (1980).

expanded his interests to attack slavery, a cause that monopolized his energies for most of the 1830s.

For his part, Finney never became as political as his acolyte Weld. But when in 1835 he published the best-selling *Lectures on Revivals of Religion*, he had become much more vocal about politics than when Tocqueville was visiting upstate New York. In 1835, Finney's preaching was still aimed at shaping mores, but it also included an appeal for direct political results: "As on the subject of slavery and temperance, so on this subject [politics], the church must act right or the country will be ruined." Finney even came close to echoing Tocqueville, but with a much more activistic conclusion: "Politics are a part of religion in such a country as this, and Christians must do their duty to the country as a part of their duty to God" (Finney 1835/1960, 297).

Tocqueville missed something significant when he did not cross paths with T. D. Weld in 1831 or register the expansion of Finney's interests by 1835. What he missed was the rapid transformation of much American Protestantism from narrowly focused religious concerns to broadly public political reform.

The same blind spot was evident during the travelers' visit to Cincinnati in early December 1831. In the months surrounding their visit, leading civic and religious figures of that city were negotiating with Lyman Beecher to assume the leadership of a new theological seminary. In a highly visible ministerial career that had already taken him from rural Connecticut to Boston's centrally located Park Street Church, Beecher (after Finney) was probably the era's best known Protestant minister. In 1830 Beecher could still fit within Tocqueville's paradigm, but just barely. During his early ministerial career, Beecher had fought hard to sustain Connecticut's Congregationalist establishment left over from the colonial era. But in comments made as Connecticut gave up its formal church-state union in 1818, Beecher had expressed Tocqueville's sentiments by claiming that disestablishment was the best thing that had ever happened for the cause of true religion and social well-being (Beecher 1865, 1:336–37). Although by 1830 Beecher had added temperance reform to his more overtly religious concerns, he was still devoting most of his energies to what Tocqueville would have styled "the building of mores."

Shortly after the Frenchmen left Cincinnati, Beecher accepted the position as head of Lane Seminary. Soon thereafter that seminary suffered a division when some of the students, inspired by Theodore Dwight Weld, came out more strongly against slavery than Beecher felt they should. The dissidents migrated northward in Ohio to found Oberlin College, where they admitted women and African American students to the student body and where they recruited Charles G. Finney as their theology professor.

Meanwhile, back in Cincinnati, where Beecher's daughter Harriet was learning about slavery as it existed in Kentucky across the Ohio River,

Beecher's apolitical stance began to melt away. For Beecher, the need to combat what he saw as the Catholic menace was the precipitating factor. In 1835 he published a book entitled *A Plea for the West* that called for all-out mobilization against Catholics, whom he saw as threatening the civic as well as the religious health of the country. This work climaxed several years of active anti-Catholic polemicizing, including at least one sermon preached at Boston in late 1830, shortly before Tocqueville and Beaumont were in the city and paying court to the Unitarian William Ellery Channing.[29] If Tocqueville had devoted the attention to Beecher he lavished on Channing, he may have understood better how religion was working to influence politics directly, rather than just indirectly, in the United States that was emerging as his journey came to an end.

Tocqueville was remarkably accurate in describing the America he witnessed personally during his visit. Yet what he missed about populations like the Methodists and movement toward a more overt religious politics was also significant. A partial explanation for this lapse was the French standard against which he was assessing American developments. With the Catholic church and its officials interwoven into every aspect of public life in France before the Revolution, and continuing to be important in public life on a scale unknown in America after the Revolution, the religious-political connections that he would have observed in 1831–32 might have seemed like only child's play.

A SHIFTING LANDSCAPE

Most important for a historical assessment of the picture of religion and politics that Tocqueville provided in *Democracy* were the altered circumstances for race and slavery that decisively altered the United States he experienced first hand. Once the dramatic occurrences of the 1830s come into view, it becomes obvious that at least some of Tocqueville's analysis drew on an America that vanished shortly after his visit was over.

An excellent point of reference for such conclusions is Tocqueville's interview with John Canfield Spencer in Canandaigua on July 17 and 18, 1831. Tocqueville found out some things about his host, but not enough. Shortly before entertaining his foreign guests, Spencer had helped prosecute three Masons who were charged with the abduction and presumed murder of a former Mason who had disclosed Masonic secrets. Spencer referred to this trial in speaking with Tocqueville, but Tocqueville did not probe the implications

29. For the timing of this sermon, see Billington (1938/1964, 70). As it happens, Beaumont concentrated more on American anti-Catholicism than did Tocqueville; see Beaumont (1958/1999, 31) and an extensive section of Beaumont (2009, 89–92).

(Zunz 2010, 219). During the time of Tocqueville's visit, Spencer was continuing his Antimasonic activity, even to the point of publishing an expose of the Masonic fraternity and playing at least some role in the activities of the Antimasonic Party (Spencer 1832).

The key circumstance was that Antimasonry became an important early vehicle for the direct intermingling of religion and politics. The charge against Masonic secrecy was that it violated the republican values of a democracy and against Masonic ideology that it substituted a vague deism for the traditional beliefs of Christian churches. The larger significance of the Antimasonic Party, with civil religion as its driving force, has been has well explained by Daniel Walker Howe: "In 1831, the Antimasons would be the first political party to hold a national convention, a practice that evangelical reform movements had pioneered. . . . The lasting contribution of the Antimasonic movement to America was a concept of party politics that combined popular participation with moral passion" (Howe 2007, 270–71). Antimasonry soon fizzled as a political movement, but the doorway it cracked open to direct religious politics remained open for several decades.

Soon thereafter religion began to exert the kind of overt political role that had been mostly absent during Tocqueville's visit. Thus, every presidential election from 1840 to 1860 would witness open religious campaigning, much unlike what occurred from 1804 to 1824 (see Carwardine 1993). Within a decade of Tocqueville's departure, denominational allegiance was the most reliable indicator of voting preference in the nation's Second Party System (see Swierenga 2007). And the strong affinity between the Democratic Party and the Catholic Church was much more visible than it had been during 1831–32 (see Hochgeschwender 2006).

Spencer's interview with Tocqueville was important for a second reason. In the course of supporting Tocqueville's conclusion about the benefits when clergy stayed clear of politics, Spencer referred to the weight that clergy could carry as educators. He told Tocqueville that it was good for ministers to be excluded from politics, because that exclusion allowed them to regain their influence in society indirectly through their role as teachers: if the clerical element is excluded from politics, "you will find that public education will slowly fall into its hands, and over time the younger generation will change its way of thinking." Tocqueville followed up Spencer's assertion by asking, "Is the clergy in charge of your public schools?" Spencer replied, "Absolutely. I know of only two counterexamples in the entire state of New York. This seems only natural to me" (Zunz 2010, 220).

To Tocqueville, the fact that clergy occupied a prime place in directing American public education confirmed his sense of Christianity working indirectly to shape mores. In America history as it actually developed, however, public education became an arena for religious combat, political activism, and occasional violence. The precipitating sparks came from Protestant anxieties. The concern that Catholic private schools subverted community morality lay behind the incineration of a convent school near Boston in 1834, shortly after Lyman Beecher had delivered another of his stem-winding anti-Catholic sermons.[30]

A second concern was more complicated. Early public schools in the United States uniformly prescribed reading from the Protestant King James Bible, which was assumed to provide nonsectarian support for the moral virtue without which a republic would collapse. When Catholics demanded a place for their own translation of scripture in the public schools, Protestants sometimes reacted violently, as during the riots in Philadelphia in spring and summer of 1844 that left numerous individuals killed and wounded, two Catholic churches burned to the ground, and great damage of mostly Irish immigrant property (Billington 1938/1964, 220–37). Where Tocqueville regarded education as part of the indirect influencing of public mores, Americans in the years immediately after his visit treated education as so directly connected to public well-being that it required direct political action. Catholic-Protestant religious differences, which in conflict over public schooling acted as anything but a check on the tyranny of the majority, were crucial.

But the most important reason for the politicization of religion and the sacralization of politics from the early 1830s was slavery. Spurred by religiously supported views on slavery, American religion was politicized with a vengeance, and politics became an arena where leading clerics tried to exert their influence directly. Religious attempts to shape mores through distinctly spiritual or narrowly moral means did not pass away; but those attempts were joined increasingly by religious efforts to influence politics directly. Had Tocqueville visited the United States even 5 years later, he would not have been able to write about religious-political connections as he did.

Events overlapping with the Frenchmen's visit were already pointing to the politicization of religion that expanded steadily from 1830 through the Civil War. As early as 1827, a Philadelphia Presbyterian minister, Ezra Stiles Ely, had created a stir by calling for an overtly Christian political party in a much-noticed Fourth of July address (Ely 1828). By the early 1830s, prominent clergy and laymen were campaigning against moving the mails on Sunday as a violation of the Christian Sabbath (see John 1995). Several ministers, including Gustave de Beaumont's fictional Daniel Nelson, took overt action to stop Cherokee Removal, a cause that another daughter of Lyman Beecher,

30. This event was treated at some length in Beaumont (2009, 92), but it is not mentioned in Tocqueville (2010).

Catherine, took up with religious fervor (see McLoughlin 1984). Timothy Dwight Weld and other temperance advocates were moving rapidly from moral suasion to political action, which spoke more generally of a broader move of the voluntary societies to legislation and the ballot (see Young 2006, 75).

Yet among all such prompts to the increased intermingling of religion and politics, the strongest was the nation's system of black-only racial slavery. Shortly before Beaumont and Tocqueville arrived in America, William Lloyd Garrison began publishing *The Liberator* and the Virginia legislature took up the possibility of providing for the emancipation of that state's slaves. In early August 1831, when the Frenchmen were traveling on Lake Huron toward Sault Sainte Marie and Green Bay, the Nat Turner Rebellion in Virginia riveted the nation's attention and ensured the victory of pro-slave forces in that state's constitutional debate. Within a year of their departure from the United States, the cause of immediate emancipation as a moral imperative sparked the founding of the American Anti-Slavery Society—which, in turn, stimulated a profusion of publications, first from the South but then soon also from the North, that defended slavery as an institution sanctioned by scripture. Then in 1837 the Presbyterians split into an Old School faction, mostly willing to leave slavery alone, and a New School party, with many adherents who looked upon slavery as a sin. The North-South division of both Methodists and Baptists in 1844 broke apart institutions that Henry Clay and John C. Calhoun, along with many others, considered the nation's strongest (see Noll 2002, 199). In other words, almost as soon as Tocqueville was back in France, his account of religion and American politics required serious adjustment—ministers increasingly took political stances, religion was increasingly brought to bear on political conflicts, and national mores concerning race were increasingly mingled with overt political religion.

To assess *Democracy in America* by what happened in the United States after Tocqueville returned to France unfairly requires him to function as a prophet as well as a political scientist. Yet if his book is to count as a perennially useful guide to the subjects he discussed, some account must be given of America as it changed as well as the America that he visited.

CONCLUSION

Obsessively chronological attention to the arguments about religion and politics in Tocqueville's *Democracy in America* forces this text into a frame alien to its own intentions. But such an attempt could still help political scientists to understand Tocqueville within the framework he chose for himself. A crucial question that both historians and political scientists must address is the character of Tocqueville's argument. Was he describing an ideal type? (That is, if religious functions as I have described it, then it will continue to support democratic liberty and check the excesses to which democracy is prone.) Or was he claiming to see something perennial in the makeup of American society and culture? (That is, since religion functions in America as I have described it, American politics will continue to be shaped by religion as "the first of [the United States'] political institutions" [Tocqueville 2010, 2:475].) Historical assessment points to the conclusion that, when the circumstances of the work's composition are in view, *Democracy in America* works much better as an ideal type than as an accurate reading of American actualities.

Many of the conclusions that Tocqueville drew in *Democracy* were advanced as simple statements of fact. Several of these statements reflected reality in 1830 and in large measure have continued to do so—for example, that the American state puts up no obstacles to religious practice, that American religious groups tolerate each other, and that Americans enjoy the legal separation of church and state. The observation that American denominations, despite their differences in dogma, teach broadly the same morality was mostly true into the twentieth century, with the significant exception of slavery, but seems less true for the recent past.

Yet a number of his conclusions perform better as conditionals than as factual generalizations. These include assertions about American religion being free of all political prejudices and about clerics not participating directly in political affairs. Such assertions may have been largely factual during the time of Tocqueville's visit, but they were soon falsified by developments in the 1830s and have been often contradicted thereafter.

The timing of Tocqueville's trip meant that he experienced direct religious-political connections at a low point in all of American history. His claims about religion in the abstract and about clergymen concretely—that they worked only indirectly to influence politics by their influence on mores—was decidedly not the case from the mid-1830s through the 1860s. Since that time these claims have been only intermittently true for religion as a whole and true for only some religious traditions even then. The question, therefore, arises, whether Tocqueville's depiction of American religion and politics is valid if one of his central assertions has only occasionally prevailed in the unfolding of later history.

An even more problematic aspect of Tocqueville's analysis comes into focus when the spotlight shifts to Gustave de Beaumont. Beaumont's *Marie* significantly states in its subtitle that this novel about slavery was a depiction of American mores. Beaumont, in other words, was underscoring the wisdom of Tocqueville's stress on mores as providing the nurturing medium for politics. But what Beaumont emphasized more strongly than Tocqueville was the way that race consciousness or race prejudice functioned in America as a religion-like force to shape the mores that influenced politics. In Beaumont's novel, race consciousness seems sometimes to act independently of religion and sometimes in cooperation.

As many students have documented, Tocqueville also wrote perceptively about race—for example, when he reported that in the North he saw "the legal barrier" that separated the races falling away, "but not that of mores. I see slavery receding; the prejudice to which it gave birth is immovable" (Tocqueville 2010, 2:553). Yet, unlike Beaumont, Tocqueville treated the nation's difficulties with race as only one among several important characteristics. For Beaumont, by contrast, it was central.

In 1835, it may have seemed narrow to focus so closely on "the condition of the black race in America and its influence on the future of the United States" (Beaumont 1958/1999, 6). Yet in pointing out the way in which slavery created separate societies North and South, and even more in contending that racial prejudice posed more intractable problems than slavery itself, Beaumont highlighted circumstances that long influenced the relation of religion and politics. Although *Marie* did not treat the religious-political dynamic extensively, Beaumont's observations were still telling. For example, at the end of Ludovic's travels designed expressly to explore American racial prejudice, he concludes, "but what caused me the greatest wonder was to find this segregation in churches. Who would have believed it? Rank and privilege in Christian churches? The blacks are either relegated to some dark corner of the building or completely excluded" (Beaumont 1958/1999, 76).[31] Moreover, when "considering this" religious subject, Ludovic exploits Tocqueville's insight about the power of American public opinion in order to expound what he calls "a sad truth": "public opinion, so charitable when it protects, is the cruelest of tyrants when it persecutes. Public opinion, all-powerful in the United States, desires the oppression of a detested race, and nothing can thwart its hatred" (77). When in the notes to the novel Beaumont detailed the anti-Catholic animus that mingled with anti-black fervor to spark the extensive New York and Philadelphia riots of July 1834, he came as close to explaining the potential for civil war as anything explicit in *Democracy*.

Nonetheless, if Tocqueville's analysis could be augmented with Beaumont's concentration on race, the application of Tocqueville's ideal type to much of American history after 1832 would actually be strengthened. Tocqueville's crucial argument can be summarized in four connected propositions: First, the religion he saw at work in the United States, though lacking in dogmatic heft

31. In both the novel and his long note on American religion, Beaumont overstated the extent to which American Catholics promoted racial integration, but he was entirely correct in suggesting that Catholic worship was less segregated than Protestant.

by comparison with Catholicism, nonetheless had internalized a fundamental fact of the universe, that "Christianity has made all men equal before God" (Tocqueville 2010, 1:24). Second, acceptance of this fundamental Christian fact was propelling a remarkable advance of genuine human liberty because it could operate so freely alongside the new nation's commitment to democratic equality of conditions. Third, the great secret of why such religion could have such effects, and, in striking contrast to Europe where religion was still entangled in political structures presupposing inequality, was that it foreswore overt political power and concentrated on shaping the mores of the people. Fourth and finally, because religion embodying this fundamental Christian principle was effectively shaping national mores, those mores were preventing democracy from degenerating into a tyranny of the majority.

By taking Beaumont more seriously in his account of the foundational racialism at work in the United States—by, that is, incorporating Beaumont's insight into the calculus of his ideal type—Tocqueville's argument not only explains a great deal of American history but also modifies Tocqueville's ideal type in such a way to fit what actually happened.

Thus, the beginnings of overt conflict over slavery in the 1830s pushed racialism to the fore alongside religion as the most powerful shaping forces on American mores. Racialism, likewise, lay behind the efforts of clergy to influence politics directly. But racialism represented a fundamental contradiction of Tocqueville's dogmatic theological proposition that "Christianity has made all men equal before God." Because racialism counteracted the workings of Christian egalitarianism upon democracy, and because racialism pushed America toward repeating the European mistake of directly intermingling a religious principle of equality with political institutions of power, American democracy in the era of the Civil War suffered from what could be called the tyranny of the majority. Southern defenses of slavery, based on racialist principles and driven by clerical activism that fulfilled the negative possibilities of Tocqueville's model, were the main evil. But a secondary evil was an all-out northern commitment to the Union, based primarily on an inegalitarian ideology of Manifest Destiny, only incidentally defending theological equality before God, and even more strikingly influenced by clergy taking direct political action. The combination of the South's great evil and the North's subsidiary evil was mass slaughter and, for the South, a scorched earth. In comparative terms, the Civil War witnessed a tyranny of the majority even more devastating, at least for the short term, than the tyranny of the majority that Tocqueville's family experienced during the French Revolution.

The effect of the Civil War on national mores was more complicated. On the one hand, the Thirteenth, Fourteenth, and Fifteenth Amendments reflected the positive potential of Tocqueville's ideal type to infuse democracy with liberty. On the other hand, the postwar acceptance of systematic racial discrimination and the relative enfeeblement of religion in competition with consumer capitalism, reflected more the negative possibilities of the ideal type as modified by the realism of Beaumont's *Marie.*

Alexis de Tocqueville's *Democracy in America* was and is a great book. The heroic labor of scholars to document the experiences of the French travelers that went into the writing of this classic have not diminished its greatness. To the contrary, they have made it possible to analyze with much greater precision the extent to which Tocqueville's *Democracy* accurately reflected the United States he visited as well as the capacity of his arguments to explain the entire sweep of American history. Their labors are the indispensable background for my conclusion: that *Democracy in America* offered a stunningly insightful depiction of the nation that the French travelers visited, but also that this great work would have been more cogent in accounting for what actually has happened in later American history if Tocqueville and Beaumont had carried out their original plan of together writing one book about democracy, liberty, and the mores of the American people.

REFERENCES

Abzug, Robert H. 1980. *Passionate Liberator: Theodore Dwight Weld and the Dilemma of Reform.* New York: Oxford University Press.

Asbury, Francis. 1958. *The Journal and Letters of Francis Asbury.* Ed. Elmer T. Clark et al. 3 vols. Nashville: Cokesbury.

Beaumont, Gustave de. 1958/1999. *Marie; or, Slavery in the United States: A Novel of Jacksonian America.* Trans. Barbara Chapman. Stanford, CA: Stanford University Press. Repr. with intro. by Gerard Fergerson (Baltimore: Johns Hopkins University Press). Originally published as *Marie ou l'esclavage aux États-Unis*, 5 eds. (Paris, 1835–42).

———. 2009. "Note sur le mouvement religieux aux États-Unis." In *Marie ou l'esclavage aux Etats-Unis, Tome II: Notes, Appendice, Annexes*, ed. Marie-Claude Schapira, 87–103. Paris: L'Harmattan.

Beecher, Lyman. 1865. *Autobiography, Correspondence, etc., of Lyman Beecher, D. D.* Ed. Charles Beecher. 2 vols. New York: Harper.

Billington, Ray Allen. 1938/1964. *The Protestant Crusade, 1800–1860.* Repr. Chicago: University of Chicago Press.

Bremer, Frederica. 1849–51/1976. *The Homes of the New World.* Abridged in *Abroad in America: Visitors to the New Nation, 1776–1914*, ed. Marc Placher. Reading, MA: Addison-Wesley.

Brown, Frederick, ed. 2010. *Alexis de Tocqueville: Letters from America.* New Haven, CT: Yale University Press.

Carwardine, Richard. 1993. *Evangelicals and Politics in Antebellum America.* New Haven, CT: Yale University Press.

Cooper, Ezekiel. 1819. *The Substance of a Funeral Discours . . . : On the Death of the Rev. Francis Asbury*. Philadelphia: Jonathan Pounder.

Damrosch, Leo. 2010. *Tocqueville's Discovery of America*. New York: Farrar, Straus & Giroux.

Dickens, Charles. 1842. *American Notes for General Circulation*. London: Chapman & Hall.

Ely, Ezra Stiles. 1828. *The Duty of Freemen to Elect Christian Rulers*. Philadelphia: W. F. Geddes.

Finney, Charles G. 1835/1960. *Lectures on Revivals of Religion*. Ed. William G. McLoughlin. Repr. Cambridge, MA: Harvard University Press.

———. 1989. *The Memoirs of Charles G. Finney: The Complete Restored Text*. Ed. Garth M. Rosell and A. G. Dupuis. Grand Rapids, MI: Zondervan.

Foster, Charles I. 1960. *Errand of Mercy: The Evangelical United Front, 1790–1837*. Chapel Hill: University of North Carolina Press.

Hochgeschwender, Michael. 2006. *Wahrheit, Einheit, Ordnung: Die Sklavenfrage und der amerikanischen Katholizismus, 1835–1870*. Paderborn: Schöningen.

Howe, Daniel Walker. 2007. *What Hath God Wrought: The Transformation of America, 1815–1848*. New York: Oxford University Press.

John, Richard R. 1995. *Spreading the News: The American Postal System from Franklin to Morse*. Cambridge, MA: Harvard University Press.

Johnson, Curtis D. 1989. *Islands of Holiness: Rural Religion in Upstate New York, 1790–1860*. Ithaca, NY: Cornell University Press.

Johnson, Paul E. 1978. *Shopkeepers' Millennium: Society and Revivals in Rochester, New York, 1815–1837*. New York: Hill & Wang.

Kammen, Michael. 1996. *Alexis de Tocqueville and "Democracy in America."* Washington, DC: Library of Congress.

Lazerow, Jama. 1995. *Religion and the Working Class in Antebellum America*. Washington, DC: Smithsonian Institution.

Marsden, George M. 1970. *The Evangelical Mind and the New School Presbyterian Experience*. New Haven, CT: Yale University Press.

Mathews, Donald G. 1969. "The Second Great Awakening as an Organizing Process." *American Quarterly* 21:23–43.

McLoughlin, William G. 1984. *Cherokees and Missionaries, 1789–1839*. New Haven, CT: Yale University Press.

Methodist Episcopal Church. 1813. *Minutes of the Methodist Conferences Annually Held in America, from 1773 to 1813, Inclusive*. New York: Hitt & Ware.

Murat, Achille. 1832/1967. *A Moral and Political Sketch of the United States of North America*. Abridged in *The Voluntary Church: American Religion Life, 1740–1860, Seen through the Eyes of European Visitors*, ed. Milton B. Powell. New York: Macmillan.

Noll, Mark A. 2002. *America's God: From Jonathan Edwards to Abraham Lincoln*. New York: Oxford University Press.

Nord, David Paul. 1996. "Free Grace, Free Books, Free Riders: The Economics of Religious Publishing in Early Nineteenth-Century America." *Proceedings of the American Antiquarian Society* 106:241–72.

———. 2001. "Benevolent Capital: Financing Evangelical Book Publishing in Early-Nineteenth-Century America." In *God and Mammon: Protestants, Money, and the Market, 1790–1860*, ed. Mark A. Noll, 147–70. New York: Oxford University Press.

Perciaccante, Marianne. 2003. *Calling Down Fire: Charles Grandison Finney and Revivalism in Jefferson County, New York, 1800–1840.* Albany, NY: SUNY Press.

Pierson, George Wilson. 1938/1996. *Tocqueville in America.* Repr. Baltimore: Johns Hopkins University Press. Originally published as *Tocqueville and Beaumont in America.*

Porter, Laura Rominger. Forthcoming. *From Church House to Statehouse: Evangelicals and the Politics of Sin in the Nineteenth-Century Upper South.*

Potts, David. 1992. *Wesleyan University, 1831–1910: Collegiate Enterprise in New England.* New Haven, CT: Yale University Press.

Schleifer, James T. 2000. *The Making of Tocqueville's "Democracy in America."* 2nd ed. Indianapolis: Liberty Fund.

Skinner, Quentin. 2002. *Visions of Politics.* Vol. 1, *Regarding Method.* New York: Cambridge University Press.

Spencer, John C. 1832. *Extract from the Proceedings of the United States Anti-Masonic Convention: Held at Baltimore, Md. Sept. 1831.* Utica, NY: Willliams.

Swierenga, Robert P. 2007. "Ethnoreligious Political Behavior in the Mid-nineteenth Century: Voting, Values, Cultures." In *Religion and American Politics: From the Colonial Period to the Present*, ed. Mark A. Noll and Luke E. Harlow, 148–68. New York: Oxford University Press.

Tocqueville, Alexis de. 2010. *Democracy in America.* Ed. Eduardo Nolla. Trans. James T. Schleifer. 4 vols. Indianapolis: Liberty Fund. Originally published as *De la démocratie en Amérique* (Paris: Flammarion, 1835, 1840).

Trollope, Frances. 1832. *Domestic Manners of the Americans.* London: Whittacker, Treacher.

Wigger, John H. 1998. *Taking Heaven by Storm: Methodism and the Rise of Popular Christianity in America.* New York: Oxford University Press.

———. 2009. *American Saint: Francis Asbury and the Methodists.* New York: Oxford University Press.

Young, Michael P. 2006. *Bearing Witness against Sin: The Evangelical Birth of the American Society Movement.* Chicago: University of Chicago Press.

Zunz, Olivier, ed. 2010. *Alexis de Tocqueville and Gustave de Beaumont in America.* Trans. Arthur Goldhammer. Charlottesville: University of Virginia Press.

Tocqueville, Pascal, and the Transcendent Horizon

ALEXANDER JECH

ABSTRACT

This article traces the contours of Pascal's influence on Tocqueville's understanding of the human condition and our appropriate response to it. Similar temperaments lead both authors to emphasize human limitations and contingency, especially our mortality, our ignorance of the most important subjects, and the effects of historical contingency on human nature, and both represent the complex internal dynamic of human nature in terms of the interplay of "angel" and "brute." They disagree over the power and significance of human action. Whereas the motif of human weakness is fundamental for Pascal, Tocqueville repeatedly affirms that, under the right conditions, human beings are "powerful and free." Beginning from Pascalian premises, and endeavoring to be more faithful to some of those premises than Pascal himself was, Tocqueville aims to illuminate the possibility of an amelioration of the human condition through a "new political science" that redeems the political realm without divinizing it.

Most students of Tocqueville know of his remark, "There are three men with whom I live a little every day; they are Pascal, Montesquieu, and Rousseau."[1] Pascal is considered a religious rather than a political philosopher and is not often invoked in discussions of politics, so the influence of the other two is more obvious and more widely commented on. Yet Pascal's influence is as profound as theirs, and although Tocqueville made a careful study of Pascal's elegant yet natural literary style, it is not merely stylistic.[2] When we examine Tocqueville's understanding of human existence and seek to get a sense of what we might call his own "religious sensibility" and his conception of the

Alexander Jech is professor of philosophy, University of Notre Dame, 100 Malloy Hall, Notre Dame, IN 46556 (ajech@nd.edu).

I would like to express gratitude to Michael Zuckert, Roger Knights, and the three anonymous referees for their helpful advice in the writing of this article.

1. Correspondence of Alexis de Tocqueville and Louis de Kergorlay, *Oeuvres complètes* (Paris: Gallimard, 1977), 13:418.

2. See the article by Kergorlay titled "Etude Littéraire sur Alexis de Tocqueville," in *Le Correspondant*, April 1861 (see annexe in *Oeuvres complètes*, 13:352–63): "As [Tocqueville] approached maturity, he attached himself by preference to other masters, to none other than Pascal for the very depth of the language, to Voltaire for the ease and the art of lightening the style."

[American Political Thought, vol. 5, issue 1, Winter 2016]

shape and limitations of human life, we constantly find him wrestling with Pascal, dialectically engaged with Pascal's arguments and positions, and developing his own more social, more historical, and more political conception of the human condition.

Since Diez del Corral's "Tocqueville et Pascal," there have been several attempts to understand Pascal's influence on Tocqueville (Corral 1965). The new critical edition of *Democracy in America* edited by Eduardo Nolla and translated by James Schleifer is helpful in making some of the most patent connections clear to the reader. The most notable and sustained of these studies is Peter Lawler's *The Restless Mind: Alexis de Tocqueville on the Origin and Perpetuation of Human Liberty*, to which my account owes something, but I regard his book as making Tocqueville too indebted to Pascal and not doing justice to the social and political aspects of Tocqueville's thought. By and large, however, Tocqueville scholarship has not made much of Pascalian influence, and so readers may wonder just to what extent the seventeenth-century scientist, Jansenist, and polemicist shaped the convictions of the nineteenth-century statesman and political theorist.

Fundamentally, what Tocqueville and Pascal share is a temperament open to certain experiences of the sublime, on the one hand, and aware of human limitations and contingency, on the other. This temperament leads them to endorse similar kinds of principles, although they do not always interpret the same experiences in the same way and do not always draw the same conclusions from them. My goal here is to identify the exact points on which Tocqueville and Pascal agree or disagree regarding the human condition and thereby to illuminate why they draw different conclusions on that subject.

On a wide number of points regarding the importance of mortality, ignorance, and the structure of human nature, there is significant agreement between the two thinkers. I shall discuss each of these points in what follows. Moreover, one great difference between Pascal and Tocqueville grows out of a point of agreement. Both believe that what different people count as "human nature" and as "justice" at any given time is heavily influenced by custom and history. Pascal addresses such themes in a variety of ways, and in fragment 159 he toys with the radically historicist idea that, our true nature having been lost in the Fall, we are now custom all the way down. Pascal's reflections on the power of custom to shape human sentiments and behavior, however, are not developed in a systematic way. Tocqueville, on the other hand, treats the historical malleability of human nature as one of his primary problematics. His science of social state functions to unify the "two distinct humanities" of "democratic man" and "aristocratic man" and to subject such historicism to a rule (*Democracy in America* 2.4.8; Tocqueville 2010, 1282; see also Zuckert 1993; Jech 2013).[3] His thought is therefore more social and more political than Pascal's.

The most important difference between them concerns their relative estimates of human power and the significance of human action. The motif of human weakness is an important part of Pascal's analysis of the human condition. "What astonishes us most," Pascal says, "is that everyone is not more astonished at his own weakness" (frag. 67). One finds Pascal returning to this theme in fragments 62, 67, 130, 182, 184, 240, 249, 540, and 643, among others. Human action is incapable of ameliorating the afflictions associated with the human condition, and action is engaged in primarily as a means of avoiding honestly facing those afflictions. For Pascal, action is frequently no more than a form of distraction or diversion (frags. 168 and 171); it is as if humanity dwelled in a doomed valley, afflicted by severe and crippling ills that will eventually destroy us, while our only cures lay beyond the impassable peaks closing us in. To solve the human condition would require transcending it, a task that requires equally transcendent power.

Tocqueville, on the other hand, repeatedly affirms that, under the right conditions, human beings are (in a turn of phrase one cannot imagine finding in Pascal) "powerful and free" (2.4.8, Tocqueville 2010, 1285). Despite agreeing with Pascal that human greatness lies entirely "in the soul," he modifies this idea so that its significance is that human greatness is especially present in action. Tocqueville arrives at this conclusion from Pascalian premises. In fact, in a crucial respect, he makes these premises more internally consistent than Pascal had done. Without denying Pascal's otherworldly conclusions, Tocqueville affirms a very different orientation to the here and now—to the temporal and finite realm. He opens up the possibility that engagement with the things of the world can amount to more than vanity and distraction. Tocqueville's statement that the Americans have "successfully blended . . . and marvelously combined" the "spirit of religion" and the "spirit of liberty" is indicative of a concern with providing an amelioration of the human condition via a harmonization of the two aspects of human nature in the form of a "new political science" that redeems the political realm without divinizing it.

3. Citations from *Democracy in America* refer to the bilingual critical edition (Tocqueville 2010). Citations from *The Old Regime and the Revolution* refer to Alan Kahan's translation (Tocqueville 1998). Citations of Tocqueville's letters are from Tocqueville (1985).

1. PASCAL'S PREMISES

Nietzsche, no friend to Christians, wrote in a letter to his friend Georg Brandes that Pascal was the "only *logical* Christian" and averred that he had learned "an infinite amount" from him (Nietzsche 1996, 327). Such testimony should lead us to expect to find a very powerful analysis of the human condition in Pascal's works, an analysis that forms the basis of his conclusion that the only solution to humanity's woes is supernatural and otherworldly and never to be achieved by human action in this world. Yet, for all the clarity and logical rigor we find in his published papers, when we examine the *Pensées*, the work where we find Pascal's observations and analysis of the human condition, we encounter an unfinished work of cobbled-together fragments, whose pages shine with brilliant observations but which sprawls out with no obvious order, in apparently disorganized and contradictory array. Is there a deeper logic here, or even a coherent conception of human life?

The reception of Pascal's work (especially the history of responses to the now-eponymous "Pascal's Wager") demonstrates the value of exercising patience on this point, for it is Nietzsche who appears to have had the more accurate sense of the *Pensées*' aphoristic fragments.[4] Time has led to a sharper and subtler understanding of what Pascal is up to. When Pascal's writing appears obscure, one must be careful not to assume that the difficulty is in his thought; instead, one must first seek to uncover the logic behind it. Here I will try to reconstruct the main lines of his conception of the human condition, especially those aspects with which Tocqueville was most engaged. I will do this first by delineating a set of "premises" Pascal develops through close observation or analysis of human behavior and then, in the next section, by turning to the conclusions that he draws from these premises.

The first premise of Pascal's argument is that the human desire for happiness is universal. As he puts it, "[man] wants to be happy, he only wants to be happy, and cannot not want to be happy" (frag. 166), and "[happiness] is the motive for men's every action, even those who are going to hang themselves" (frag. 181).

1. All human beings necessarily wish to be happy, and all other desires are subordinate to this wish.

This is our dearest desire; nonetheless, we suffer from a deep lack of clarity regarding the nature of happiness. Happiness consists in peace or rest, while

4. See Hacking (2006) for a good example of how the development of probability theory, on the one hand, and a better understanding of Pascal's manuscript, on the other, have led scholars to a much subtler appreciation of the precise nature and function of Pascal's Wager.

we consistently seek it out through activity (frag. 166). We do not understand happiness well because we intuitively or subconsciously recognize that our condition makes its achievement impossible. When happiness is impossible, our happiness is best served if we avoid dwelling on its impossibility, because doing so would make us even worse off and more miserable than before: "men have decided for their own happiness not to think about it" (frag. 166).

Tocqueville agrees that we all desire happiness, although he does not espouse the very strong, rather "classical" description of this desire expressed in Pascal's premise. He appears to hold a weaker version of the premise instead. In *Democracy in America* Tocqueville states that "personal interest" is the "only fixed point in the human heart" (1.2.6, Tocqueville 2010, 391), and elsewhere he says that all human beings possess an "ardent passion" for happiness (Tocqueville 1985, 63), but he also denies that all our actions are performed for the sake of self-interest (2.2.8, Tocqueville 2010, 921). "Interest" is not quite what Pascal means by "happiness," but we can settle here by saying that Tocqueville agrees at least that we all pursue happiness and desire it. He also agrees that happiness is not truly possible (Tocqueville 1985, 63).

Now, why does Pascal think that our happiness is so elusive, and so poorly understood? Pascal is an antisystematic thinker. He distrusts the vanity involved in system building, which serves the pride of the philosopher (frag. 175). Human nature consists of "two different natures" (frag. 144), both "instinct" and "reason," "passion" and "thought," "greatness" and "baseness," the "angel" and the "brute," combined in a confused mixture we cannot comprehend (frags. 164 and 230). It is dangerous to understand only one of these: we must understand both our "greatness" and our "baseness" to think and live as we ought (frags. 153 and 513). Yet philosophers for the most part have tried to reduce human beings into one of these alternatives: "Some wanted to renounce the passions and become gods, the others wanted to renounce reason and become brute beasts. But neither group succeeded" (frag. 29; see also Dreyfus 2012). From the Platonists, Stoics, and Epicureans of antiquity down to Descartes and Hobbes in Pascal's own time, philosophers were guilty again and again of oversimplifying the mixture that is humanity in order to render it more theoretically tidy and unified. They unknowingly agree with Dostoevsky's Dmitry Karamazov that human nature is "much too prodigious" and should be "cut down to size" (Dostoevsky 1994, 136).

Pascal refuses either simplification; human nature contains both "baseness" and "greatness," and we are thoroughly contradictory (frag. 230). Thus,

2. All human beings are a mixture of a rational nature and an animal nature, each with its own principles.

He also denies that we can, or should aim to, become wholly one or the other. We can never escape the needs or properties associated with the half we try to suppress, and the attempt to do so only corrupts the aspect we pursue: "Man is neither angel nor brute, and the unfortunate thing is that he who would act the angel acts the brute" (frag. 358). Human happiness requires that both sides of our nature be fulfilled, not just one or the other. We fail at achieving happiness when either the brute's or the angel's desires are denied (frags. 110 and 166) or when the war between these two aspects prevents us from finding any repose (frags. 29 and 168).

3. Human happiness requires fulfilling both our rational and our animal nature and harmonizing these with each other.

Tocqueville not only accepts premise 2, the mixture principle, but adopts Pascal's language as well, referring to humanity as being divided between the "angel" and the "brute" (2.2.16, Tocqueville 2010, 963). Tocqueville further accepts that each of these elements has its own distinct needs and desires (2.2.12, Tocqueville 2010, 940; 2.2.15, Tocqueville 2010, 956). Thus, Tocqueville also accepts premise 3. It is unhealthy for humanity to live too much as angels or as brutes. Tocqueville noted that the colonists in the West Indies succumbed to the temptations of bestiality and suffered for it (1.1.1, Tocqueville 2010, 38), but he also pointed out that those who live too much within the realm of thought also suffer for it (2.1.10, Tocqueville 2010, 781–82), tacitly chiding Pascal for failing to live by his own principles. The wish to satisfy only the angel or only the brute is a self-destructive urge that legislators ought to combat (2.2.15, Tocqueville 2010, 956). One also thinks of his mixed judgment on the leading figures of the French Revolution, those extraordinary figures who understood the theory of politics much more than they understood true statesmanship, who excelled more in "genius" and in "conceiving vast plans" than in "common sense" and the achievement of "great tasks"—and who consequently fell short of "true glory" (*The Old Regime and the Revolution* 1.3.8, Tocqueville 1998, 246).

Unfortunately, we are incapable of fulfilling the desires of either aspect of human nature. The rational aspect of our nature desires to know the truth but is trapped between ignorance and knowledge (frag. 230). We cannot help wanting to know the truth about human existence, but its accomplishment is impossible (frag. 110). Human reason is calculative, moving from premises to conclusions, and perfect in itself when its method is sound (Pascal 1995, 196–97), but incapable of securing its first premises, which it acquires from "nature" (Pascal 1995, 194). What we regard as nature, however, is subject to custom and frequently misleads us (frag. 164). It is subject to the "uncertain balance between truth and pleasure . . . in the deepest interior of a human being," in such a way and to such a degree that a person rarely knows which he or she is following (Pascal 1995, 195). The attempt to use our finite intellect in order to comprehend an infinitely great and infinitely divisible universe disorients our reason, which requires a resting point (frag. 230). For Pascal, human science necessarily includes a "void" within it, "at its foundation" (Khalfa 2003, 133). Moral knowledge is incomparably more important to us than scientific knowledge (frag. 57), but the difficulty, or impossibility, of knowing ourselves or our true nature makes it even more elusive (frags. 230 and 576). We are unsure even of how far our ignorance goes, because neither skepticism nor dogmatism can be established (frag. 164). The lack of a fixed point leaves us with the realization that for all reason can show us, every aspect of human life is contingent and accidental. The kind of cosmic order that the philosophers have sought, which would give us a clear sense of human identity and purpose, is entirely absent; the universe is "silent" (frag. 229).

Can one live well by embracing the brute? Pascal does not take this option seriously, or perhaps does not take himself to be addressing those who would seriously consider pursuing a life like this. We cannot eliminate the angel, the rational aspect of human nature, but we can make it serve the brute by devoting it to searching out the means for securing the brute's desires and existence. In Tocqueville's phrase, the angel is capable of teaching the brute and showing it how to meet its needs, even to the point of constructing a sort of morality that secures our brutish desires. Even in this role, the rational side of human nature shows its greatness (frag. 138). But the rational aspect of human nature distorts the brute's simple desires: the interaction of the rational and animal aspects of humanity produces the imagination, which renders the desires of the brute fantastical, unlimited, and incapable of satisfaction (frag. 78). Furthermore, reason reveals to the brute that we must die. Death undermines contentment, for it is the most inescapable of our ills and our knowledge of its inescapable and unpredictable arrival is itself an enormous evil (frag. 681). Knowledge of death is so miserable that we require constant diversion or distraction to escape from its misery (frag. 166).

Furthermore, the desires rooted in the two aspects of our nature conflict with each other (frag. 514). They draw us in different directions and require different things of us; the difficulty of reconciling them is what has led philosophers to their inaccurate simplifications of human nature (frag. 29). The two aspects of ourselves do not fit together well; taken as a whole, man is a monstrous, incomprehensible being (frags. 163 and 164). Pascal therefore concludes,

4. We are incapable of fulfilling or even harmonizing the desires natural to human nature.

Tocqueville largely accepts premise 4. He understands mortality as an evil we innately desire to escape, which impinges especially on our desire for material things and therefore conflicts with the desires of the "brute" (1.2.9, Tocqueville 2010, 482). He is aware of the power of general ideas but is also aware of the cost associated with them (2.1.3, Tocqueville 2010, 727). He believes that we are incapable of achieving either happiness or knowledge; Tocqueville says that we have an innate desire to engage in "the search for absolute, demonstrable truth," but pursuing this "impossible" quest succeeded only in throwing him into "a horrible state," "the unhappiest time of his life." The "inextricable doubts" he encountered so disoriented him that he felt "the floor tremble under his feet" and saw "the walls that surround him move." Despite our immense desire to know and to understand our own existence, our lack of certainty regarding "the immense majority of points that it is important for us to know" is "one of the most inflexible laws of our nature" (Tocqueville 1985, 64). Fundamentally, we do not understand our place in the universe or the significance of our existence; we experience our lives as contingent, and our reason is sufficiently weak that we cannot live without dogmatic beliefs (2.1.2, Tocqueville 2010, 712–15). Pure thought is too difficult for us.

Human beings therefore occupy an unpleasant position. Can they ameliorate or, better, correct this condition? Can the being nature left in painful perplexity overcome its condition by its own efforts at reform and enlightenment?

Pascal's answer is a firm "No": the causes of human misery escape human control. Our misery is matched by our weakness. The nature of our ignorance is itself a cause of our remaining in ignorance; our ignorance is not simple, so that our ignorance of a moral standard itself prevents us from identifying the moral standard. "We need a rule" to determine which starting point to begin from, but "reason is pliable in either direction," and so "there is no rule" (frag. 455). We have no power to overcome human mortality. And no one has yet found a means of making the passions and reason live with each other, nor is it clear how someone could.

5. We lack the power to change the human condition so as to make it possible to fulfill the desires natural to human nature or to harmonize our two aspects.

The wretchedness of the human condition, combined with our powerlessness to make it anything else, lies at the root of the great restlessness that marks human nature. According to Pascal, our desire to be happy and our incapacity to become so force us to continually engage in an absurd attempt to undo what cannot be undone, the corruption of human nature. The only remedy available requires turning to God for help, which is contrary to our passions. Therefore, we "doggedly refuse to face our misery" (Kolakowski 1995, 133) and seek distractions instead.

Does Tocqueville agree? In a pessimistic mood late in life, he remarks that "this singular being we call man" has been "granted just enough enlightenment to see the wretchedness of his condition but not enough to change it" (letter to Bouchitte, January 8, 1858, as quoted in Lamberti 1989, 157). But this is not his dominant mood, as we will see in a moment. First, however, let us see the conclusions that Pascal draws from these premises.

2. PASCAL'S CONCLUSIONS

Pascal, we sense, is not an optimist about the human condition. From his premises he concludes,

> C1. Human beings are necessarily wretched and miserable beings.

We are wretched because we lack happiness; this wretchedness is necessary because we lack the power to seriously change the conditions that prevent our happiness.

Where does this wretchedness come from? According to Pascal, we were created with another nature but have fallen from that nature, and we now live with the consequences of inheriting a corrupted form of humanity, "like a fruit bred from a rotten seed" (Pascal 1995, 222). Our "unsatisfied desires for certainty, happiness, and rest" point us back to a state of perfection we have lost (Lawler 1993, 76). According to Pascal, this is the only, or at least the best, explanation for humanity as we find it, and Christianity alone provides a philosophy that makes sense of our contradictory nature (frag. 690).

> C2. The reason why human beings are wretched and weak is that human nature has been corrupted from its original form.

It is natural to then ask, can we never escape or improve this condition? Pascal's answer is that we ourselves can never improve this condition (frag. 67); it can, however, be improved by another—that is, by God. The natural means at our disposal all fall short. However, supernatural grace, of the kind Pascal experienced firsthand in "the night of fire" and recorded in the "Memorial" (Pascal 1995, 178), has the power to change human nature. In this life, the change is partial, although Pascal argues that saints, even in this life, are happy (frag. 389). But even saints remain weighted down with corruption until the resurrection of the dead. A full cure and harmonization of human nature will not be achieved until then.

Pascal, then, argues that only a transcendent power could cure the human condition. Moreover, because our malady must be healed by grace and not by us, there is nothing in the realm of action, within the near horizon, that can ameliorate our condition. One can train the body, the "automaton," so that it is accustomed to the ways of grace, but without grace this offers little help regarding the fundamental ills of human life. We can and should seek grace, but we cannot "win" it or perform any action that would overcome these ills. Thus,

C3. We are capable of no form of action that could cure or significantly ameliorate human wretchedness and weakness.

C4. Human wretchedness and weakness can therefore be cured only by receiving supernatural grace from a transcendent source, that is, God.

For Pascal, then, the human end is, in principle, unachievable by action and received only by grace. His conclusions drain the political realm of its significance: rather than being a domain in which to manifest the human *telos*, its primary significance is instead to contain the sinful self-love of individuals, which, each conflicting with every other, must be subjected to force in order for any peace to exist at all (frags. 119 and 135). Even the classical authors, according to Pascal, knew better than to ascribe any significance to action and politics. Their political theories were created "to provide rules for a madhouse" and "connived with [rulers'] delusions in order to restrain their madness to as mild a form as possible" (frag. 457). "The proper function of power," Pascal says, "is to protect" (frag. 650): it is not for the sake of the human good, which lies beyond its power to achieve, seeing as it can end neither ignorance, nor mortality, nor the deep conflict within our nature. The "glory" of the political realm is nothing but the vain attempt to substitute another life, one lived in the eyes of others, for the unhappiness of our actual life (frag. 707).

For Pascal, then, man is a being with instincts for action. He has drives that point and prod him toward a certain set of goals, but he has been set loose within an environment in which all of those goals are set at an infinite distance. Weak, corrupt, and ignorant, man's one chance of gaining the human end requires a transcendent power that could transport him beyond the limits of his own horizon.

Pascal's conception of the human condition can be summarized as follows:

1. All human beings necessarily wish to be happy, and all other desires are subordinate to this wish.
2. All human beings are a mixture of a rational nature and an animal nature, each with its own principles.
3. Human happiness requires fulfilling both our rational and our animal nature and harmonizing these with each other.
4. We are incapable of fulfilling or even harmonizing the desires natural to human nature.
5. We lack the power to change the human condition so as to make it possible to fulfill the desires natural to human nature or to harmonize our two aspects.

From these premises, Pascal derives the following conclusions:

C1. Human beings are necessarily wretched and miserable beings.
C2. The reason why human beings are wretched and weak is that human nature has been corrupted from its original form.
C3. We are capable of no form of action that could cure or significantly ameliorate human wretchedness and weakness.
C4. Human wretchedness and weakness can therefore be cured only by receiving supernatural grace from a transcendent source, that is, God.

3. THE MIXTURE THAT IS HUMAN NATURE: TOCQUEVILLE'S CRITIQUE OF PASCAL

Tocqueville agrees with Pascal in conceiving of human nature as a combination of two factors (premise 2) and in thinking that happiness requires harmonizing these with each other (premise 3). He also accepts that we are not happy (conclusion C1) but seems to think it better to be content without happiness and to fight our "foolish passion" for it (Tocqueville 1985, 63). In accepting these, he also makes a criticism of Pascal of far-reaching significance (2.1.10, Tocqueville 2010, 781–82): according to Tocqueville, Pascal attempted to live too much in thought; his life was inhuman because it gave too little place to "the brute." We might be tempted to say that this criticism has no theoretical significance; after all, Tocqueville criticizes Pascal the man on the basis of Pascal's own principles. However, consider premise 5: does not

Pascal's estimation of human power have great implications for how we think of action, which is to say, to what kind of use we may put "the brute"? The most obvious significance of our animality, in contrast to our spirituality, is embodiment: we have bodies and are therefore beings who do things in the world; we are beings who act, not merely thinkers. But what sort of action are we to engage in? Pascal's conception of politics is deeply apolitical; only private life seems to retain any true significance (frag. 650). His view of human life encourages "individualism" (2.2.2, Tocqueville 2010, 881–84). Even in the religious realm Pascal does not carve out a significant role for action. The fragments concerned with "Christian Morality" have surprisingly little to say about the type of activities Christians should engage in, and Pascal devotes remarkably little space to developing his potent metaphors of the Church as a "republic" or as "a body of thinking members" (frag. 403). Similarly, the sacramental practices he recommends unbelievers engage in (on the suppositions that "faith is catching," as Hacking [2006, 67] puts it, and that it is necessary to give "belief" the "immediacy and authority of 'sentiment'" [Moriarty 2003, 156]) help prepare the body—or, as he terms it here, "the machine"—to follow the Christian way of life, but these practices are empty without grace, and they do not manifest the "greatness" that marks thought. Although Pascal asserts that "we are as much automaton as mind" (frag. 661), his thought tilts injudiciously far toward the spiritual factor.

One must be careful here. Pascal's view is not, as some might take it, that the soul is good and the body bad, but that humanity is subject to a double duality of body (or automaton) and soul (or mind), on the one hand, and nature and corruption, on the other. The mind or soul is the source of human greatness but is not thereby identified with goodness. For Augustine, whom Pascal follows closely in his theology, human corruption arises in the soul, in the sin of pride, and not in the body. The corruption of the body is the punishment of the sin of the soul (Augustine 1998, 606). The duality of mind and automaton is established in creation and would be as much a part of a perfect humanity as a fallen one. Greatness is the exclusive prerogative of the mind, or of thought. By comparison, the body is petty or base. As created, however, both are good. As fallen, both are evil. Thus, he believes that wickedness can manifest greatness, as when he says, "When wickedness has reason on its side, it becomes proud, and shows off reason in all its lustre" (frag. 458). We are necessarily both mind and body, and thus for Pascal salvation does not come through the mind, but through the heart (frag. 680).

Tocqueville treats these two dualities differently. Like Kierkegaard and Dostoevsky, religious thinkers influenced by Pascal, he sought a form of activity in which the two aspects of human nature, soul and body, could be harmonized and that would escape the charge of vanity. Unlike them, Tocqueville is concerned specifically with redeeming the political realm and with identifying a way that action might share in the "greatness" Pascal associated with "thought" or the "angel." According to Tocqueville, in the right conditions we are "powerful and free" and capable of engaging in action that manifests greatness in a way ruled out by Pascal's understanding of our condition. Perhaps we cannot cure the human condition; but if Tocqueville is correct, such action allows us then to significantly improve it. He is after a means not "to transcend" but "to preserve and reform this life" (Lawler 1993, 82). He rejects premise 5, at least as it stands.

This leads Tocqueville to make modifications elsewhere. Premise 4 is modified as follows: the ultimate harmonization and correction of the human condition is impossible in the temporal realm, but action manifesting the greatness of thought does effect a partial improvement and harmonization. Tocqueville is silent concerning conclusion C2, inferring neither Pascal's Christian nor Rousseau's historical version of the "corruption" claim. Thus, the second duality disappears from view; he is less Augustinian than Pascal and less anti-Augustinian than Rousseau. Tocqueville's view of conclusion C4 seems to be that if the human condition can be fundamentally transformed, it can be cured only through such a means (1.2.9, Tocqueville 2010, 482). But his modification of premise 5 leads him into a direct confrontation with conclusion C3: action cannot effect the kind of cure described in conclusion C4, in which the ultimate fulfillment of human desires is envisioned and the distressing conflict of angel and beast is completely overcome; it can, however, do much more to affect our condition than Pascal believed, and it is in such action that Tocqueville found the best cure for our restlessness and the fulfillment of our need for harmony between angel and beast. It may be that conclusion C1 is not as sure as it seems.

4. FREE ACTION AND ACTION MANIFESTING GREATNESS

Alongside our deplorable ignorance, our mortality, and the perpetual disturbance between the two conflicting aspects of human nature, then, we also find a fourth important part of the human condition: our capacity to engage in a form of action realizing the greatness of thought. Such action, originating in the categories of thought rather than through the necessities of the body, is a form of free action. Thus, for Tocqueville, human beings must be free to manifest greatness; and unless we believe ourselves free, we will not become the sort of people or engage in the sort of projects that manifest greatness.

Tocqueville's category of action manifesting greatness can be understood by examining some of his examples of it: an aristocrat's extravagant vices

(2.2.11, Tocqueville 2010, 936); the making of magnificent tombs (1.1.1, Tocqueville 2010, 43); Renaissance painting (2.1.11, Tocqueville 2010, 795); the American Pilgrims' founding of a new colony where they would be free to worship (1.1.2, Tocqueville 2010, 54); the actions of the American statesman George Washington in the founding and in establishing the direction of American foreign policy, a greatness most completely expressed in his resistance to the exaggerations of popular passion (1.1.8, Tocqueville 2010, 190; 1.2.5, Tocqueville 2010, 371); and the actions of the French Revolutionary generation during the first stage of the Revolution (*The Old Regime and the Revolution* 1.3.8, Tocqueville 1998, 244).

Like Aristotle, Tocqueville distinguishes greatness as a quality of action from other qualities, such as goodness (Aristotle, *Poetics* 1450b25). Actions manifesting greatness can be admired under that category despite being either vicious or deeply problematic in other ways. Today we admire the Pyramids, the Great Wall, and other monuments raised by despotic powers despite the conditions under which they were created and even the ends they were meant to serve; Tocqueville likewise distinguishes between the question of whether an action arose in thought and the question of whether it arose from a thought that was true or even good.

Let's begin with Tocqueville's famous statement that what set apart the American Pilgrims who colonized New England was their aim: rather than being "forced by necessity," they had left behind relatively comfortable material and social circumstances "to obey a purely intellectual need"; they suffered the "deprivations of exile" and settled in a "rough and neglected" land that required them to exert tremendous effort, all for "the triumph of an *idea*" (1.1.2, Tocqueville 2010, 54). Tocqueville observes that the greatness of this action has been enough to make Plymouth Rock, an insignificant boulder, into an "object of veneration" (57). He concludes, echoing Pascal, by saying that "the power and the greatness of man lie entirely in the soul" (57).

The main elements of Tocqueville's conception of greatness-in-action appear here: (1) the action was not motivated by material necessity, or at least not directly necessitated by instinct or by material needs; (2) the action originated "in the soul," that is, in an idea or ideal that itself manifests greatness in the form of virtue, wisdom, beauty, or something similar; and (3) it required considerable effort and power or mastery to realize the idea in the world. Different actions may display these qualities to varying degrees, but the most impressive human achievements, from Tocqueville's perspective, seem to need all three qualities to a high degree. (And so he might have judged the Pyramids of Giza more impressive than the Great Wall because they were not constructed to fulfill a natural necessity such as defense.)

The other paradigms of greatness-in-action cited by Tocqueville correspond to the example of the Pilgrims, manifesting all three of these qualities as well. In each case, the action does not aim at meeting a material need or natural necessity. The construction of tombs, the production of fine art, and the pursuit of "liberty, equality, and fraternity" do not fill the stomach or clothe the body. Further, each arises from an idea or ideal having its origin in thought. Modern painters, such as Jacques-Louis David, are exact anatomists, but their painting does not display greatness; they "copy small objects that have only too many originals in nature." Renaissance painters, on the contrary, "looked above themselves" for "great subjects"; Raphael "sought something better than nature" for his art, and rather than merely providing "an exact portrait of man," he "gave us a glimpse of divinity in his works" (2.1.11, Tocqueville 2010, 795). Finally, all these examples require great mastery to be achieved. None could be executed without overcoming significant difficulties and without showing extraordinary character and personal qualities, above all, displaying mastery—a mastery of the material environment that allows the actor or actors to bridge the gap between the realm of thought, where the idea or ideal arose, and the realm of the body, where this idea is now to be realized and achieved. As Pascal wrote, "only mastery and control create glory" (frag. 648).

Actions manifesting greatness are, like humanity itself, mixed. Their peculiar mixture can be understood by comparison with two different sorts of mixed actions. Tocqueville considers the Pilgrims' actions to have manifested greatness. Their lofty goal was reinforced by the nature of the efforts required in colonizing New England: the difficulty of settling in the rough landscape, the requirement that life must struggle with death, meant that the settlers' efforts to meet their material needs always required the soul's involvement as well. They constantly had to develop and exercise virtues and qualities belonging to the soul in order to successfully transform their surroundings into a livable environment. Thus, not only did they set out with the object of realizing an idea, but even their material needs served to reinforce their "soulish" orientation, while preventing them from becoming as excessively soulish as Pascal, with whom they shared theological kinship.

But if the Pilgrims were so challenged by their environment as to require the constant development and use of the powers of the soul by natural necessity, as it were, the Americans of Tocqueville's time presented a different aspect. They too were engaged in constant practical activity—the unending pursuit of greater wealth. But what was the end of this pursuit? What pressure led to this constant activity, if the natural environment was no longer so threatening? The American social state is democratic, which is to say, it is marked by widespread socioeconomic equality: society is filled with many weak individuals whose fortunes vary constantly rather than a few classes whose power remains constant from generation to generation. Thus, material goods are available to anyone, but only with effort, and these are never secure. This uncertainty and the general enjoyment of "mediocre fortunes," coupled with the "natural and instinctive taste" for material well-being, produce desire and fear: desire to possess greater material wealth and the fear of losing what one has (2.2.10, Tocqueville 2010, 931, 933). This gives the passion for material gain a particularly powerful grasp on the soul (931).

Restlessness, however, is not the effect simply of the uncertainty attached to Americans' material possessions. Americans' devotion to material well-being starves the soul, so that its needs are not met (2.2.12, Tocqueville 2010, 940). The pursuit of material wealth may "distract it from itself" but cannot prevent it from becoming "bored, restless, and agitated" (940). In a few individuals, this leads to the formation of "bizarre sects" and "religious madness" (940); in these instances, the angel strives to break free from the brute altogether and, not knowing itself or its limits, runs "beyond the limits of common sense" (941).

The starving of the soul produces other effects in the greater population. "The man who has confined his heart solely to the goods of this world" (2.2.13, Tocqueville 2010, 944) is driven into a kind of irrationality. Knowing that he has only "a limited time" (944) to enjoy goods "so precious, so incomplete, and so fleeting" (2.2.10, Tocqueville 2010, 933), he is "goaded" by the knowledge that life is running out and that death will cut short his enjoyment of these transient goods (2.2.13, Tocqueville 2010, 944): "at every instant he is afraid of ceasing to live before enjoying them" (943). In fact, despite the American's vaunted philosophy of "interest well-understood," he seems to regularly miscalculate: despite constant anxiety about spending more effort in obtaining a good than its enjoyment is worth (945), he is caught up in "useless pursuit" that does not end in the enjoyment of his goods, or in "felicity," but in the intervention of "death" (944). For the average individual in a democratic society, then, the starving of the soul produces a kind of heightened material activity that is driven on by the fear of death—not of death per se, but of death's curtailing of enjoyment—which is, when strictly examined, irrational in itself and productive of "melancholy" and "disgust with life" (946).

What is the difference between these cases? In both, the American is put to constant labor to achieve the needs of the body; yet in one, this yields the improvement of the powers of the soul, and in the other, their impoverishment. The early Americans, we note, enjoyed a more aristocratic social state, the later Americans a more democratic one; religion and the conviction that humanity includes "a non-material and immortal principle" were more natural to the former than the latter (2.2.15, Tocqueville 2010, 958). Such convictions must be "protected carefully as the most precious heritage of aristocratic centuries" (958), and this is why Tocqueville shortly argues that democratic legislators must, to the greatest extent possible, strive to inculcate "the taste for the infinite, the sentiment of the grand, and the love for non-material pleasures" (957). The lofty and austere character of a Washington presents such an example, but the conditions necessary for preparing such individuals have dwindled in subsequent generations. The early Americans, the Pilgrims, had an ultimate goal rooted in the soul: the establishment of an idea. The more they had to strive with their environment to realize this idea, the more it supported their endeavor by strengthening their character. But for the later Americans, these ends appear insignificant, and their constant pursuit of material goods drowns the soul in narrow and petty concerns.

One should not miss the very Pascalian use that Tocqueville makes of the fear of death here. That fear is closely associated with the pursuit of material goods, which, by their nature, can be enjoyed only in this life. The Americans Tocqueville describes seem trapped in a vicious cycle: the more they pursue these goods, the more uneasiness they experience and the more frantically they need to pursue the goods, precisely because of the latter's instability and transitory nature, so that finally the Americans live entirely in their pursuit and, to the extent that they enjoy what they possess, seem to do so by accident. They are actively increasing the discordance between the two elements of human nature in themselves and intensifying the ills of the human condition by increasing the fearfulness of death.

This explains Tocqueville's severe language regarding those who teach materialism. Because materialism encourages, and would even justify, Americans in this behavior, we should "consider the men who profess [these harmful theories] as the natural enemies of the people" (2.2.15, Tocqueville 2010, 957). We cannot know the answers to the ultimate questions, such as whether materialism is true, but Tocqueville thinks that we can and do know what the results are of following that doctrine. Because Tocqueville's adherence to several key features of Pascal's conception of the human condition is often not apparent, his condemnation of materialism can surprise the reader. Tocqueville sees the propagation of materialism as increasing the inherent misery of the human condition and driving us away from what is "great" and worthwhile in human life.

Since a democratic social state is conducive to materialism and hostile to belief in any kind of spiritual reality, the fate of democratic peoples—their ability to respond appropriately to the human condition and to engage in activities manifesting greatness—appears to hinge on whether they can preserve their sources of spiritual belief. This is why Tocqueville recommends that democratic legislators pay careful attention to the preservation of religion: "it is when religion is not speaking about liberty that it best teaches Americans the art of being free" (1.2.9, Tocqueville 2010, 472), he says, and we must combine this with his statement that "it is necessary that all those who are interested in the future of democratic societies unite, and that all in concert make continual efforts to spread within these societies the taste for the infinite, the sentiment for the grand and the love for non-material pleasures" (2.2.15, Tocqueville 2010, 957). This is achieved, above all, by combating materialism and preserving any "belief in a non-material and immortal principle" (958). We must preserve the possibility of action like that undertaken by the Pilgrims, rather than limiting ourselves to the pursuit of materialistic consumption.

We are now in a position to better understand why greatness-in-action forms Tocqueville's great exception to Pascal's picture. He believes that actions and activities that manifest greatness somehow ameliorate our condition. But why?

5. THE AMELIORATIVE POWER OF GREATNESS-IN-ACTION

Tocqueville agrees with Pascal that our existence is marked by severe ills and that we are unable to fundamentally transform our condition to avoid them. However, he parts from Pascal in believing that there are ways of significantly improving our condition, through engaging in action that manifests greatness. The question is, why believe that engaging in such action alters our condition?

Tocqueville never wears his theories on his sleeve. This is why his philosophical sophistication has been so underestimated (as noted, e.g., in Lawler 1993, 98); he leaves the work of excavation and reconstruction to his reader. Let us, then, put things together. The body has needs and desires intrinsic to it; the soul also has its needs and desires. In pursuing material goods we generally serve the body; in pursuing spiritual goods we serve the soul. When the soul is starved in the pursuit of material goods, its uneasiness gives a frantic character to the pursuit of material well-being. On the other hand, the body is neglected for the pursuit of pure spiritual goods. The body suffers, and a Pascal wears out his body too soon, so that he dies "of old age before reaching forty years of age" (2.1.10, Tocqueville 2010, 782). But there are activities in which the two of these come together and, to some extent, harmonize with one another: activities arising in the soul, in a great idea or ideal of some kind, and achieved through mastery exercised in the material realm. These aim at a goal that combines physical and spiritual qualities and, in their greatness, achieve a lasting existence that endures beyond the life of the actor. Those who engage in these activities also acquire a kind of knowledge—not the knowledge that consists of abstract, general concepts, of which Tocqueville is so dismissive, and not the knowledge of those ultimate truths that Tocqueville despaired of ever finding, but a knowledge rooted in things and in action, a knowledge that is both precise and practical and related to matters of importance.

Let's begin with the question of harmonizing the two aspects of human nature. What is it about activities manifesting greatness that brings the elements of human nature together? It is not that activities manifesting greatness manage to meet both types of needs at once: painting a great masterpiece is no means to care for the body. Very few activities manifesting greatness would have the accidental quality of also caring for the body's needs. Constructing a great work of architecture or founding a republic that will endure the ages might be actions of this type: although aiming to realize an idea, they also do something for the body. But this is not generally the case, and Tocqueville attaches little importance to such coincidences, so we need to consider a different sort of harmonizing that occurs in these activities.

Greatness-in-action harmonizes the soul and the body, the spiritual and physical aspects of ourselves, by embodying an idea or making the ideal real, through the use of the body. Accomplishing this task requires great mastery of the physical realm in which the work is to be accomplished—a practical, embodied knowledge of the material realm in which the idea is to be realized. Exercising this mastery is an affair of the body, involving it in the constant pursuit of the ideal put before it by the soul. In pursuing this ideal, the body is ennobled and participates in greatness insofar as it realizes the achievement of its sublime goal, whereas the body is despised and negated by philosophers and contemplatives who seek greatness in pursuing answers to the eternal questions, in contemplation, or in other purely spiritual activities, so that it is finally "worn out" by someone like Pascal who accomplishes this too completely. In the effort to embody the ideal, the body is an active participant that, through the exercise of mastery, is constantly harmonized with the soul in the activity of embodiment. In these activities we are whole.

Soul and body are therefore harmonized in the activity itself in which each pursues the same end. But does such activity really do nothing to satisfy the needs and desires of our bodily aspect, except by accident? The most fundamental of the body's needs is the instinctive aversion to death; it is this instinct that is, ironically, frustrated the most when a person is wholly devoted to pursuing material goods, since these are only good in being enjoyed, and enjoyment ends when the body dies and can only begin when pursuit ceases. The stationary peasant gets more enjoyment from the little he has than the restless American who devotes himself to always obtaining more (2.2.13,

Tocqueville 2010, 942–43). Not only the activity itself, but also the result of greatness-in-action ameliorates the human condition by leaving behind either a great product or the memory of something great. When someone embodies the ideal in something that exists here and now, in some monument, or institution, or event that will be remembered, the person leaves behind something that will endure beyond death. Tocqueville agrees with Pascal that ultimately we lack the power to overcome death, remarking that, "of all the works of man, the most durable is still the one that best recounts his nothingness and woes!"—that is, the tombs that we build for the dead, which sometimes endure long beyond the memory of the people who made them (1.1.1, Tocqueville 2010, 43). The power to abolish death transcends human capacities. Within the circumscribed horizon of what lies within our power, however, it is possible to achieve something significant and worthwhile that will endure beyond us, an aspect of glory that escaped Pascal.

In such action we also escape the fundamental ignorance that marks our condition. We resort to general ideas in our inability to properly grasp and understand "the immensity of details" involved in attempting "to examine and to judge individually all the particular cases" connected to a topic (2.1.3, Tocqueville 2010, 726). Our "imperfect, but necessary procedure" is to give similar cases the same name, and therefore to treat distinct but analogous beings, facts, and rules as if they were exactly the same (727). But when it comes to action, the matter is different; when it comes to what people deal with "everyday" and "in a practical way," they must "enter into details" and acquire a very "deep knowledge" and "infinite skill" (2.1.4, Tocqueville 2010, 739; 1.2.11, Tocqueville 2010, 174). This obtains great significance when it comes to political matters: a people that "has only been able to think about the best way to conduct politics" will necessarily be very poor at it (2.1.4, Tocqueville 2010, 738). One that "has always run public affairs by themselves" will, on the contrary, not be overly taken up by theories that only approximate reality (*The Old Regime and the Revolution* 1.3.1, Tocqueville 1998, 201; *Democracy in America* 2.1.4, Tocqueville 2010, 739). Such a people will instead have a grasp of the elements of politics rooted in experience with the matter itself.

Can such knowledge compensate for our ignorance of fundamental principles? To be sure, it is hard to see how a fine and exact knowledge of wheat prices would do so, but should we say the same of the knowledge related to greatness-in-action? If statesmanship, for example, manifests greatness in it, then must we not attribute added importance to knowledge related to statesmanship, above all to the kind that is well acquainted with action itself, and not just the theoretical knowledge of it that Tocqueville criticized Diderot for (*The Old Regime and the Revolution* 1.3.2, Tocqueville 1998, 206)? And likewise to the knowledge related to these other kinds of action that manifest greatness? Since we know best what we are most frequently and actively engaged with, this knowledge will not suffer from the looseness and falsifying abstraction that afflicts so much of our theoretical knowledge; and since it relates to something that is great, sublime, or otherwise significant, this knowledge will not be something petty. Just as the endurance of greatness-in-action falls short of immortality but greatly exceeds that of purely material goods, so too the knowledge of matters related to greatness-in-action falls short of the knowledge of first principles we desire but cannot have, but it greatly exceeds the other kinds of knowledge we can obtain—it exceeds our theoretical knowledge by being true and more precise, and it exceeds our other practical knowledge by relating to matters with greater significance and importance.

In this way, then, we can see how Tocqueville could conclude that engaging in action that manifests greatness can indeed ameliorate the human condition. Such action strikes at each of the particular woes associated with our condition and, although not completely victorious in vanquishing them, establishes a rampart against them and secures a place within which human beings can become more whole and, to some extent, triumphant over our ignorance and mortality.

It also helps us to understand why we should regard liberty as particularly important—and why liberty cannot be identified either with simply providing individuals with security in their private pursuits (as Aron [1965, 190] mistakenly concludes) or with the collective actions of a large mass of individuals. Liberty as Tocqueville understands it secures the possibility of individuals freely coming together in action (see Boesche 1987, 154–55). Some kinds of greatness-in-action can be achieved by a single individual or by a few friends. Great goals, however, frequently require the cooperation of many individuals acting together. Liberty as Tocqueville understands it—a liberty that provides individuals with institutional and social contexts in which to freely initiate and freely participate in action together with others—does not guarantee that it will be used for the sake of great and significant goals. Such liberty is, however, frequently one of its necessary conditions. A liberty that secures only the pursuit of individual interests, or a liberty that only allows individuals to come together for the sake of electing a national leader, would never suffice to secure this possibility for individuals. Besides threatening to produce conditions favorable to tyranny, such arrangements are objectionable in that each throws individuals back upon themselves and divorces them from a context in which they could participate in action that manifests greatness, so that they "[fall] gradually below the level of humanity" (2.4.6, Tocqueville 2010, 1259).

Without denying Pascal's transcendent ultimate solution to the ills of human existence, then, Tocqueville provides a this-worldly response to our condition, a way of confronting it in the here and now. His political solution is imperfect; politics is still partially a diversion (Lawler 1993, 118). In a certain way, tombs, which testify to our "nothingness," are a symbol for all types of greatness-in-action. Nonetheless, if Tocqueville is correct, then we may cede much to Pascal without ceding all. It may be true that humanity is afflicted by significant, even crippling, ills of ignorance, mortality, and disorder, and that the only cure for these lies at an infinite distance from us, beyond peaks we can never scale and a transcendent horizon we can never cross. But within the domain that is within our power there are palliatives available and modes of existence that manifest some of the grandeur that Pascal argued was lost in Adam, including liberty and political action—not beyond the unclimbable peaks but among the foothills whose ascent is, sometimes, within our power.

REFERENCES

Aron, Raymond. 1965. *Main Currents in Sociological Thought.* Vol. I. Translated by Richard Howard and Helen Weaver. New York: Basic Books.

Augustine. 1998. *The City of God against the Pagans.* New York: Cambridge University Press.

Boesche, Roger. 1987. *The Strange Liberalism of Alexis de Tocqueville.* Ithaca, NY: Cornell University Press.

Corral, Diez del. 1965. "Tocqueville et Pascal." *Revue des Travaux de l'Academie des Sciences Morales et Politiques.*

Dostoevsky, Fyodor. 1994. *The Karamazov Brothers.* Translated by Ignat Avsey. Oxford: Oxford University Press.

Dreyfus, Hubert. 2012. "'What a Monster Then Is Man': Pascal and Kierkegaard on Being a Contradictory Self and What to Do about It." In *The Cambridge Companion to Existentialism*, ed. Steven Crowell, 96–110. Cambridge: Cambridge University Press.

Hacking, Ian. 2006. *The Emergence of Probability.* 2nd ed. New York: Cambridge University Press.

Jech, Alexander. 2013. "'Man Simply': Excavating Tocqueville's Conception of Human Nature." *Perspectives on Political Science* 42 (2): 84–93.

Khalfa, Jean. 2003. "Pascal's Theory of Knowledge." In *The Cambridge Companion to Pascal*, ed. Nicholas Hammond, 122–43. New York: Cambridge University Press.

Kolakowski, Leszek. 1995. *God Owes Us Nothing.* Chicago: University of Chicago Press.

Lamberti, Jean-Claude. 1989. *Tocqueville and the Two Democracies.* Cambridge, MA: Harvard University Press.

Lawler, Peter Augustine. 1993. *The Restless Mind: Alexis de Tocqueville on the Origin and Perpetuation of Human Liberty.* Lanham, MD: Rowman & Littlefield.

Moriarty, Michael. 2003. "Grace and Religious Belief in Pascal." In *The Cambridge Companion to Pascal*, ed. Nicholas Hammond, 144–61. New York: Cambridge University Press.

Nietzsche, Friedrich. 1996. *Selected Letters of Friedrich Nietzsche*. Edited by Christopher Middleton. Translated by Christopher Middleton. Indianapolis: Hackett.

Pascal, Blaise. 1995. *Pensées and Other Writings*. Translated by Honor Levi. Oxford: Oxford University Press.

Tocqueville, Alexis de. 1985. *Selected Letters on Politics and Society*. Edited by Roger Boesche. Translated by Roger James Toupin and Roger Boesche. Berkeley: University of California Press.

———. 1998. *The Old Regime and the Revolution*. Vol. 1. Edited by François Furet and Françoise Mélonio. Translated by Alan S. Kahan. Chicago: University of Chicago Press.

———. 2010. *Democracy in America*. Bilingual ed. Edited by Eduardo Nolla. Translated by James Schliefer. 4 vols. Indianapolis: Liberty Fund.

Zuckert, Michael. 1993. "On Social State." In *Tocqueville's Defense of Human Liberty*, ed. Peter Augustine Lawler. New York: Garland.

On Individualism, Authority, and Democracy as a New Form of Religion: A Few Tocquevillian Reflections[1]

AURELIAN CRAIUTU
MATTHEW N. HOLBREICH

> Faith in common opinion will become a sort of religion whose prophet will be the majority. (Tocqueville 2010)

1. A PROBLEM OF LIBERAL MODERNITY?

Three and a half decades ago, in his influential book *After Virtue* (1981), Alasdair MacIntyre advanced one of the most trenchant arguments against liberalism, which elicited a wide array of responses and heated debates in academic circles. The values and principles of economic and political liberalism, he argued, are based on an emotivist and relativist culture that uncritically celebrates the absolute autonomy of the individual will and fosters the gradual but inevitable decomposition of the social fabric. The main culprit, in MacIntyre's view, is liberal individualism, the dominant doctrine of the past three centuries that has shaped our norms and beliefs and had a strong influence on our social institutions and values. As society becomes atomized, so the story goes, it eventually turns into a mere "collection of citizens of nowhere" (MacIntyre 1981, 147) detached from each other and pursuing interests that are often at odds with the common good. "The barbarians are not waiting be-

Aurelian Craiutu is Professor of Political Science, Indiana University, Bloomington, IN 47405 (acraiutu@indiana.edu). Matthew Holbreich is the Resident Scholar at the Zahava and Moshael Straus Center for Torah and Western Thought, Yeshiva University, New York, New York, 10033 (mholbreich@yu.edu).

1. An earlier version of this chapter was originally presented (by Aurelian Craiutu) at the conference "Combining the Spirit of Religion and the Spirit of Liberty: Tocqueville's Thesis Revisited" organized at the University of Notre Dame, September 29–30, 2011. We would like to thank the organizers of that conference and, in particular, Michael Zuckert for his useful comments on previous drafts of this chapter.

yond the frontiers," MacIntyre warned his readers; "they have already been governing us for quite some time and it is our lack of consciousness of this that constitutes part of our predicament" (245).

MacIntyre's critique of liberal modernity still resonates today, and the debate is unlikely to be settled anytime soon. In an interesting exchange published in the August 2012 issue of *First Things*, Patrick Deneen reiterated some of MacIntyre's concerns when arguing that liberalism remains unsustainable in spite of the optimism of many of its champions who uncritically celebrate individual autonomy and choice.[2] "The first revolution, and the most basic and distinctive aspect of liberalism," Deneen (2012) argued, "is to base politics upon the idea of voluntarism—the free, unfettered, and autonomous choice of individuals" seen as radically independent and autonomous persons who can choose to engage in social relations only based on their explicit consent. By grounding all relationships between autonomous individuals in a voluntaristic logic, liberalism, in Deneen's view, is ultimately unable to constitute social norms needed to sustain the practice and experience of self-governance in democratic communities. Neither MacIntyre nor Deneen seems to believe that this is a uniquely American phenomenon, and they both criticize liberalism generally, often referring to the "liberal project."[3] They regard the modern predicament as an expression of liberalism's deeply individualistic roots, which illustrate, in their view, the challenges posed by modern individualism, characterized by a clear preference for individual autonomy and a deep-seated skepticism toward any forms of self-limitation and self-restraint.

Individualism, negatively perceived, has long been a concern of those skeptical of the elevation of individual autonomy to the rank of supreme philosophical and political principle. It might be useful to remember that the concept of individualism was invented in the crucible of postrevolutionary France as the country began its transition to modern industrial society in the early 1800s. As Konraad Swart (1962, 77) showed in a seminal article published five and a half decades ago, the perplexing variety of meanings associated with individualism and the present-day confusion about its real meaning have a long history that dates back to the early nineteenth century, when the word was invented. Individualism was then a term used to designate simultaneously the political doctrine associated with the rights of man, the economic doctrine of laissez-faire liberalism, and the cult of romantic or Protestant individualism.

2. Deneen's essay "Unsustainable Liberalism" and Daniel J. Mahoney's and Paul Griffiths's responses, published in the August 2012 issue of *First Things*, are available at http://www.firstthings.com/article/2012/08/unsustainable-liberalism#print.

3. It is worth noting that critics of modern forms of narcissism such as Christopher Lasch have sometimes been inclined to believe that this is a predominantly American phenomenon.

Some (like Joseph de Maistre) attributed the evils associated with individualism to the French Revolution and Protestantism, which they criticized for furthering the atomization of society and undermining its foundations. Others, like Marx, denounced individualism as the engine of economic liberalism and regarded it as the main culprit for the large-scale disruption and alienation brought forth by modern capitalism. Most of these critiques shared the view that individualism was responsible for the waning of traditional social structures, values, and norms and thus represented a serious threat to the entire political and social order.

This story has been widely discussed in academic circles and is relatively well known. What some have described as a loss of traditional norms and values has been characterized by others as a step toward full individual autonomy, liberated from the shackles and constraints of an older hierarchical world. What we would like to do here is to highlight a counternarrative about liberal democracy's relationship to individualism by using the insights of two leading representatives of nineteenth-century French social and political thought whose writings have rarely been connected to each other. In order to examine the relationship between democracy, individualism, authority, and religion, we focus on Abbé de Lamennais's critique of individualism and Alexis de Tocqueville's analysis of democratic life, between which, we argue, exist important affinities as well as differences. By juxtaposing Tocqueville's views on democratic individualism to those held by a major critic of modern liberal democracy such as Lamennais, we demonstrate that Tocqueville departed from him in both his diagnosis of the democratic problem (the perils of individualism) and his proposed solution ("civil" religion). Whereas Lamennais believed that the essential problem of democracy was the erosion of authority and that a primary task of modern life was to reestablish it by means of "true" religion, Tocqueville demonstrated how a new form of authority emerged in modern democratic society and how this democratic authority was self-generating and tended to become all-powerful, requiring proper limitation, not reinforcement. We also show how Tocqueville, long seen as a critic of individualism and egoism, took issue with them while also arguing that individualism does not prevent the establishment of a new form of "religion" (sui generis) along with the appearance of new forms of conformity to common opinion. Tocqueville claimed that democratic values and principles such as equality and individual autonomy are dogmatically held in such a way that the common allegiance to them produces a particular faith in democracy that takes on the characteristics of a new form of "religion." While Lamennais assumed that genuine belief in Christianity was central to any solution to indifference and atomization, Tocqueville held a more complex view. He praised democratically modified forms of traditional religion while also noticing that belief in them, like the belief in democratic values, was essentially "dogmatic" in the original meaning of the term.

In the first part of our paper, we draw on the pioneering work of Lucien Jaume on Tocqueville, with a focus on the latter's analysis of democracy as a new form of religion.[4] In the second part, we show how individualism triggers a shift in the nature of religion in modern society by dint of which traditional attributes of religion such as hope, transcendence, and belief are transferred from the otherworld to democracy itself and, sometimes, to its organ of power, the state. In the final section, we explore a tension at the heart of Tocqueville's analysis of religion in America that sheds fresh light on the original theme of this essay, the relationship between individualism, authority, and democratic religion.

2. AUTHORITY AND INDIVIDUALISM IN LIBERAL DEMOCRATIC SOCIETIES

It is not a mere accident that the term *individualisme* gained wide currency in Saint-Simonian circles in the 1820s in France. Konraad Swart traced the first usage of this concept back to an issue of *Le Producteur, journal de l'industrie, des sciences et des beaux-arts* in 1826.[5] Within a few years, the term *individualisme* came to be seen as a metaphor for the disintegration of society and was employed by a variety of authors writing from different ideological and methodological perspectives to express dissatisfaction with the postrevolutionary order. The denunciation of individualism was a major trope in the writings of many critics of democracy from that period, who warned and feared that its principles would erode authority and produce anarchy.

As a result of the outstanding Tocquevillian scholarship published in the past three decades, it is now well established that Tocqueville was quite familiar with conservative critics of liberal democracy, including Lamennais. While he disagreed with their overall assessment and rejection of political democracy, Tocqueville paid special attention to one of their key concerns: the fate of authority in democratic times. Conservative critics of democracy worried that the new forms of democratic individualism were likely to subvert social and moral authority, paving the way to anomie and anarchy. Tocqueville took distance from these criticisms while giving voice to his own concerns. Unlike those antiliberal thinkers who believed that individualism would erode communal ideals and was therefore inherently schismatic, dissociative, and unsustainable, he argued that democratic individualism was bound to create new and power-

4. For a review of Jaume's excellent book, see Craiutu (2010).
5. See Swart (1962, 79).

ful forms of authority that restrain and limit the individual will, though not always in salutary ways. He also added that individualism, somewhat paradoxically, feeds into and ultimately promotes the power of mass opinion; rather than undermining authority, individualism, Tocqueville argued, recreates it on a new basis.

As Lucien Jaume suggested, exploring the intellectual dialogue between Félicité Robert de Lamennais (1782–1854) and Tocqueville allows us to understand the latter's views on authority in modern democracy. Lamennais was the author of several influential books and one of the most vocal Catholic writers in early nineteenth-century France. Although he shared some of the ideas advanced by ultraconservatives such as Joseph de Maistre and Louis de Bonald, he was closer to the agenda of French liberal Catholics;[6] for some time, he edited *l'Avenir*, an influential journal best remembered today for its motto "God and Liberty."[7] Among those who became particularly close to Lamennais during this period were two distinguished liberal Catholics, the young Count Charles de Montalembert and Father Henri Lacordaire (the latter succeeded Tocqueville at the *Académie Française* in 1861). Lamennais's most important work was the four-volume *Essai sur l'indifférence en matière de religion* (1817–24), which earned him the reputation of the new Bossuet and a visit to the Vatican in 1824, where he was warmly received by Pope Leo XII (his relations with the Vatican would deteriorate later).[8] The encyclical of Pope Gregory XVI, *Mirari Vos*, issued in 1832, was critical of Lamennais's ideas and signaled how far apart Lamennais and his former friends at the Vatican had become. Lamennais further radicalized his ideas in his *Paroles d'un croyant* (1834), a book that marked his complete break with the official church. Despite his differences with the Holy See, he was never formally excommunicated, and he continued to consider himself a Catholic in 1836.[9]

Lamennais published his *Essay on Indifference about Religious Matters* between 1817 and 1824. Tocqueville certainly knew of the work because he sent its author a copy of the first volume of *Democracy in America* (1835) accom-

6. Antoine comments on the intellectual dialogue between Tocqueville and the French liberal Catholics and insists on the differences among them (Antoine 2003, 208–11). For more information on Lamennais and liberal Catholicism, see Reardon (1975, 62–112). The political ideas of Lamennais, Montalembert, and Lacordaire are also discussed in a special chapter in Jaume (1997, 193–237).

7. For more details on the context, see Jennings (2011, 298–343).

8. Lamennais's first volume of his *Essai* was originally published in 1817 and received wide acclaim; three more volumes followed between 1818 and 1824. In what follows, we use the four-volume edition of this work published in 1830. For more information, see Reardon (1975, 66–78).

9. Lacordaire severed all ties with Lamennais in 1832, and Montalembert did the same soon thereafter. On the relationship between these thinkers, see Reardon (1975, 107–12) and Jaume (1997, 193–237).

panied by a note in which he wrote that no one professed deeper respect or warmer admiration for Lamennais's character and writings than him. Despite the hint of possible disingenuous flattery characteristic of a young author wishing to gain public approval for his first book, it is likely that Tocqueville had learned a great deal from Lamennais's writings and had good reasons for reading and admiring them.

The multivolume *Essay* provides a thorough critique of modern individualism. It begins with a description of the profound transformation at work in modern society, the roots of which can be traced back to Descartes and the *philosophes*. Lamennais critiqued the philosophical and individualistic foundations of modernity that, in his mind, paved the way for universal doubt and social anarchy. He decried the waning of sacred principles and fixed laws, along with the disappearance of what he called *public reason*. More generally, he lamented the instability of public institutions and moral life, which tends to produce a culture of doubt and uncertainty.[10] Lamennais believed that the social and political chaos manifested by dysfunctional social and political institutions mirrored a moral disorder at the heart of which is the belief that individual reason and will ought to be seen as the sole criterion of truth. Where every individual becomes his own law, Lamennais argued, the rational consequence is likely to be widespread anarchy. In reality, he insisted, individual reason is always inferior to social reason and must unconditionally submit to it: "Authority, or the general reason, or what all men are agreed upon, is the rule for governing the judgments of the individual man."[11] Once *la raison publique*—that is, the mixture of traditions, customs, social knowledge, and precepts that govern social interaction—is weakened to the point of being destroyed, there is nothing that can prevent or diminish the confusion between truth and falsehood. This explains, in Lamennais's view, the growing chaos in society and the rising uncertainty in ideas, doctrines, and institutions.[12] Under these circumstances, individuals tend to become restless and confused, and in an attempt to rid themselves of the fear of living with uncertainty, they come

10. Here is the original passage: "Des lors, plus de principles certains, plus de maximes ni de lois fixes; et comme il n'y a rien de stable dans les institutions, il n'y a rien d'arrêté dans les pensées. Tout est vrai, et tout est faux. *La raison publique, fondement et règle de la raison individuelle, est détruite*" (Lamennais 1830, 2:ii; emphasis added).

11. This passage, taken from Lamennais's *Défense de l'Essai sur l'indifférence* (1821), is quoted in Reardon (1975, 71). In the foreword to the fourth edition of the *Essai*, Lamennais admitted, "Chercher la certitude, c'est chercher une raison infaillible; et son infaillibilité doit être crue, ou admise sans preuves" (quoted in Reardon 1975, 73n48).

12. "On n'aperçoit qu'un chaos d'idées inconciliables," wrote Lamennais (1830, 2:iii). Also interesting is the original parallel that Jaume (2008) draws between Tocqueville's ideas and those of Alexandre Vinet, with special emphasis on individualism, authority, and the constitution of society. A defender of Protestant liberalism, Vinet opposed "individuality" to individualism and provided a trenchant critique of public opinion in modern society.

to espouse "terrible beliefs" that can only bring about spurious and false certitudes.[13]

Lamennais interpreted these changes as nefarious consequences of the existence of what he took to be a number of principles of division within the new democratic society. Two philosophies, he claimed, compete for supremacy in the modern world: one of them tends to bring people together, while the other separates and isolates them. The first protects individuals by forcing them to follow social norms, while the second contributes to the slow destruction of society by making the legitimacy of social norms conditional upon individual judgment and consent. The first principle emphasizes generality, authority, common beliefs, and duties to a universal and invariable law; the second principle emphasizes particularity, individual interests, and independence. According to the individualistic mind-set, duties are subordinated to rights and general norms and beliefs to individual opinion. Each individual conceives of himself as self-sufficient and autonomous and obeys only the laws he has prescribed himself, considering individual reason as the sole ground of epistemic certainty. Once this process of individualization of society begins unfolding, it is irreversible and tends to lead to general anarchy. As a result, Lamennais argued, the very existence of society is gradually called into question, as constant change, doubt, and pervasive social mobility work in tandem to undermine established traditions, customs, social norms, ways of life, and mores.[14]

The same idea can also be found in another book written by Lamennais in 1825, which predated and anticipated (to some extent) Tocqueville's analysis of democracy a decade later. The character of modern democracy, in Lamennais's opinion, is constant mobility. Everything changes at a startling speed that reflects, in turn, the constant evolution of passions, opinions, and interests. Not surprisingly, the institutions and laws themselves are in permanent flux, thus contributing further to the acceleration of social and political life.[15] Ac-

13. These are Lamennais's own words: "Quand les esprits sont dans le vague, ils s'inquiètent; dans leurs ténèbres et dans leur éffroi, ils se font des croyances térribles" (1830, 2:iv).

14. Here is the original paragraph: "Deux doctrines sont en presence dans le monde; l'une tend à unir les hommes, et les autres a les *séparer*; l'une conserve les individus en rapportant tout à la societe, l'autre détruit la société *en ramenant tout à l'individu*. Dans l'une tout est général, l'autorité, les croyances, les devoirs; et chacun n'existant que pour la société, concourt au maintien de l'ordre par une obéissance parfaite de la raison, du cœur et des sens à une loi invariable. Dans l'autre tout est *particulier*; et les devoirs sont plus que les intérêts, les croyances que des opinions, l'autorité n'est que l'indépendance. Chacun, maître de sa raison, de son cœur, de ses actions, ne connaît de loi que sa volonté, de règles que ses désirs, et de frein que la force. Aussi, dès que la force se rélâche, la guerre commence aussitôt; tout ce qui existe est attaqué; la société *entière est mise en question*" (Lamennais 1830, 2:v–viii; emphasis added).

15. Here is what Lamennais wrote in *De la religion considerée dans ses rapports avec l'ordre politique et civil* in 1825: "Le caractère de la démocratie est *une mobilité continuelle*; tout sans cesse y est en mouvement, tout y change, avec une rapidité effrayante, au gré des passions et des opinions. Rien de stable dans les principes, dans les institutions, dans les lois"

cording to Lamennais, the driving forces behind this profound transformation are extreme individualism, doubt, and religious indifference. Doubt, he opined, contributes to the erosion of "a common fund of recognized truths, proclaimed rights, and a general order which nobody imagined could be turned upside down" (Lamennais 1830, 2:x). Today, Lamennais continued, all links between individuals are broken and people find themselves alone, mere monads surrounded by many other free-floating monads, separated from each other. Faith in the existence (or possibility) of a common good has disappeared, and individuals no longer know what to do or what to believe in. They move in too many directions at once, and their actions create instability in opinions and institutions.[16] As such, Lamennais claimed, the root of evil has a new name and face: it is an extreme form of individualism marked by the undisputed reign of individual will, which recognizes no other authority than itself.[17]

The numerous references to *la raison sociale*, a key concept in Lamennais's works, are far from accidental and deserve special attention in the present context. As we have seen, he believed that the attacks on and the extinction of social reason would, in the end, lead to social disintegration and anarchy. To avoid the latter, Lamennais believed that modern individuals must acknowledge the existence of a "social reason" superior to—and placed above—all individual wills. While elevating social reason above individual reason, Lamennais did not condemn the latter in the same way as Joseph de Maistre or Louis de Bonald had done before him by taking Protestantism (broadly defined) to task for undermining the foundations of modern society. Lamennais condemned first and foremost the universal drive to absolute individual independence and autonomy, a tendency that, he believed, went beyond the borders of Protestantism (it could also be found in the writings of secular authors such as Rousseau).[18] In Lamennais's view, this extreme form of individualism was threatening to corrupt society and destroy the set of common doctrines along

---

(as quoted in Jaume 2008, 123; emphasis added). A similar idea of *la démocratie mouvante* was advanced by Charles de Rémusat, a young member of the group of the French Doctrinaires, in several articles published in 1825–26. For more details, see Roldán (1999) and Craiutu (2003, 28–29, 108–10).

16. The original paragraph reads as follows: "Tous les liens sont brisés, l'homme est seul; la foi sociale a disparu, les esprits, abandonnés à eux-mêmes, ne savent où se prendre; on le voit flotter au hasard dans mille directions contraires. De là, un désordre universel, une effrayante instabilité d'opinions et d'institutions" (Lamennais 1830, 2:x–xi).

17. Writes Lamennais, "Il y a au fond des cœurs, avec un malaise incroyable, comme un immense dégôut de la vie, et un insatiable besoin de destruction" (Lamennais 1830, 2:xi).

18. "On ne croît que soi, on n'aime que soi, on ne rapport rien qu'à soi; et qu'est-ce que cela, sinon le renversement de la société? Car la société consiste dans la croyance de certains vérités sur le témoignage général. . . . Société signifie union, et là où tout se sépare et devient individuel, chacun des lors se trouve dans l'impossibilité de se défendre contre tous, ou dans l'impossibilité d'exister" (Lamennais 1830, 2:xiv).

with the necessary social solidarity and unity without which no society could properly function.

Lamennais concluded that, in order to survive and prosper, modern society needed a new form of authority capable of keeping the emerging intellectual anarchy at bay. Accordingly, he tried to imagine the possibility of a new form of authority in modern democratic societies capable of tempering and restraining individual wills and providing some form of certainty. A central role would have to be played, he believed, by true religion. Authority, Lamennais insisted, is "the general means offered to people to discern the true religion," which relies on "the greatest visible authority" (1830, 2:191). All philosophies, he went on, lead to universal doubt, and, as such, they tend to subvert social and political authority. And yet, Lamennais added, absolute doubt is simply impossible for human beings, and human reason, when letting itself be guided only by skepticism and doubt, places individuals into a state contrary to their nature, since we are naturally made to believe (192). We all start our lives by obeying and believing what our parents, society, and tradition ask us to do. Without those ideas that we are bound to receive and obey without questioning, we are powerless and unable to think or act properly.

At first glance, there are significant affinities between Tocqueville and Lamennais, with regard to both their diagnosis of the pathologies of democracy and their use of religion (however defined) as a solution to the problems of liberal democracy. But it is important to point out that they held different opinions about the nature of democracy and the relationship between democracy, individualism, and religion. A former student of Guizot, whose lectures on the history of civilization in Europe he assiduously followed in 1828, Tocqueville sought to unearth the historical roots of the progress of democracy understood as a progressive equalization of conditions. In an unpublished note that can be found in the critical edition of *Democracy in America*, Tocqueville offered the following account of this process. "In the Middle Ages," he wrote, "it was believed that all opinions had to follow from authority" and that philosophy took "the characteristics of a religion." In the eighteenth century, "the extreme of the opposite state was reached" and people claimed "to appeal for all things only to individual reason and to chase dogmatic beliefs away entirely" (Tocqueville 2010, 3:709 n. u). The situation began to change at the outset of the nineteenth century. "Today," Tocqueville added, "the movement still continues in the minds of a second order, but the others understand and accept that received beliefs and discovered beliefs, authority and liberty, individualism and social force are needed at the very same time. The whole question is to decide the limits of these two things" (709–10). It is worth noting that while Tocqueville and Lamennais disagreed about the extent of the latter, they agreed on the fact that the rise of democratic individualism requires proper limits.

On several important points, Tocqueville's analysis of the pathologies of modern life seems very similar to Lamennais's diagnosis of modernity. For example, in a note for the opening chapter on the philosophical method of the Americans, Tocqueville describes the ultimate consequences of this change in a tone that reminds us of Lamennais's critical diagnosis of modern society as increasingly devoid of true authority. Tocqueville points out the "general revolt against all authority," which he equates with the "attempt to appeal to individual reason in all things" (2010, 3:708 n. t). He then goes on to add that while this "essentially democratic" phenomenon had begun in the eighteenth century, it had taken a much more radical form in the age of democracy when conditions had become increasingly equal. This development is important because it makes possible, somewhat paradoxically, a new form of servitude—soft despotism—in the age of democracy. One of the consequences of the rise of individualism, in Tocqueville's (and Lamennais's) view, is that each individual becomes accustomed to having "only confused and changing notions" on the fundamental questions regarding personal and social life. Individual opinions tend to be, for the most part, poorly defended and easily abandoned, and one sees the authority of former beliefs challenged, eroded, or destroyed without being replaced by anything similar. Tocqueville was anxious about this intellectual anarchy and commented on the negative consequences of the spread of a new form of skepticism that, he believed, was a bad omen for the future. "We see on this point more disorder than we will ever see" (708 n. t), he wrote. Although he refers here to disorder rather than indifference—Lamennais's concept—it would not be an exaggeration to claim that the overall social and moral condition described by Tocqueville shared a lot in common with the intellectual vacuum denounced by Lamennais in his *Essai sur l'indifférence en matière de religion*.

The two thinkers also shared a similar concern that commercial democratic society could become entirely absorbed in material affairs and thus would neglect the spiritual and transcendent aspects of life. They both traced in part the democratic tendency to selfishness and solipsism to the philosophy of the Enlightenment, although they differed in their general assessment of the latter. These themes are all quite apparent in the beginning of the second volume of *Democracy in America* (1840). There Tocqueville begins with the philosophical (Cartesian) method of the Americans, which seeks all truth "by yourself and in yourself alone" and appeals to the "individual effort of their own intellect" (2010, 3:829). These concerns are echoed and deepened in Tocqueville's chapter "Individualism in Democratic Countries," where he laments and seeks to counter the tendency of democratic life to produce the habits of "withdrawal to the side with his family and his friends, so that, after thus creating a small society for his own use, he willingly abandons the large society to itself" and "encloses him within the solitude of his own heart" (4:882, 884). In sum, although there were important differences in their understanding of democracy and individualism, both Tocqueville and Lamennais feared that democracy, if left unchecked, would produce social disintegration, civic apathy, and extreme privatization such that the social interests of citizens would be restricted to the narrow circle of their families and friends.

But the confluence between Lamennais and Tocqueville only goes so far, both in their analysis of democratic pathologies and in their recommended solutions. It is true that Tocqueville thought that individualism was a dangerous tendency of democratic modernity, but his analysis of individualism feeds into his deeper concern about democratic conformity, a topic not examined by Lamennais. It is in his analysis of democratic conformity that Tocqueville reveals his genius and offers a different account of democracy's problems than Lamennais. In the first volume of *Democracy in America*, Tocqueville expressed his deep concern that the loss of secondary bodies and the tendency of democracy to take equality to extremes could lead to a tyranny of the majority that would exclude dissent and restrain free thought. As a proof of his concern, he claimed that in the United States, there is less freedom of the mind than anywhere else in the world. These concerns were repeated and amplified in the first part of the second volume of *Democracy in America*, where Tocqueville explained how a culture with a strong individualistic Cartesian mind-set may not produce the intellectual independence that Lamennais feared, but a paradoxical conformity to mass opinion. In an unpublished note, Tocqueville remarked that "it is to the mass alone that each individual hands over the care of forming for him opinions that he cannot form for himself on a great number of matters" (2010, 3:711 n. a). He further wrote that "as citizens become more equal and more similar, the tendency of each blindly to believe a certain man or a certain class decreases. The disposition to believe the mass increases, and more and more it is opinion that leads the world" (718). While Lamennais feared the dissolution of all beliefs and predicted the appearance of a new form of anarchy in the Western world, Tocqueville thought that no such dissolution and anarchy would occur in a society characterized by the increasing equalization of conditions. Rather, he argued, it was likely that democratic times would engender a greater degree of conformity than aristocratic centuries, a trend that worried him a great deal, as demonstrated by the unpublished notes collected in the critical edition of *Democracy in America* compiled by Eduardo Nolla.

Tocqueville's concern about democratic conformity reveals how his analysis of modernity departs from Lamennais on another crucial topic: the nature of authority in modern society. If Tocqueville's analysis of democracy gave the pride of place to equality and liberty, the fate of authority in modern times was also of great interest to him as it was to Lamennais, who, as we have already seen, thought that the great danger in democratic times would be the erosion of authority and the ensuing intellectual and moral crisis. Tocqueville was more optimistic than Lamennais in this regard. He understood that authority is always located somewhere in society or above it, since the inflexible law of the human condition is such that individuals cannot form all their opinions by themselves. They are "always brought and held together by some principal ideas; and that cannot happen without each one of them coming at times to draw his opinions from the same source and consenting to receive a certain number of ready-made beliefs" (Tocqueville 2010, 3:713). In the absence of such shared principles, there can be no common beliefs, and consequently no collective action is possible.

Tocqueville took issue with the opinion that dogmatic beliefs are incompatible with and contrary to the ethos of a democracy that promotes individual autonomy and choice. Individuals living in democratic times, he argued, have neither the time nor the necessary strength of mind to develop their own opinions on all the matters that interest them. Hence, they are forced to rely on ready-made opinions that they "receive on trust and without discussion" (Tocqueville 2010, 3:712), that is, as dogmas to be accepted without questioning, as opinions that people accept because they lack the time to look for something better. Such dogmatic beliefs, necessary at all times, are particularly important in democratic societies as "supports necessary for the weakness of men" (712 n. c) thrown into the vortex of social life. Hence, even in democratic societies in which equality applies even to the intellect, authority must always be found somewhere in the intellectual and moral world even if its place is variable. "Thus," Tocqueville concludes, "the question is not to know if an intellectual authority exists in democratic centuries, but only to know where its repository is and what extent it will be" (717). Since authority is no longer found in or tied to aristocratic persons, the danger in democratic times is that there would be no other source of authority than a monolithic and potentially intolerant public opinion. If this is correct, then the danger of democratic times is not, as Lamennais thought, the spread of corrosive individualism and indifference toward religion; it is rather the fact that individualism feeds into the power of mass opinion and undermines freedom of thought, empowering the majority to do as it will, sometimes even endangering the rights of minorities. For Tocqueville, therefore, the problem of modernity is not simply that unchecked individualism tends to erode authority and subverts order. Rather, the real problem is that it can lead to too much authority and order that might in the end threaten individual liberty.

3. DEMOCRACY AS A NEW FAITH AND FORM OF "RELIGION"

But what kind of authority is bound to emerge in democratic times, and why would it be detrimental to individual liberty? Is authority in the strong sense of the word even possible in a democratic society composed of free and independent individuals who instinctively apply the philosophical precepts of Descartes to their daily choices? If so, what would be the foundation of social order in such a society?

Tocqueville based his answers to these questions on his understanding of how individualism interacts with religion, as well as on his reflections on the choice between liberty and equality in democratic societies.[19] Note the language he chose to describe the new authority in democratic times. Tocqueville pointed out that the foundational tenets of democracy—the autonomy of the individual and the equality of all—are held in ways analogous to religious belief and with the same fervor. It is not a mere coincidence that Tocqueville employs quasi-religious vocabulary to describe the nature of authority in democratic life, using terms such as the majority as "prophet" and the state as a "shepherd of the flock." In his view, democracy not only erodes traditional forms of religious belief but also can itself become the simulacrum of traditional religion.

This religious terminology comes fully to light in the second volume of *Democracy in America*, where Tocqueville explores the consequences of the appearance of new forms of democratic authority. Democracy's primary beliefs are religiously held insofar as they resemble tenets of faith, generate fervent emotions, and become sources of general meaning.[20] Individuals place all their hopes in the possibility of democracy itself, and the government, the organ that fulfills democratic longings, becomes the source of hope, the divine shepherd that guides the flock.[21] At the same time that democracy becomes more akin to a religion, it "extricate[s] religion from [traditional] forms, practices, and figures, as men become more democratic" (Tocqueville 2010, 3:742 n. a); in so doing, democratic faith surreptitiously replaces traditional faith while continu-

19. On this issue, see Antoine (2003, 148). The claim to originality must be taken, however, with a necessary grain of salt, since, as Jaume demonstrated, Tocqueville drew on a number of authors who also argued that the religious sentiments or instincts are constitutive of human nature and that faith represents, as it were, the "permanent state of humanity." If the latter is Tocqueville's phrase, its spirit can also be found mutatis mutandis in the writings of Joseph de Maistre and René de Chateaubriand, to name only two of his most famous contemporaries.

20. For a more extensive discussion on this sacralization of democracy, see Deneen (2005, 87–90). Deneen comments, among others, on John Dewey's important essay "Christianity and Democracy" (1892), which is relevant in the present context.

21. It is important to point out that Tocqueville was uneasy about this phenomenon and was far from endorsing it.

ing to display some of its characteristics. On this view, democracy should not be described as movement away from faith to secularism; in reality, it only transfers the hopes, longings, and beliefs from one sphere (traditional religion) to another (the secular realm of democratic politics).[22] Against the background of the gradual erosion and displacement of traditional institutions and practices in modern society, democratic principles and values acquire a new status and image. In democratic societies, the new form of faith in equality and public opinion grants the majority an aura of divinity by investing it with the attributes of a powerful and infallible prophet. Thus, the wisdom and reason of the majority represent the hope and democratic promise to ease suffering and produce universal freedom and well-being.

This quasi-religious symbolism of democracy, a powerful and seductive combination of belief in progress and secular hope in the universality of democratic principles, has been a constant feature of the American political discourse on democracy, whose roots can be traced back to Walt Whitman and whose echoes can be found even in the 2005 second inaugural address given by President George W. Bush. It was anticipated by Tocqueville himself, who, unlike the great American poet, drew mixed conclusions about its coherence and logic. In the final chapter of the first volume of *Democracy in America*, Tocqueville described the new republican religion as follows: "In the United States, the religion of the greatest number itself is republican; it subjects the truths of the other world to individual reason, as politics relinquishes to the good sense of all the responsibility for the interests of this one; and it agrees that each man should freely take the path that will lead him to heaven, in the same way that the law recognizes the right of each citizen to choose his government" (2010, 2:633–34). As Tocqueville himself acknowledged, "religion itself reigns there much less as revealed doctrine than as common opinion" (3:720). He elaborated on this point in a long and very interesting note (which he chose not to include in the final text), where he distinguished between "true" religion and the new democratic religion in which the majority enjoys virtually absolute power. Tocqueville writes, "A religion is a power whose movements are regulated in advance and that moves within a known sphere, and many people believe that within this sphere its effects are beneficial, and that a dogmatic religion better manages to obtain the desirable effects of a religion than one that is rational. The majority is a [illegible word] power that moves in a way haphazardly and can spread successively to everything. *Religion is law, the omnipotence of the majority is arbitrariness*" (721 n. r;

22. It is revealing that after arguing for the need to have a new type of religion, Tocqueville added, "Necessity of gaining the favor of the majority" (2010, 3:742 n. a).

emphasis added). Tocqueville was worried that the new form of democratic faith, based simultaneously on the authority of the individual and that of public opinion, contains within itself the potential seeds of arbitrariness and despotism. He believed that this new form of democratic faith must be countervailed by traditional religions and dogmas that rely on a different type of authority and place the object of man's desires beyond and above the goods of this world.

In another revealing note written for the same chapter ("Of the Principal Source of Beliefs among Democratic Peoples"), Tocqueville stressed the link between traditional forms of religion and the modern democratic faith as follows: "New sources of beliefs. Authority. Sources of beliefs among democratic peoples. To put in, before or after the chapters in which I treat the influence of equality on philosophy and religion. Religion—authority. Philosophy—liberty. What is happening in the United States in the matter of religion is proof of this. [Illegible word] difficulty for men to stop at common ideas. Remedy for that in the future. This difficulty is something more *revolutionary* than *democratic*" (2010, 3:711–12 n. b). The equation between religion and authority in this passage is as striking as that between philosophy and liberty. The two concepts must, of course, be interpreted metaphorically, as demonstrated by another important note, in which Tocqueville explained, "By philosophy I mean all that the individual discovers by the individual effort of his reason. By religion I mean all that he accepts without discussing it. So philosophy and religion are two natural antagonists. . . . Philosophy is needed and religions are needed" (713 n. e). Liberty and authority, he wrote in yet another note, "will always divide the intellectual world into two parts. These two parts will be more or less unequal depending on the centuries. Authority can be exercised in the name of one certain power or in the name of another; but authority itself will continue to exist" (724 n. s).

In these fascinating notes, Tocqueville emphasizes that all societies—and, above all, the democratic ones—need a balance between what he called "religion" (authority) and "philosophy" (liberty), both of which are essential to the preservation of liberal pluralism in modern society. If one were to prevail at the expense of the other, society would succumb to either despotism or anarchy. The question that preoccupied Tocqueville is whether or not modern democracy can achieve such a happy union between authority and liberty, or, in his terms, between "religion" and "philosophy." The stakes could not be higher since, depending on the survival of this union, liberty or servitude would prevail in modern society. Viewed from this perspective, Tocqueville suggests, the new forms of democratic authority that are held analogously to religious beliefs need to be moderated through corresponding countervailing elements that would protect individual freedom. The paradox is that only traditional religion can successfully complement and temper the democratic faith.

Tocqueville explores the complex balancing between traditional and democratic faith in a seminal note that deserves to be quoted in full here:

> Faith in common opinion is the faith of democratic nations. The majority is the prophet; you believe it without reasoning. You follow it confidently without discussion. It exerts an immense pressure on individual intelligence. The moral dominion of the majority is perhaps called to replace traditional religion to a certain point or to perpetuate certain ones of them, if it protects them. *But then religion would live more like common opinion than like religion.* Its strength would be more borrowed than its own. All this can be supported by the example of the Americans. Men will never be able to deepen all their ideas by themselves. That is contrary to their limited nature. The most [illegible word] and the most free genius believes a million things on the faith of others. So *moral authority* no matter what you do must be found somewhere in the moral world. Its place is variable, but a place is necessary for it. Man needs to believe dogmatically a host of things, were it only to have the time to discuss a few others of them. This authority is principally called *religion* in aristocratic centuries. It will perhaps be named *majority* in democratic centuries, or rather *common opinion.* (2010, 3:720 n. p; emphasis added)

From the many possible interpretations of this fragment we would like to emphasize only one for the moment. Tocqueville believed that democracy should not be regarded as a turn away from religion, but rather as an avatar or metamorphosis of religion broadly defined.[23] While he acknowledged this development, he was also deeply ambivalent about it. He was concerned that democratic individuals are expected "to believe without reasoning" and that the new democratic faith becomes faith in equality and public opinion, which is but the voice of the majority. These dogmatic beliefs accepted without questioning, Tocqueville noted, become the locus of the new moral authority in democracy. There is a deep irony here that did not escape his perceptive eye. Tocqueville understood that a new form of democratic faith is needed in modern society, but he also grasped that this new type of faith may in fact under-

23. For a close analysis on this topic, see Jaume (2011). On the complex relationship between democracy and religion in general, see Gauchet (1985), Gauchet (2002, 27–108, 401–64), and Taylor (2007). On Tocqueville's views on religion, see, inter alia, Zuckert (1981), Lawler (1993), Antoine (2003), and Kahan (2015). The relation between sovereignty and religion in Tocqueville is analyzed in Holbreich (2011).

mine democracy in the long run. What makes the American case interesting and puzzling, in his view, is that democracy seems to regulate itself here through its own internal tensions and contradictions. How is this possible? We explore this issue in the next section, in which we focus on the dilemmas of Tocqueville's "religious functionalism."

4. THE DILEMMAS OF TOCQUEVILLE'S RELIGIOUS FUNCTIONALISM[24]

Tocqueville predicted that in an age of increasing individualism, in which true individuality is becoming rare, "faith in common opinion will become a sort of religion whose prophet will be the majority" (2010, 3:724). It would, however, be a new faith that no longer seeks to leave the earth behind in search for a better world. "But then," he added, "religion would live more like common opinion than like religion" (724). This is a striking phrase that might help us understand how, in Tocqueville's view, the authority of revealed religion tends to be gradually replaced by the authority of public opinion in democratic societies.

It is worth repeating that Tocqueville felt uneasy about this transition and was not entirely optimistic about unconditional religious deference toward public opinion and its self-proclaimed prophet, the majority. He was certain that the new democratic religion would be different from the religions of the past. If it might fail to satisfy the deepest longings of those who crave the revelation of a genuine *mysterium tremendum*, it would still be a powerful form of religion in keeping with the inclinations of the democratic mind. As Tocqueville explained, the sources of this new type of religion must be looked for in equality, an all-powerful principle in democratic societies that commands universal respect and allegiance. He saw, however, that the gradual tendency to replace traditional faith with belief in the infallibility of the majority was not inevitable, and he thought that it could be effectively countered through wisely chosen policies. In the United States, for example, Tocqueville noticed that traditional religion acts as a healthy antidote to some of the pernicious tendencies of democratic life; yet, at the same time, religion is forced to make doctrinal and pastoral accommodations to the democratic spirit. Tocqueville also realized that religion in the United States was held more or less dogmatically largely because religious traditionalism was an inherited belief held with the same

24. It is worth stressing that Tocqueville's functional account of religion is complex and not devoid of some important tensions. His description of democratic man owes much to Pascal and thus can be described as a secularized version of the latter's Christian anthropology. An excellent account of the affinities between Tocqueville and Pascal can be found in Díez del Corral (1989, 227–71); see also Lawler (1993, 73–150) and Kahan (2015, 16–30).

dogmatism with which the Americans believed in the legitimacy and infallibility of the majority. Paradoxically, the Americans were able to effectively use traditional religion and practices to counter the new religion of democracy mainly because they did it unthinkingly or instinctively.

Tocqueville feared that religions that have as their object eternal truths might dilute their substance if they were to give in too much to the new democratic Zeitgeist.[25] In particular, he was concerned about the rise of pantheism in democratic societies, a concern that he expressed in the (short) seventh chapter of the first part of the second volume of *Democracy in America*. It is no accident that the discussion of pantheism comes after two important chapters on the principal source of beliefs among democratic peoples and the Americans' preference for general ideas. By pantheism, Tocqueville did not have in mind the classical definition of this term, that is, a doctrine that equates God with the forces and laws of the universe. The key observation he made was that in democratic times, people have a strong tendency to espouse general ideas and search for rules "applicable indiscriminately and in the same way to several matters at once" (Tocqueville 2010, 3:728). Pantheism thus tends to become a popular doctrine in democratic societies because it mirrors—and springs from—the new egalitarian social condition. While promoting equality and individual independence, the democratic *état social* tends to make individuals isolated and powerless and encourages them to seek compensation in general ideas and causes:

> In centuries of equality, all men are independent of each other, isolated and weak; you see none whose will directs the movements of the crowd in a permanent fashion; in these times, humanity always seems to march by itself. So in order to explain what is happening in the world, you are reduced to searching for some general causes that, acting in the same way on each one of our fellows, therefore lead them all voluntarily to follow the same route. That also naturally leads the human mind to conceive general ideas and causes it to contract the taste for them. (733–34)

Tocqueville then pointed out the disturbing implications of this powerful inclination that tends to make individuals obsessed with single causes and unity at the expense of particularity and leads them to embrace determinism. First, pantheism represents a formidable if invisible threat to preserving liberty and human greatness in democratic societies. "Among the different systems by the aid of which philosophy seeks to explain the world," Tocqueville opined,

25. See Tocqueville (2010, 3:751).

"pantheism seems to me the one most likely to seduce the human mind in democratic centuries. All those who remain enamored of the true grandeur of man must join forces and struggle against it" (2010, 3:758). Second, pantheism tends to foster fatalism and thwarts the people's ability to change or reform the world in which they live because it attributes to individuals "almost no influence on the destiny of the species, or to citizens on the fate of the people" (853). At the same time, it gives "great general causes to all the small particular facts" and tends to present all events as "linked together by a tight and necessary chain"; thus, it ends up "by denying nations control over themselves and by contesting the liberty of having been able to do what they did" (853). As such, third, pantheism tends to foster uniformity and centralization of power among democratic peoples who have seen the principle of equality triumph among them.

Religions, Tocqueville argued, must always hold firm in this regard. They may not compromise the principal opinions that constitute their fundamental beliefs, but they should be at the same time flexible enough with regard to the incidental notions linked to them. This middle ground seems to have been his preferred solution for reconciling religion (authority) and philosophy (liberty) and for combating the nefarious effects of pantheism: "As men become more similar and more equal, it is more important for religions, while still keeping carefully out of the daily movement of affairs, not unnecessarily to go against generally accepted ideas and the permanent interests that rule the mass. . . . In this way, by respecting all the democratic instincts that are not contrary to it and by using several of those instincts to help itself, religion *succeeds* in struggling with advantage against the spirit of *individual independence* that is the *most dangerous* of all to religion" (Tocqueville 2010, 3:752–53; emphasis added).

The example of America also taught Tocqueville another important lesson about religion in democracy: religion can act as a countervailing power to the mixture of this-worldly attitudes, excessive individualism, and materialism that can be found in democratic times. Tocqueville noticed the Americans' melancholy demeanor amid their material abundance and attributed it in part to their restlessness. The equality of conditions opens up new opportunities for everyone while increasing at the same time the competition for a limited set of resources. Since democracy tells everyone, in the spirit of equality, that there is no limit to one's right to pursue one's desires as long as they do not harm others, democratic life is bound to promote disappointment and unhappiness when individuals realize that they cannot, in fact, achieve everything that democracy promises them: "When all the prerogatives of birth and fortune are destroyed, when all the professions are open to everyone, and when you can reach the summit of each one of them on your own, an immense and easy career seems to open before the ambition of men, and they readily imagine that they are called to great destinies. But that is an erroneous view that experience corrects every day" (Tocqueville 2010, 3:946). The main point here is not that democratic mass opinion tends to promote extreme forms of worldliness, materialism, and commercialism. In reality, democracy engenders unlimited hope about its own ability to deliver prosperity and social mobility, and democratic institutions are rarely able to fulfill that promise.[26]

Hence, democratic faith needs to be moderated and purified of its excesses because the dogmas of democratic life alone, such as the autonomy of the will, the power of the individual, and the equality of all, do not automatically engender universal bliss or happiness. Democratic faith itself produces a cycle of disappointment out of which it cannot easily escape without external help. It oscillates between effusive optimism and dejected disappointment, promoting and feeding off of ceaseless restlessness. To shift the locus of transcendence from the divine to the majority and to put one's full faith in democracy and its foundational assumptions is, according to Tocqueville, an error. The democratic faith and dogmas, even if the majority is their prophet, must be limited by countervailing tendencies that arise from traditional religion.

Nonetheless, traditional religion can only combat materialism, commercialism, and social disintegration so long as it does not become fully captured by the democratic egalitarian spirit. "It must be recognized," Tocqueville wrote, "that equality, which introduces great advantages into the world, nevertheless suggests . . . very dangerous instincts to men; it tends to isolate them from one another and to lead each one of them to be interested in himself alone. It opens their souls excessively to the love of material enjoyments. The greatest advantage of religions is to inspire entirely opposite instincts" (2010, 3: 745). When recommending religion as an antidote to democratic conformity, Tocqueville reveals, in fact, both his distance from Lamennais and the affinity with him. Certainly Tocqueville and Lamennais both cared to preserve traditional religion in the democratic era, but they did so for significantly different reasons. Tocqueville thought that organized, institutional, and traditional religion was a counterweight to the democratic inclination to materialism, while Lamennais was above all concerned with the pernicious effects of individualism and the unlimited use of individual reason. Yet they both believed that in order to survive, liberal democracy must be spiritualized somehow. In an unpublished foreword to the second volume of *Democracy in America*, Tocqueville pointed out his desire to make his readers understand that "democracy cannot give the happy fruits that they expect from it except by combining it

26. On this issue, see also Manent (1996) and Mitchell (1999).

with morality, spiritualism, beliefs" (693 n. f). He also thought that religion was "the most precious heritage of aristocratic centuries" (958) and expressed his admiration for the ways in which the Puritans combined the spirit of liberty and the spirit of religion in America.

While Tocqueville accepted the need for institutionalized religion as an antidote to democratic pathologies, he praised it primarily (though not exclusively) for its functional value rather than because revealed Christianity was the true religion, as Lamennais argued. Of course, we cannot know for certain what Tocqueville's personal beliefs were; they have been a subject of much speculation and are beyond the scope of this essay. Suffice it to say that he did not endorse a conventional view of civil religion,[27] and he was surprisingly critical of Catholic liberal parties, which, in fact, endorsed many ideas that he also shared. Tocqueville distanced himself from liberal Catholics such as Lacordaire and Montalembert and criticized the papal hierarchy of Pope Pius I. Moreover, he had no place for dogmas such as the Immaculate Conception and never spoke about original sin in his works. Personally, he was plagued by inner doubt and terrified by it (along with old age, decrepitude, and illness). "If you know a recipe for belief," Tocqueville once wrote, "for God, give it to me. . . . If will alone were sufficient for belief, I would have been devout a long time ago; or rather I would always have been devout, for doubt has always seemed to me the most unbearable of the ills of the world; I have constantly judged it to be worse than death and inferior only to illnesses."[28]

It may then be argued that Tocqueville embraced a rather nebulous form of spirituality plagued by uncertainty and doubt, different in both tone and substance from Lamennais's belief that Christianity was the right religion for the French. Tocqueville's primary concern was with human liberty and greatness, and only secondarily with the truth content of the religious beliefs of democratic peoples. When discussing materialism, Tocqueville's first concern is not that it is false, but that the doctrine itself is "pernicious."[29] He went even farther to claim, "Assuredly metempsychosis is not more reasonable than materialism; but if it were absolutely necessary for a democracy to make a choice between the two, I would not hesitate, and I would judge that citizens become brutalized less by thinking that their soul is going to pass into the body of a pig than by believing that it is nothing" (Tocqueville 2010, 3:958). All religions, even the most false and dangerous ones, Tocqueville claimed, can lift our attention skyward, make us believe we are more than just material entities, and

27. On Tocqueville's civil religion, see Kessler (1994) and Beiner (2010, 249–58).

28. Tocqueville (1983, 29); an English translation can be found in Tocqueville (2010, 2:480 n. t).

29. See Tocqueville (2010, 3:957).

impose duties on us that take us out of ourselves and give us a sense of larger vistas.[30]

Nonetheless, Tocqueville did not think that every form of religious worship accomplished the goal properly. He noted that "there are very false and very absurd religions" (Tocqueville 2010, 3:744), even though he shied away from discussing metaphysical truths. "I have neither the right nor the will to examine the supernatural means that God uses to make a religious belief reach the heart of man. At this moment I am envisaging religions only from a purely human viewpoint" (746). He preferred to draw two distinctions, one about the content of beliefs, and one about religious practice. In terms of content, Tocqueville admonished religions to make doctrinal and pastoral concessions to the animating spirit of democratic life. He recommended, however, that they remain "within the limits that are appropriate to them and must not try to go beyond them" (746), thus refraining from commenting on political matters. They should attempt instead to purify the search for well-being, but they should not seek to eradicate it. For this reason, he thought that Islam and other forms of comprehensive religious practice would face strong headwinds in democratic times. Democracy requires that religious doctrines conform to equality, and it also demands that religious practices lay less emphasis on obscurantist rituals. In that category, he originally was going to mention as examples indulgences, pilgrimages, and relics, but he later changed his mind.

At the same time, Tocqueville thought that communal practices and rituals are important in limiting the excesses of individualism in democratic societies. He claimed that he "firmly believe[s] in the necessity of forms" and drew a distinction between institutionalized, regularized, and ritualized religion and episodic, de-ritualized religion characteristic of bucolic gatherings in the West during the Second Great Awakening.[31] Throughout the second volume of *Democracy in America*, Tocqueville contrasted two sets of religious contexts. The first is the traditional Christian service, whether Catholic or Protestant, broadly conceived. The second are unorthodox forms of democratic worship, such as spontaneous gatherings in the western woods or forms of mysticism. What distinguishes the traditional practice from the bucolic spiritual gatherings is that man's religious impulse is filtered through what Tocqueville called *formes*, a word that is close to a shorthand for *formalités*, the idea that there are sanctioned rules and practices for religious worship and social interaction. While those formalities can degenerate into obscurantism, Tocqueville insisted that formalized worship encourages more sophisticated and durable forms of religious practice. The democratic ethos scorns formalities and wants an im-

30. See Tocqueville (2010, 3:746).
31. See Tocqueville (2010, 3:750).

mediate, direct experience of the divine. Americans do not care, for instance, about the "details of worship" (Tocqueville 2010, 3:750) and tend to believe that iconography hides rather than illuminates. True to his Cartesian subjectivity, democratic man thinks the direct spiritual experience to be more meaningful and true than one filtered through conventional religious authorities. Tocqueville was perfectly happy if this religious impulse for immediacy remained within the broad confines of traditional Christian worship. The number of Protestant sects in America did not worry him at all.[32]

Tocqueville's main concern was what might happen when the desire for immediacy and directness manages to completely break loose from traditional religious contexts. This is when democracy gives rise to bizarre sects, religious follies, and odd forms of spiritualism. Tocqueville does not deny that man can have a direct and meaningful experience of the divine outside of a traditional service, or that all meaningful spiritual practices are only transmitted through hierarchy (after all, he seems to have had an unstructured quasi-religious experience in the wilderness of Michigan). The central point is that these forms of worship are not durable and do not establish stable religious contexts that might structure man's religiosity. Religion "is the one [area] in which it is most difficult for each person, left to himself, to come to fix his ideas solely by the effort of his reason" (Tocqueville 2010, 3:743). The solitary experience of the divine does not always provide answers to enduring primordial questions.

Tocqueville's concern, then, is that extreme democratic forms of religiosity cannot give rise to fixed and stable ideas, but deliver man's actions to change and condemn them to "a sort of disorder and impotence" (2010, 3:743). Since the unorthodox religious experience is much more fluid and indeterminate, it is more easily co-opted by democratic fads. Rather than acting as a regularized oppositional force to democratic life, it is merely a caesura that has little lasting effect. Therefore, when Tocqueville says that religion places a "salutary yoke on the intellect" and stops the "free ascent of the mind in all directions" (744), what he means is that a traditional religious context aids us in formulating our questions about the divine and in structuring and regularizing our religious practice. Tocqueville's fear, as opposed to Lamennais and the more conservative Maistre, is not that the world is going to become completely atheistic

32. It is worth noting that after 1840, in all of his writings on America and especially in his correspondence with his American friends, Tocqueville no longer mentioned religion as a pillar of democracy. While Tocqueville earlier believed that religion properly practiced could provide the foundation for sound mores and encourage a virtuous form of materialism in an age of individualism and skepticism, by the mid- to late 1850s this belief appears to have waned. In his fascinating correspondence with his American friends from that period, Tocqueville no longer made mention of America's originality in combining liberty and religion, a major trope in the first volume of *Democracy in America*. On this issue, see Craiutu and Jennings (2009, 26–33).

if man starts asking allegedly forbidden questions and asserts his individual will. Tocqueville thinks that man is by nature a religious animal and will always exhibit and search for one form of spirituality or another. The real question for him is whether spiritual practices will be bizarre, idiosyncratic, and sporadic with little lasting effect, or whether democratic man's spiritual life will be more sophisticated and effective. The answer to this question, in his view, depends on the extent to which man's spiritual life is regularized and institutionalized in traditional and durable religious communities and contexts.

Tocqueville wondered whether structured and traditional forms of Christian religious life could be maintained against the advance and power of democratic norms and values. If left unchecked, democratic faith, he feared, would overtake and replace traditional faith. He worried that institutionalized, ritualized religion would be either entirely subsumed into the democratic movement or displaced by idiosyncratic forms of democratic spiritualism. On the latter point, Tocqueville's experience of democracy in America convinced him that mysticism, religious communitarianism, and other forms of ecstatic but episodic religions might take on greater prominence in democratic centuries.[33] Following Pascal, he professed his appreciation for a religious "middle" between the "angel" and the "beast," along with his admiration for the English, a people famous for its middlingness even in religious matters.[34] While Tocqueville believed that overall political liberty enlivens religious passions more than it extinguishes them, and that free institutions are often the natural and, sometimes, indispensable instruments of religious passions, he was concerned about the effect of extreme religious passions as much as about the propensity toward an extreme detachment from earthly passions (as preached by Thomas à Kempis, the author of *The Imitation of Jesus-Christ*). In Tocqueville's view, in America, the passing of time and the increase of well-being had deprived the

33. See Tocqueville (2010, 3:940).

34. Here is Tocqueville again: "J'ai toujours cru qu'il y avait du danger même dans les passions les meilleures quand elles devenaient ardentes et exclusives. Je n'accepte pas la passion religieuse; je le mettrai même en tête, parce que poussée à un certain point, elle fait, pour ainsi dire et plus qu'aucune autre disparaître tout ce qui n'est pas elle et crée les citoyens les plus inutiles ou les plus dangereux au nom de la morale et du devoir. Je te confesse que j'ai toujours consideré un livre comme *l'Imitation de Jesus-Christ* par exemple, quand on le considere autrement que comme un enseignement destiné à la vie claustrale, comme souverainement immoral. Il n'est pas *sain* de se détacher de la terre, de ses intérêts, de ses affaires, même de ses plaisirs, quand ils sont honnêtes, au point que l'auteur l'enseigne et ceux qui vivent de la lecture d'un semblable livre ne peuvent guére manquer de perdre tout ce qui fait les vertus publiques en acquérant certains vertus privées. Une certain préoccupation des vérités religieuses n'allant pas jusqu'à l'absorption de la pensée dans l'autre monde, m'a donc toujours paru l'état le plus conforme à la moralité humaine sous toutes ses formes. C'est ce milieu dans lequel on reste plus souvent ce me semble chez les Anglais que chez aucun autre people que je connnaisse" (1977, 328).

religious element of three-quarters of its original strength. This was, Tocqueville believed, a natural phenomenon that could not be arrested or reversed in modern society. Once political liberty is well established and operates in a peaceful environment, it encourages people to pursue and develop a taste for well-being that eventually diminishes and may even extinguish religious passions.

At the same time, Tocqueville worried that religious pulpits would simply be the mouthpiece of democratic values, but he did not think that, for that matter, religion should be antidemocratic as it happened to be in France during the Old Regime. "As men become more similar and more equal," he wrote, "it is more important for religions, while still keeping carefully out of the daily movement of affairs, not unnecessarily to go against generally accepted ideas and the permanent interests that rule the mass. . . . In this way, by respecting all the democratic instincts that are not contrary to it and by using several of those instincts to help itself, religion *succeeds* in struggling with advantage against the spirit of *individual independence* that is the *most dangerous* of all to religion" (Tocqueville 2010, 3:752–53; emphasis added). For religion to act effectively as a counterweight to the self-defeating tendencies of democracy, it needs more than ritual and structure and must avoid the pitfalls of pantheism. In other words, it must preach beliefs that are not simply spiritual analogs of commercialism and individualism. This, Tocqueville surmised, was no easy task in a conformist environment like America, where, he thought, religion is believed and practiced more because it is a mass opinion and phenomenon than because of its intrinsic doctrinal content.

This is where Tocqueville's views on religion betray their complexity to the point of appearing paradoxical. The belief in the equality of all is a new democratic faith supported by common opinion in such a way that it takes on the trappings of a religion, and religion itself, the very thing meant to counter the pernicious tendencies of democracy, is also believed because it is mass opinion. There is, Tocqueville feared, a certain degree of hypocrisy in American religious belief and practice: it is done because it is what people do. "You are free to think that a certain number of Americans, in the worship they give to God," he wrote, "follow their habits more than their convictions. In the United States, moreover, the sovereign is religious, and consequently hypocrisy must be common" (Tocqueville 2010, 2:473). American public opinion then contains an internal inconsistency of which it is not fully aware: it is a form of dogma that has political or functional value only so long as it is believed.[35] Tocqueville saw the mass opinion that favored religious institutions and practices as ben-

35. Among those who saw Tocqueville's account of religion as problematic were Lively (1962) and Zetterbaum (1967); for a different opinion, consider Zuckert (1981).

eficial. But if that is the case, Tocqueville might have seen religion more as a salutary myth, beneficial only so long as it is believed, and it is "believed" only because being religious in America is a form of acquiescence to social pressure. To the extent that democratic mass opinion in favor of religion erodes, Tocqueville's solution itself becomes tenuous. The conjunction of the erosion of the mechanism of religious influence in American society and the erosion of religious consensus gave some cause for Tocqueville to worry about the future of religion in democratic societies in general.

5. CONCLUSION

Tocqueville never relinquished the conviction that "if [man] does not have faith he must serve, and, if he is free, he must believe" (2010, 3:745). He appreciated religion for what it brings, prizing it mostly as a salutary dogma, while also admitting that at times it could serve as a vehicle of eternal truths. This double feature of his thought, public recommendation and private doubt, forces Tocqueville to adopt a posture in which he thinks it is best for the masses to believe that which he himself doubts. Such a view seems able to attract few adherents today.

But Tocqueville is valuable as a guide for us today insofar as he is worried about public thought that encourages individualized forms of spiritual experience shorn of tradition, institution, and ritual. Tocqueville would therefore be broadly sympathetic to contemporary defenses of spiritualism insofar as he thought that materialism was morally corrosive and an unfit doctrine for a regime that encouraged freedom.[36] But Tocqueville was far less concerned with defending the truth or reasonableness of theism and did not think that philosophy could do much good in maintaining public faith broadly defined. It is hard to counter one's skepticism about moral standards or uneasiness in the face of an infinite universe that might lack a center merely with philosophic arguments, however ingenious they may be. Tocqueville sarcastically ridiculed the physiocrats for wanting a regime that has "for religion only a philosophy, and for an aristocracy none but intellectuals" (1998, 213). While he recommended the need for civil religion, he was concerned that the dogmatic character the latter took in America might ultimately prove inferior to genuine religious belief.[37] From this point of view, Lamennais may, in fact, have been

36. Two such examples can be found in Platinga (2000) and Nagel (2012).

37. On the general issue of civil religion in America, see Bellah (1967) and Hammond (1994). Kessler (1994) and Beiner (2010) argued that Tocqueville believed that America had, in fact, a robust "civil" religion. According to Beiner, "the religious life of the American citizens described by Tocqueville does exactly what Rousseau says a civil religion should do: It fosters good citizenship, attaches the citizenry to the laws and institutions of the political

right that religious indifference could be combated only by traditional religious faith and not by enlightened self-interest, however well understood, or by religious social conformity. The latter will ultimately be only another mouthpiece of democratic dogmas, and a dangerous one.

Be that as it may, Tocqueville helps us see that it is misleading to think that the world will be divided simply between indifference or secular atheism and agnosticism or pietistic religiosity. On this issue, he provided a more complicated portrait of modern life than Lamennais insofar as he grasped the extent to which foundational tenets of democracy are themselves held in the same manner as religious beliefs. It is not so much that hope is lost as that a shift occurs in the entity that provides hope. The ultimate consequence of the spread of democratic norms and values is therefore the replacement of traditional religious beliefs with new forms of faith. The locus of faith shifts from transcendent otherworldliness to the autonomy of the individual will, then collectively to the will of the (majority of the) people, and then, ultimately, to the state as their organ (incarnation) of democratic hope.

As such, secular atheism does not adequately give voice to the mix of hope and dogmatism that characterizes the new democratic faith. Tocqueville's analysis of democracy as a new form of religion challenges precisely the crudest version of the secularization thesis and what Charles Taylor called "subtraction stories" (2007, 22), that is, narratives that explain modernity's trajectory as one of loss or liberation from previous religious narratives. The development of equality and the emergence of democracy, Tocqueville reminds us, do not inevitably lead to atheism and do not necessarily attack the core of religion. The political and the religious can work—and do often work—hand in hand. Far from seeking to emancipate itself from the chains of religion, modern democracy contributes to a metamorphosis of faith.

Correspondingly, the fullness of democratic life is to be looked for not beyond human life, but essentially within it. It is important to note that the latter point, along with Tocqueville's insistence on the compatibility between democracy and religion in America, was, in fact, meant to be a lesson addressed to his French audience still sharply divided on the issue of religion. Postrevolutionary France offered the spectacle of a constant struggle between those who believed

---

community, and serves a thoroughly patriotic purpose" (2010, 250). As his correspondence from the 1850s shows, beginning with 1852, Tocqueville noticed obvious signs of decline in America and was no longer sure whether religion could stave it off. It is also worth pointing out that in a letter to his friend Francisque de Corcelle from July 29, 1857, in which Tocqueville spoke admiringly of England, he praised that country's "perfect accord between religious and political morality" (2003, 1253). A similar reference to the relationship between religion and liberty in England can be found in Tocqueville's letter to Louis de Kergorlay from August 4, 1857 (translated in Tocqueville 1985, 355–57).

that modern democracy could not function without religion and those who believed that religion was a relic of the past, incompatible with modern democracy. Tocqueville showed their compatibility, but not in the way that conservatives thought that religion would survive in modern society.

Democracy, Tocqueville concluded, redefines the form and role of religion, but in so doing, it relies on inherited traditional religious principles and practices to achieve the degree of self-restraint and prudence necessary for social cooperation. Those religious practices may themselves be dogmatically upheld out of social conformity. And yet, the good news that Tocqueville conveys is that, while the barbarians may be waiting at the gates, as MacIntyre and others have warned us, we do have sufficient resources to fight them. If Lamennais doubted this point, Tocqueville insisted, in Pascal's footsteps, that unbelief is a historical accident while faith alone, however defined, is the permanent state of humanity.

Will the future vindicate his optimism? And if so, will the new forms of faith be compatible with democracy or inimical to it? These are bound to remain open questions, and the best homage we can pay to Tocqueville is to pose them and invite our readers to find their own answers.

REFERENCES

Antoine, Agnès. 2003. *L'Impensé de la démocratie: Tocqueville, la citoyenneté, et la religion*. Paris: Fayard.

Beiner, Ronald. 2010. *Civil Religion: A Dialogue in the History of Political Philosophy*. New York: Cambridge University Press.

Bellah, Robert N. 1967. "American Civil Religion." *Daedalus* 96:1–21.

Craiutu, Aurelian. 2003. *Liberalism under Siege: The Political Thought of the French Doctrinaires*. Lanham, MD: Lexington.

———. 2010. "French Liberalism and the Aristocratic Sources of Liberty." *History of European Ideas* 35 (3): 385–90.

Craiutu, Aurelian, and Jeremy Jennings. 2009. "The Third Democracy." In *Tocqueville on America after 1840*, ed. and trans. Aurelian Craiutu and Jeremy Jennings, 1–39. New York: Cambridge University Press.

Deneen, Patrick J. 2005. *Democratic Faith*. Princeton, NJ: Princeton University Press.

———. 2012. "Unsustainable Liberalism." *First Things*, August. http://www.firstthings.com/article/2012/08/unsustainable-liberalism#print.

Díez del Corral, Luís. 1989. *El pensamiento político de Tocqueville*. Madrid: Alianza.

Gauchet, Marcel. 1985. *Le désanchantement du monde. Une histoire politique de la religion*. Paris: Gallimard.

———. 2002. *La démocratie contre elle-même*. Paris: Gallimard.

Hammond, Philip. 1994. "American Civil Religion Revisited." *Religion and American Culture: A Journal of Interpretation* 4 (1): 1–23.

Holbreich, Matthew N. 2011. "Between Sovereignty and Freedom: Tocqueville and the Project of French Liberalism." PhD diss., University of Notre Dame.

Jaume, Lucien. 1997. *L'individu effacé ou le paradoxe du libéralisme français*. Paris: Fayard.

———. 2008. *Tocqueville: Les sources aristocratique de la liberté*. Paris: Fayard, 2008. Translated by Arthur Goldhammer as *Tocqueville: The Aristocratic Sources of Liberty* (Princeton, NJ: Princeton University Press, 2013).

———. 2011. The Avatars of Religion in Tocqueville." In *Crediting God: Sovereignty and Religion in the Age of Global Capitalism*, ed. Miguel Vatter, 273–84. New York: Fordham University Press.

Jennings, Jeremy. 2011. *Revolution and the Republic: A History of the Political Thought in France since the Eighteenth Century*. Oxford: Oxford University Press.

Kahan, Alan S. 2015. *Tocqueville, Democracy, and Religion: Checks and Balances for Democratic Souls*. Oxford: Oxford University Press.

Kessler, Sanford. 1994. *Tocqueville's Civil Religion: American Christianity and the Prospects for Freedom*. Albany, NY: SUNY Press.

Lamennais, Félicité de. 1830. *Essai sur l'indifférence en matière de religion*. 4 vols. Paris: Tournachon Molin & Segun.

Lawler, Peter A. 1993. *Tocqueville: The Restless Mind*. Lanham, MD: Rowman & Littlefield.

Lively, Jack. 1962. *The Social and Political Thought of Alexis de Tocqueville*. Oxford: Oxford University Press.

MacIntyre, Alasdair. 1981. *After Virtue*. Notre Dame, IN: University of Notre Dame Press.

Manent, Pierre. 1996. *Tocqueville and the Nature of Democracy*. Trans. John Waggoner. Lanham, MD: Rowman & Littlefield.

Mitchell, Joshua. 1999. *The Fragility of Freedom: Tocqueville on Religion, Democracy and the American Future*. Chicago: University of Chicago Press.

Nagel, Thomas. 2012. *Mind and Cosmos: Why the Materialist Neo-Darwinian Conception of Nature Is Almost Certainly False*. New York: Oxford University Press.

Platinga, Alvin. 2000. *Warranted Christian Belief*. Oxford: Oxford University Press.

Reardon, Bernard. 1975. *Liberalism and Tradition: Aspects of Catholic Thought in Nineteenth Century France*. Cambridge: Cambridge University Press.

Roldán, Darío. 1999. *Charles de Rémusat: Certitudes et impasses du libéralisme doctrinaire*. Paris: L'Harmattan.

Swart, Konraad W. 1962. "'Individualism' in the Mid-nineteenth Century." *Journal of the History of Ideas* 23 (1): 77–90.

Taylor, Charles. 2007. *A Secular Age*. Cambridge, MA: Harvard University Press.

Tocqueville, Alexis de. 1977. *Œuvres Complètes, XIII: 2, Correspondance d'Alexis de Tocqueville et de Louis de Kergorlay*. Ed. André Jardin and Jean-Alain Lesourd. Paris: Gallimard.

———. 1983. *Œuvres Complètes, XV: 2. Correspondance d'Alexis de Tocqueville et de Francisque de Corcelle. Correspondance d'Alexis de Tocqueville et de Madame Swetchine*. Ed. Pierre Gibert. Paris: Gallimard.

———. 1985. *Selected Letters on Politics and Society*. Trans. Roger Boesche and James Toupin. Berkeley: University of California Press.

———. 1998. *The Old Regime and the Revolution*. Ed. François Furet and Françoise Mélonio. Trans. Alan S. Kahan. Chicago: University of Chicago Press.

———. 2003. *Lettres choisies. Souvenirs*. Ed. Françoise Mélonio and Laurence Guellec. Paris: Gallimard, Quarto.

———. 2010. *Democracy in America*. 4 vols. Ed. Eduardo Nolla. Trans. James T. Schleifer. Indianapolis: Liberty Fund.

Zetterbaum, Marvin. 1967. *Tocqueville and the Problem of Democracy*. Stanford, CA: Stanford University Press.

Zuckert, Catherine. 1981. "Not by Preaching Alone: Tocqueville on the Role of Religion in American Democracy." *Review of Politics* 43 (2): 259–80.

Part III

THE TOCQUEVILLE THESIS: THEORETICAL PERSPECTIVES

Tocqueville's Pendulum: Thoughts on Religion, Liberty, and Reason in Democratic Times[1]

EDUARDO NOLLA

> C'est un métier que de faire un livre, comme de faire une pendule: il faut plus que de l'esprit pour être auteur. (La Bruyère 1823, 11–12)

Time is of the essence.

Yet, it is an impossible task to define that continuum that we mean by time. These days, physicists are once again trying, and failing, to explain what it is, and if Einstein was right, it might not even exist.

Saint Augustine's confession remains very much relevant: "For what is time? Who can easily and briefly explain it? Who can even comprehend it in thought or put the answer into words? Yet, is it not true that in conversation we refer to nothing more familiarly or knowingly than time? And surely we understand it when we speak of it; we understand it also when we hear another speak of it. What, then, is time? If no one asks me, I know what it is. If I wish to explain it to him who asks me, I do not know" (Augustine 1955, 195). This, not by chance, makes one think about a similar reflection by Tocqueville about the difficulties of defining liberty, which is his central and most important concept, his *idée mère*, as he frequently put it. An unpublished note for *Democracy in America* reads, "Religion, liberty. Image of the pendulum."[2] He will not use

Eduardo Nolla is Professor of Political Theory and Director of Fundación Ortega y Gasset - Gregorio Marañón, Calle Fortuny, 53, 28010 Madrid (enolla@mac.com).

1. In order to place the quotes in context, references to unpublished fragments from the working manuscript of *Democracy in America* are followed by the matching page number in the 2010 Liberty Fund edition (Tocqueville 2010). This edition, in four volumes, uses the same page numbers as the two-volume English-only edition published by Liberty Fund in 2012, as well as Eduardo Nolla's Spanish translation in one volume published in Madrid by Trotta in the year 2010.

2. Yale Tocqueville Collection (hereafter YTC), CVh, 1, 64. The secondary bibliography on Tocqueville's ideas about religion is extensive and established. I would like to point out some interesting and less known works, such as Heimonet (1999, 303–41), Antoine (2003),

this simile in his book. It would have been totally out of character if he had done so.

The famous Parisian pendulum of Léon Foucault was installed and opened to the public in the Panthéon in March 1851. The original sphere of the pendulum crashed on April 6, 2010, at the Musée des Arts et Metiers in Paris, and was irreparably damaged (Tresch 2011, 31–35).

Tocqueville disliked machines. You will not find them in his books; you will not find them in his notes or correspondence. A trivial and obvious remark by an American Indian on his two-barrel hunting rifle (the fact that it was less precise in aiming than a one-barrel gun) will astonish him during his American trip. The famous American traveler was never keen on technology or inventions. The image of a clock or a clockwork apparatus would thus have been surprising to find in his book.

Machines always have for him and Gustave de Beaumont negative connotations. Beaumont wrote to his father on June 3, 1831, that he and Tocqueville dreaded being "examining machines" living only half of lives, without a heart.[3] The same idea is found in Tocqueville's letter to Kergorlay of July 23, 1827: "I am afraid of becoming a law machine, like so many of my fellow human beings" (Tocqueville 1977, 1:108). It is also found, for example, in his letter of July 25, 1831, to Alexandrine, where he describes himself as "a reasoning machine."[4]

Tocqueville hated and mistrusted mechanisms, seeing in them unreliable and dangerous contraptions. The world was to him in July of 1850 a "large and respectable machine, which breaks down a little every day" (Tocqueville 1866a, 153–54). Centralization, one of the developments of modernity he most hated, was described by him as "a machine admirably organized in the interest of those who govern but always defective and frequently detestable from the point of view of social interest which, after all, is the only one to be used when judging human institutions" (317).

The images that Tocqueville enjoys and uses in his writings are very different. They speak of movement, flow, and change and are frequently wrapped in veils or mist, hidden behind curtains. "All the objects of this life appear to us only like certain decorations of the opera that you see only through a curtain that prevents you from discerning the contours with precision" (Tocqueville 2010, 841 n. v). Floods, roads, walks—such are his visualizations. Rivers appear frequently, and Tocqueville describes them as roads that leave no traces, no history (1353). In addition, they are not only nearly always moving things; they are also at the mercy of chance. "With difficulty, the human mind manages in a way to

Abbruzzese (2005, 91–168), and De Sanctis (2005, chap. 8). On the role of beliefs in ideas on religion, see Johnston (1995), Sloat (2000), and Yenor (2004).

3. YTC, BIa1.

4. YTC, BIa2.

draw a great circle around the future; but within this circle chance, which escapes all efforts, is in constant motion. In the portrait of the future chance always forms the obscure point where the sight of intelligence cannot penetrate" (574). And again: "In all human events there is an immense portion abandoned to chance or to secondary causes that escapes entirely from forecasts and calculations" (574 n. b). Even in full light, objects are difficult to see: "It is one of the singular defects of our mind not being able to judge objects even seeing them clearly and in full sunlight if it cannot place another object next to it."[5] Most frequently, things are found in "impenetrable shadows" (Tocqueville 2010, 840).

Yet if, from a purely Tocquevillian point of view, one would have to use the image of a machine, none could be used suitably except that of the pendulum. In fact, it can properly describe Tocqueville's basic theoretical principle and perhaps his most cherished idea (Tocqueville 1983, 2:206), that of the balance between liberty and religion.[6]

* * *

Moving pendulums mark the passage of time, and "there is a time for everything," as the Bible says (Eccles. 3). There is also free time. Much can be learned from what political thinkers do in their free time. Socrates, the main character of Plato's dialogues, spent time drinking, eating, and talking with friends. Aristotle seems to have collected all kinds of stuff. Hobbes played tennis until very late in his life, although he maintained that Machiavelli would have been a better player. Rousseau, the *garçon horloger*, as Voltaire called him, gathered herbs. Nietzsche played the piano. Karl Marx endlessly smoked cigars.

We know that Tocqueville's favorite pastimes were reading travel books, particularly if they had maps, and traveling. One can also speculate that in his trips he spent long hours looking at the clouds.

Clouds and clocks. Karl Popper divided the world into these two large parts. He added a third, a World 3, as he called it, formed by the ideas and abstractions that we create and that surround us, as Bertrand Russell explained. Clocks can be described, taken apart, replicated, and explained. Clouds are chaotic, with no

5. Letter to [Freslon], July 30, 1854. YTC, DIIIa.

6. That religion was nevertheless an extremely important element of Tocqueville's theory in the 1835 *Democracy* can be seen in the use of the terms *religion* and *religious*. The comparison is not exact or scientific since the data for the Liberty Fund edition are the result of my own choices as the editor, but I think it is suggestive. In the original standard French edition, *religion* and *religious* are used 36 times in the first volume and 122 in the second. This is almost 340% more in the second part. In the Liberty Fund critical edition, the numbers are 259 in the first and 306 in the second, just 110% more. Tocqueville used the word *liberty* 406 times in *Democracy in America* (268 in the first volume and 136 in the second) and the words *despotism*, *servitude*, and *tyranny* a total of 252 times (176 in 1835, 76 in 1840). In the Liberty Fund edition, *liberty* is used 993 times (461 in the first, 532 in the second). *Despotisme*, *servitude*, and *tyrannie* are used a total of 735 times (356 in the first, 379 in the second).

fixed limits, impossible to be described precisely, constantly changing and moving. As Victor Hugo once poetically put it, clouds are birds that never sleep.

Karl Popper never understood Tocqueville even though the Frenchman's idea of liberty has much to do with both clocks and clouds. In dealing with his idea of liberty and the relevance of Tocqueville to the present, we also need to consider whether we can deal with the difficulties of clouds.

Let us talk first about clocks. Tocqueville's idea of liberty in the first *Democracy* coincides with much of what is typical in classical clockwork liberalism. Thus, liberty is linked to the townships, which are "primary schools of liberty," associated with small states and local liberties. Its workings require the existence of the rule of law, individual rights, the sovereignty of the people, separation of powers, liberty of association, trial by jury, and decentralization.

These are all predictable, mechanical elements in a liberal theory of liberty, but Tocqueville already in the first part of his book goes further and announces that liberty is something saintly and great that cannot exist without mores or religious beliefs. He also points out that liberty is inefficient, slow, and inconstant and that it lacks a single universal definition. Liberty does not come from books either: "True enlightenment arises principally from experience, and if the Americans had not been accustomed little by little to governing themselves, the book learning that they possess would not be a great help today in succeeding to do so" (Tocqueville 2010, 493). This is the big thesis about liberty for Tocqueville, that it cannot be perfectly explained in treatises, it cannot be acquired exclusively in books. It is learned by practice. The point and key to the whole of his work is in the famous connection established between religion and liberty in the chapter about the "point of departure," which, as we shall see, is a rather complex and multifaceted relation.

But it is in the second part of *Democracy in America* where the theme of liberty becomes, well, cloudy. This explains in great part Tocqueville's problems with language and definitions. How do you describe a cloud? Generally, by comparison with recognizable shapes. Comparative analysis is, as we know, one of Tocqueville's basic research tools. Liberty is in part 2 more strongly linked to mores and beliefs, to intellectual dependency, and, simultaneously, to liberty of thought and enlightenment. It is revealed as not exclusively proper to democracies, but also suitable and originating in aristocracies.

Liberty is also described, more than once or twice, as difficult, slow, and in danger from individualism and from democratic obsession with material well-being. It is a passion, as well as a habit at risk from war and bureaucratic despotism, dangerously friendly with the desire for order and predictability. It can also be destroyed by the obsession with equality.

All of this is linked to the paradox that in order to be free, humans need to accept a certain kind of tyranny:

> A man who would undertake to examine everything by himself would only be able to give a little time and attention to each thing; this work would keep his mind in a perpetual agitation that would prevent him from penetrating any truth deeply and from settling reliably on any certitude. His intelligence would be independent and weak at the very same time. So, among the various subjects of human opinions, he must make a choice and adopt many beliefs without discussing them, in order to go more deeply into a small number that he has reserved to examine for himself.
>
> [<In this manner he is misled more, but he deceives himself less.>][7]
>
> It is true that every man who receives an opinion on the word of others puts his mind into slavery; but it is a salutary servitude that allows making a good use of liberty. (Tocqueville 2010, 715–16)

This is Tocqueville's main point. In order to be free you must also be salutarily enslaved. You understand something only if you do not try to understand everything. "The last proceeding of reason is to recognize that there is an infinity of things which are beyond it. It is but feeble if it does not see so far as to know this" (Pascal 1958, 103).

One of Pascal's most famous *pensées* captures Tocqueville's attitude toward reason, at least in part, as we shall see. "I know only two states bearable for peoples as for men: dogmatic beliefs [v: ignorance] or advanced knowledge, between these two extremes are found doubt and all miseries" (Tocqueville 2010, 713 n. d). The excesses of reason bring intellectual individualism, and the extremes of religion bring intellectual dogmatism and immobility. There must be a permanent tension and relation between both concepts, a pendulous constant movement from liberty to religion, from thought and reason to dogmatism and faith. This condition is more complicated than it appears at first sight. Tocqueville is convinced that the eighteenth-century philosophical method can prove the truth of the Christian dogma. This conviction, which is much more evident in his drafts and notes than in the final version of his book, takes him to the logical conclusion that a handful of intellectuals are capable of some kind of rational, natural religion. "I am firmly persuaded that if you sincerely applied to the search for the true religion the philosophical method of the XVIIIth century, you would without difficulty discover the truth of the dogmas taught by Jesus Christ, and I think that you would arrive at Christianity by reason as well as by faith" (707 n. s). It is also this conviction of the demonstrability of the principles of Christianity that persuades him of the fact that intellectual anarchy, as he calls it, is proper only to times of revolution (708 n. t).

7. For an explanation of the symbols used in the edition, see Tocqueville (2010, xxxix).

Tocqueville admits the need for both discovered and accepted truths; he knows that this places the individual in a condition of limited liberty, but the only choice left would be to place the source of accepted truths in the hands of the majority. This is unacceptable for Tocqueville.

By limiting the scope of the philosophers' enquiries, religion prevents philosophical excesses, namely, abstract and too general political theories. Religion also becomes a spur to practical political action. "I doubt that man can ever bear complete religious independence and full political liberty at the same time; and I am led to think that, if he does not have faith, he must serve, and, if he is free, he must believe" (Tocqueville 2010, 745). He sees only some not very hopeful options (in an unpublished note): "During democratic centuries one can predict that man will only place the origin of his beliefs in himself, in his reason or in the collective reason of his fellows. Inside humanity and not over or further away from it, equally too weak to [illegible word] a prophet, too proud to subject himself to him. It is not the time of revelations or prophets."[8]

Human beings, unable to find by themselves explanations for everything, fall into doubt. And doubt leads the citizens of democracies to find comfort in material well-being. In 1842, after the publication of the second part, he wrote, "It was not only the isolation of minds that was to be feared, but also their incertitude and their indifference. Since everyone was trying to find truth in its own way, many were going to arrive at doubt, and with doubt the love for material enjoyments entered naturally in the souls, a love that is so disastrous for liberty and so cherished by those that want to rob it from men."[9]

The combined result of doubt and materialism makes them believe blindly in majorities: "Man needs to believe dogmatically a host of things, were it only to have the time to discuss a few others of them. This authority is principally called *religion* in aristocratic centuries. It will perhaps be named *majority* in democratic centuries, or rather *common opinion*" (Tocqueville 2010, 720 n. p). And in another place: "Common opinion, like religion, gives ready made beliefs and relieves man from the unbearable and impossible obligation to decide everything each day by himself" (721 n. p).

He had already found this danger in America. In an unpublished note, he explains, "America, moral force of [the] majority. *Faith* they have in it. It's a real religion."[10] When this happens, religion moves into the world of politics and provokes immobility, dogmatism, and absence of liberty and discussion: "What these days excites the passions of men is the earth, not heaven. The world of temples is the political world."[11] Taken to its extreme condition, majority rule

8. YTC, CVj, 1, 10.
9. YTC, BIIIb, 12.
10. YTC, CVj, 1, 10.
11. YTC, CVh, 4, 65.

can bring societies, as Tocqueville explains in his speech to the Academy in 1842 (Tocqueville 1866b, 15–16), to a kind of political pantheism.

Tocqueville remains very much aware of the difficulties involved in defending religion as an indispensable element for rational thought and a free political regime. In an unpublished variant for the introduction of the first *Democracy*, Tocqueville explained,

> Many complain about the development of democracy as if it were a recent fact while there is none as old and as continuous in history. See France. From the 13th century on you will see democracy taking over society little by little.
>
> What were medieval *communes* if not the first trials of equality of citizens before the law? What were priests but the founders of equality of men in front of God? Our kings themselves from that time on what did they do if it was not to establish the equality of subjects before the prince?
>
> The first, most complete ideas of democracy come from Christianity itself because it is Christianity that has founded the equality of men in front of god and created an intellectual society where all is organized according to the order of intelligences. But great revolutions, the conquest of the Roman Empire prevented this principle from leaving the sanctuary and entering mores and laws. On the contrary, with the Barbarians inequality of conditions was promoted to its last consequences. Christianity, which could not stop the glebe, nevertheless prevented slavery. But as time passed, the principle of equality among men gradually developed and starting in the 13th century, democracy has never stopped taking hold of society.[12]

Like Bossuet in his *Histoire des variations des églises protestantes*, both Tocqueville and Beaumont defended the idea that the Reformation would eventually lead to a kind of natural religion (Beaumont 1973, 73).[13] Tocqueville also thought that the enlightened and better-educated classes would move toward deism while the poor would either embrace Catholicism or, in the absence of all beliefs in an afterlife, fall resolutely and exclusively into the doctrine of private interest.

Tocqueville had another misgiving about Protestantism. He thought that it was too much in accordance with the individual rationality of democracy and that it gave an undue weight to reason. "Their reason," he wrote to Kergorlay

12. YTC, CVh, 3, 23.
13. In his letter to Ernest de Chabrol of October 26, 1831. YTC, BIa2.

in speaking about Protestants, "is a heavy load that they joyfully sacrifice. They become Catholics."[14]

There is another difficulty with Protestantism: it coincides too much with the democratic social condition, while Catholicism has the advantage of combining aristocracy (an untouchable dogma and infallible pope) and democracy (equality among all the members of the congregation except the priest). Thus, Tocqueville saw the benefits of religion for democracy to follow best from a common faith, which would necessarily be that of Christianity, and most desirably Catholicism. He saw this to be possible in the United States because American Catholicism addressed itself to reason, was less rigid regarding its rituals, and had abandoned the pompous language that it used in Europe. In an unpublished note in *Democracy in America* he explains, "This is another idea. Religions must be more mobile in democratic centuries than in the others."[15]

It would be unfair to think that Tocqueville did not foresee that his theory about the tension between liberty and religion might not work. "When you look closely, you notice that what makes absolute governments last and act is religion, and not fear; religion, principle of strength that they use, but that is not in them. When a nation still enslaved ceases to be religious, there is no human means to keep it bundled together for long. In summary, I am profoundly convinced that there is no lasting strength except in the collaboration of human wills. So to apply this force to the preservation of societies, men must have an interest in this world or the other" (Tocqueville 2010, 159 n. y).

An interest in the other world but also a possibility of an interest in this one? This is an idea that he deals with more in his drafts and correspondence than in his final text, as is frequently the case with Tocqueville. In the drafts, he pondered those elements that could take the place of Christianity: nonreligious virtue, honor, utility, or patriotism (Tocqueville 2010, 290 n. b). If Christianity loses its grip, there are some possible solutions he envisages; one is the nonreligious teaching of virtue. However, Tocqueville thinks that it will not work. Speaking of Seneca, Tocqueville explains, "His morality, it's true, is generally very pure and advances already the presence of Christianity. But what can be done with a morality that ends in the void? One would reluctantly preach men to die in the name of virtue when one believes that they die totally?"[16] Another substitute might be patriotism (Tocqueville 2010, 1100 n. j), a thoughtful new form of patriotism that is fitting to democracies. In an unpublished note, he asks himself, "What would be left to a government that would obtain its force

14. Letter of to Louis de Kergorlay, June 29, 1831. YTC, BIa2.
15. YTC. Unpublished note in the manuscript (Tocqueville 2010, 750).
16. In a letter to Freslon dated December 29, 1855. YTC, DIIIa.

neither from patriotism nor from religion?"[17] But American patriotism particularly irritated him, and he saw in it a hidden form of individual egoism. The problem remains also of how to engender it.

In democracies it was the role of the lawmakers to create common ideas for all citizens in order to connect their minds and hearts: "So the great object of law-makers in democracies must be to create common *affairs* that *force* men to enter into contact with each other. Laws that lead to this result are useful to all peoples; to democratic peoples they are necessary. Here they increase the well-being of society; there they make society continue to exist, for what is society for thinking beings, if not the communication and connection of minds and hearts?" (Tocqueville 2010, 891 n. k). Honor appears to be another way of obtaining generally accepted rules of behavior: "To act by *virtue*, that is to do what you believe good without other motive than the pleasure of doing it and the idea of complying with a duty. To act by *honor*, that is to act not with absolute good or evil in view, but in consideration of what our fellows think of it and of the shame or the glory that will result from it. The rule of the first man is within himself, it is *conscience*. The rule of the other is outside, it is *opinion*" (1096 n. e). Tocqueville dislikes public opinion and rejects honor as a replacement for religion. He doesn't think that it would succeed in democratic societies.

Another idea that haunts Tocqueville is that of utility. Perhaps utility could be used as a rule for social and political behavior. "Who can know if to God's eyes what is useful is not beautiful?" he asks himself in a note.[18] The reflection doesn't go much further. The principle of utility was for Tocqueville too near the clockwork principles of Cartesianism.

It may be possible, as a last resource, that enlightenment and education would allow the masses to arrive at the reasonableness of the Christian faith. Tocqueville doesn't think so: "I do not consider elementary knowledge as the most potent means to educate the people; it facilitates the study of liberty for them, but it does not give them the art of being free" (Tocqueville 2010, 493). No, knowledge by itself would not be enough. And so he seems to despair: "Isn't doubt the final condition of the people?" he asks himself in a side note in the manuscript of the book.[19]

It is tempting to try to elucidate this anguish with the help of Tocqueville's own religious beliefs, which have been the topic of many heated discussions. It may be good at this point to recall Tocqueville's own reluctance to define or explain himself in this point. Beaumont, his closest friend, confessed to Senior,

17. YTC, CVh, 4, 22.
18. YTC, CVa, 41.
19. YTC. Unpublished note in the manuscript (Tocqueville 2010, 304).

"He avoided any discussion related to religion. It is possibly the only topic that we haven't discussed in forty years of friendship" (Tocqueville 1867, 503).

***

Tocqueville's pendular movement between liberty and religion is another form of his theory of mores. "Mathematical truths need observations and facts in order to be proven. But to get and believe in moral truths, mores are needed."[20] But can mores be created? Can they be taught? Who establishes them? How can they be general and universally accepted in societies that have grown in disbelief and difference?

"Is the social state the result of ideas or are the ideas the result of the social state?" Tocqueville asks himself in a draft. He never gives an answer (Tocqueville 2010, 749 n. f).

Tocqueville states, "In order to have the government of democracy, one needs *citizens*, persons interested in public life who have the *ability* to take part in them and *wish* to. Capital point to which one must always return."[21] The question is, how do you produce citizens?

There is also a second difficulty equally important in the tension between liberty and reason. What defines existence for Tocqueville is traveling, movement, passing through time: "Man comes out of nothing, passes through time, and goes to disappear forever into the bosom of God" (Tocqueville 2010, 840). And in a letter to Kergorlay dated on February 3, 1857, 2 years before his death:

> I compare man in this world to a traveler who walks towards a colder and colder region and who is forced to move more and more as he travels farther. The great illness of the soul is coldness. And in order to fight this terrible evil one must not only keep the movement of one's mind brisk with work, one most also at this age not live on what one has acquired but make an effort to acquire more things, and not to rest on ideas on which one will soon find oneself as if asleep and overwhelmed by them. One must constantly put oneself into contact and fight the ideas one adopts with the ideas one rejects, the ideas one has had in youth with those suggested by the society and times in which one lives. (Tocqueville 1977, 2:324–25)

While existence is change, movement, political theories are attempts to transform time's continuum into discreet, comprehensible, static mechanisms. Here is where the image of the pendulum speaks to Tocqueville: In order to

20. In his 1852 speech to the Academy. YTC, DIIIb, 4–5, 14.
21. YTC, CVe, 65.

exist, a pendulum needs to stay in permanent, unstoppable movement. While repeating the same mechanical movement, it ticks different, unrepeatable moments of time and life. A pendulum precludes the existence of a moment of equilibrium. The pendulum is no more if it does not move. There is no rest possible if time is to exist. A stopped pendulum is like a 1, the unity, the uniformity. When there is immobility, there is uniformity and general, universal ideas. On the contrary, a pendulum in action is a perpetual aporia. Its heartbeat tick perfectly reflects the paradoxes of time. A stopped pendulum is time frozen into a second, a minute, an hour, the tyranny of the unity and the present, "time out of joint" (*Hamlet* 5.186–90), what Tocqueville most abhors.

He writes in a draft for the second *Democracy*, "Danger of allowing a single social principle to take without objection the absolute direction of society. General idea that I wanted to make emerge from this work" (Tocqueville 2010, 740 n. d). The idea is repeated in other places: "Do not adopt a single social principle no matter how good it seems. Do not use a single form of government. Keep away from unity."[22] There are different historical and theoretical engines. Some can be assimilated to one-stroke motors, today no longer fashionable, where all change is determined by a single universal cause. The sheer possibility of engines of this kind has always been discussed. Much more popular have been the three-stroke Hegelian-type historical engines that propel history and humankind in a universal three-step dance to their unavoidable end. Tocqueville's is a two-stroke engine. Tick/tock.

In this kind of explanation, events are explicated by the constant movement or tension between two irreducible principles or ideas. Tocqueville is an expert in this kind of complex multicylinder combustion theoretical machine. All his theory works according to this unique mechanical principle. Aristocracy–democracy, liberty–equality, religion–reason, political centralization–administrative decentralization, judge–jury, private–public, mores–laws, angel–beast—Tocqueville builds an unending and complex tension between different pairs.

Simplicity is for Tocqueville not the mark of greatness; rather, it is a sign of human weakness and belongs to an intermediate phase in human development. Tocqueville wants to combine a number of different means to obtain a great end, which essentially is imitating God: "So God, if I can express myself in this way, puts the idea of grandeur and perfection not in executing a great number of things with the help of a single means, but in making a multitude of diverse means contribute to the perfect execution of a single thing" (Tocqueville 2010, 740 n. d). The two-step dialectic, for Tocqueville, comes from God. He thinks that religion, order, and morality on the one hand and liberty and equality on

22. YTC, CVk, 2, 55.

the other hand are saintly and need to be put together because God has instilled them in man's nature (Tocqueville 1866a, 432). "The mind of man left to itself leans from one side toward the limited, the material and the commercial, the useful, from the other it tends without effort toward the infinite, the non-material, the great and the beautiful" (Tocqueville 2010, 769 n. g). If the process stops, man is taken away from life, and the present imposes all its weight on him.

Tocqueville's own intellectual production deals with the future (*Democracy in America*) and the past (*The Old Regime and the Revolution*). He defends the claim that those who live only in the present are prepared for all kinds of tyrannies. Only those who remember can love, have passions and mores, and be free. Aristocratic individuals lived in the past for the future. Tocqueville would like democratic citizens to live in the present, thinking of the past and the future.

In bad democracies, time has stopped, there is no movement, no tick tock, no change, no thought: "Since nothing stirs around them, they readily imagine that everything is in its place" (Tocqueville 2010, 760). And again: "The latter owe nothing to anyone, they expect nothing so to speak from anyone; they are always accustomed to consider themselves in isolation, and they readily imagine that their entire destiny is in their hands. Thus, not only does democracy make each man forget his ancestors, but it hides his descendants from him and separates him from his contemporaries; it constantly leads him back toward himself alone and threatens finally to enclose him entirely within the solitude of his own heart" (884). That is, in the wrong kind of democracy, individuals know only the present, having no past and, as a result, no future. In democracies, Tocqueville's new science of politics needs to put human ends in a distant future, through the use of powerful and strong passions linked to religion, or patriotism, but probably not honor. In democracies, there is the danger that past and future disappear, killed by the omnipotence of the present. It is also in the matter of time that religion becomes an indispensable element for history. "Religions give the general habit of behaving with the future in view. In this they are no less useful to happiness in this life than to felicity in the other. It is one of their great political dimensions" (966). The Americans' need to conquer the wilderness and their tendency toward materialism risk locking them in the present. "For the American the past is in a way like the future: it does not exist" (643 n. n). The advantage of Americans over Europeans was, we know, that Americans had religious beliefs. "It is a great spectacle that of the most enlightened and freest people being simultaneously the most religious," wrote Tocqueville in his manuscript.[23]

23. YTC. Unpublished note in the manuscript (Tocqueville 2010, 472).

* * *

This brings us to the question of whether or not there can be a Tocquevillian liberalism in present times. If his theory of a swinging movement from liberty to religion and back is his liberalism, there is a relevant old saying that states that a person with one watch is always sure of the time while a person with two watches is never certain of the correct time. Politics is nothing but a discussion about what is the correct time, that is, how we decide among different social and political options.

It is easy to dismiss Tocqueville's idea about religion and liberty as coming from an outdated French Catholic. But if we ask ourselves the questions that Tocqueville asked himself, the result may be humbling. When speaking about the coincidence of religion and liberty, he presented the condition under which "in the moral world, therefore, everything is classified, coordinated, foreseen, decided in advance. In the political world, everything is agitated, contested, uncertain; in the one, passive though voluntary obedience; in the other, independence, scorn for experience and jealousy of all authority" (Tocqueville 2010, 70). What if we turn the scheme around? Could it be said that today we live in a world where passive and voluntary obedience have moved to the arena of politics and in the moral world all is agitated, contested, and uncertain? Do we see ourselves reflected in Tocqueville's prediction in an unpublished note of a new world where "everyone advances randomly and talks without being heard and there is neither a common enterprise nor a common sentiment, not even common ideas"?[24]

Tocqueville has taught us a number of important even if painful things. First, liberty is not merely a set of social, political, and legal structures but mainly a passion, a sentiment or feeling to be created or regenerated every day by art more than by science. We want solutions, not problems. Tocqueville's theory requires daily unrelenting dedication to problems that need a solution even if they have no fixed solution.

Second, liberty requires confusion, movement, challenge, and linking the private with the public. "Men in democracies are naturally led to concentrate on their interests. To draw them away from their interests as much as possible, to spiritualize them as much as possible, and finally if possible to connect and merge particular interest and general interest, so that you scarcely know how to distinguish the one from the other. That is the political side of the work that must never be allowed to be entirely lost from view" (Tocqueville 2010, 871 n. a).

Third, for Tocqueville, liberty requires us to accept servitude or limitations. We can be free only if we accept limits on the scope of our thoughts and actions.

24. YTC, CVd, 4.

To be free, we need to compromise. Émile Faguet expressed it clearly by stating that an anarchist is nothing but an uncompromising liberal.

Fourth, liberty is learned in practice, by exercising political rights, through associations, political parties, local politics, and the press. It requires both effort and time. These are both limited commodities these days.

Tocqueville's liberalism remains valuable because it is provocative, goes against the grain, and forces us to face problems with no answers. Will it be used to produce better democratic societies? Time will tell.

REFERENCES

Abbruzzese, Salvatore. 2005. *La sociologia di Tocqueville. Un'introduzione*. Soveria Mannelli, Calabria: Rubbettino Editore.

Antoine, Agnès. 2003. *L'impensé de la démocratie. Tocqueville, la citoyenneté et la religion*. Paris: Fayard.

Augustine. 1955. *Confessions*. Trans. and ed. Albert C. Outler. Grand Rapids, MI: Christian Classics Ethereal Library.

Beaumont, Gustave de. 1973. *Lettres d'Amérique*. Ed. André Jardin and George W. Pierson. Paris: Presses Universitaires de France.

De Sanctis, Francesco. 2005. *Tempo di democrazia. Alexis de Tocqueville*. Naples: Edioriale Scientifica.

Heimonet, Jean-Michel. 1999. *Tocqueville et le devenir de la démocratie: la perversion de l'idéal*. Paris: Harmattan.

Johnston, William E., Jr. 1995. "Finding the Common Good amidst Democracy's Strange Melancholy: Tocqueville on Religion and the Americans' 'Disgust with Life.'" *Journal of Religion* 75:44–68.

La Bruyère, Jean de. 1823. *Les caractères*. Vol. 1. Paris: Chez Lefèvre.

Pascal, Blaise. 1958. *Pensées*. New York: Dutton.

Sloat, James M. 2000. "The Subtle Significance of Sincere Belief: Tocqueville's Account of Religious Belief and Democratic Stability." *Journal of Church and State* 42 (4): 759–99.

Tocqueville, Alexis de. 1866a. *Oeuvres complètes*. Vol. 7, *Nouvelle correspondance*. Ed. Gustave de Beaumont. Paris: Michel Lèvy Frères.

———. 1866b. *Oeuvres complètes*. Vol. 9, *Études économiques, politiques et littéraires*. Ed. Gustave de Beaumont. Paris: Michel Lèvy Frères.

———. 1867. *Oeuvres complètes*. Vol. 6, *Correspondance d'Alexis de Toqueville*. Ed. Gustave de Beaumont. Paris: Michel Lèvy Frères.

———. 1977. *Oeuvres complètes. Correspondance d'Alexis de Tocqueville et de Louis de Kergorlay*. 2 vols. Paris: Gallimard.

———. 1983. *Oeuvres complètes. Correspondance d'Alexis de Tocqueville et de Francisque de Corcelle. Correspondance d'Alexis de Tocqueville et de Madame Swetchine*. 2 vols. Paris: Gallimard.

———. 2010. *Democracy in America*. 4 vols. Ed. Eduardo Nolla. Trans. James T. Schleifer. Indianapolis: Liberty Fund.

Tresch, John. 2011. "The Prophet and the Pendulum: Sensational Science and Audiovisual Phantasmagoria around 1848." *Grey Room* 43:16–41.

Yenor, Scott. 2004. "Natural Religion and Human Perfectibility: Tocqueville's Account of Religion in Modern Democracy." *Perspectives on Political Science* 33 (1): 10–17.

Checks and Balances for Democratic Souls: Alexis de Tocqueville on Religion in Democratic Societies

ALAN S. KAHAN

ABSTRACT
For Tocqueville, well-balanced souls were as important to freedom as a well-balanced constitution. Such spiritual checks and balances were essential, in his view, for the preservation of political freedom and individual human greatness. Religion was the prime source of such spiritual checks and balances, offering a parallel source for the checks and balances to democracy provided by secular mechanisms such as associations and self-interest well understood. Tocqueville envisaged religion from two different viewpoints, utilitarian and perfectionist. From a utilitarian perspective, religion helped to limit democratic societies and preserve them from excess. From a perfectionist standpoint, it encouraged human beings to become great. Not all religions, however, were equally capable of performing these functions.

We are all accustomed to the idea of checks and balances among the three branches of government, as well as the role they play in preserving freedom. In this article I argue that, for Tocqueville, religion plays a similar role for the democratic soul, providing it with checks and balances that, in an indirect way, do as much for the preservation of freedom as any political constitution. For Tocqueville, well-balanced souls were as important to freedom as a well-balanced constitution. I further argue that Tocqueville envisaged religion from two different viewpoints, utilitarian and perfectionist, and that these two perspectives were embodied in the checks and balances he thought religion provided the democratic soul. I then discuss Tocqueville's views about which

Alan S. Kahan is professor of British civilization, Université de Versailles/St. Quentin-en-Yvelines, 47 Blvd. Vauban, 78047 Guyancourt Cedex, France (alan.kahan@uvsq.fr).

I would like to thank the University of Notre Dame and the Liberty Fund for inviting me to participate in the conference "Combining the Spirit of Religion with the Spirit of Liberty: The Tocqueville Thesis Revisited," from which this article grew, and all the participants in the conference, but especially Michael and Catherine Zuckert, for their comments and questions.

[American Political Thought, vol. 4, issue 1, Winter 2015]

religions are capable of fulfilling this function and what the implications might be for the role of religion today.

The connection between religion and freedom in *Democracy in America* is explicit, but it does not lend itself easily to clear and accurate conceptualization. Tocqueville intentionally treated religion in *Democracy in America* in a diffuse manner. Having deliberately decided not to write a single large chapter or set of chapters on religion, he instead scattered several short chapters and many more brief discussions on and references to religion throughout the book's two volumes (Schleifer 2000, 9–10, 10n26). This makes it is easy to go astray or overlook important points. This tendency is unfortunately strengthened by the temptation embraced by many commentators to emphasize those aspects of Tocqueville's views most in accord with their personal religious views. In analyzing what Tocqueville says and doesn't say about religion, Tocqueville's own interests and constraints must be given priority.

How does Tocqueville arrive at the view that the role of religion is to provide checks and balances to the democratic soul? This view is based on Tocqueville's view of human nature. For Tocqueville human beings, regardless of whether they are situated in an aristocratic or a democratic society, are a compound of the angel and the beast, a combination of idealistic and materialistic elements.[1] Religion must always take both into account, or it will be unable to influence the mass of humanity. However, in different circumstances, it must lean one way or the other. In aristocratic societies, which, according to Tocqueville, are naturally biased toward the ideal, a way must be found to bring people down to earth, to emphasize the material, beast-like parts of human nature. In democratic societies, on the contrary, the role of religion is to tear people away from the materialism that is natural to those societies and lead them to higher goals. Although Tocqueville "adore[s] the angel, and would like to see it predominate at all costs," he does not think this path possible for religion or for humanity.[2] Rather, he is looking for a way between the two extremes, angel

1. The image of human nature being a combination of the angel and the beast/animal comes from Pascal's *Pensées*, where it is used at several points. The closest to Tocqueville's use is in no. 358 in the des Granges edition (in English, Pascal 1966, no. 114; 117, 119). Usually translated something like "Man is neither angel nor beast; and the misfortune is that he who would act the angel acts the beast," a more literal translation comes closer to Tocqueville's meaning: "he who would make the angel makes the beast" (*le malheur veut qui veut faire l'ange fait la bête*). The relationship between Tocqueville's religious thought and Pascal's is complex and cannot be fully treated here. In summary, while Tocqueville accepted many of Pascal's premises, he derived radically different conclusions from them.

2. Tocqueville to Kergorlay, August 5, 1836, in Tocqueville (1951–), 15, 1:389, hereafter *OC*.

and beast, a path "which will lead neither to Heliogabalus[3] nor to St. Jerome; for I hold it as certain that one will never lead the bulk of human beings to either the one or the other, and still less toward the latter than the former." Religion therefore must find a way to help people balance the angel and the beast within, ideally tilting in favor of the angel, although whether this tilt can be assured, at least with the majority, is left open by Tocqueville. In general, he opts for moderation. A religion that can fulfill this prescription is what one might call "religion properly understood," by analogy with Tocqueville's well-known concept of "self-interest properly understood."[4]

Thus far, Tocqueville's comments apply to human beings' need for spiritual balance, regardless of whether or not they live in aristocratic or democratic societies. What is common to the role of religion in both aristocratic and democratic societies is that it must play the role of a regulator between angel and beast, providing checks and balances. What differs are the elements of human character that must be checked and balanced, as well as the means religion might use for doing so. As Tocqueville put it, "All the art of the legislator consists in clearly discerning in advance these natural inclinations of human societies, in order to know where the effort of the citizens must be aided, and where . . . to slow it down. For these obligations differ according to the times. Only the end toward which humanity must always head is unchanging; the means to reach that end constantly vary" (Tocqueville 2010, 3:955). Indeed, Tocqueville refers in *Democracy* to aristocratic and democratic nations as being "like two distinct humanities, each of which has its particular advantages and disadvantages, its good and its evil which are its own" (4:1282).[5] Angel and beast find very different opportunities to express themselves depending on their social situation.

As a result, Tocqueville does not shrink from suggesting that in certain circumstances he would have been a partisan of the beast, that is, a defender of material concerns against the spiritual. If he had been born in an aristocratic society like medieval Europe, obsessed with the next world, Tocqueville wrote in *Democracy*, he would have tried to encourage "the pursuit of well-being," otherwise the bugbear of *Democracy*, and attempted to stimulate people's physical needs and their desire to satisfy them (Tocqueville 2010, 3:956). On

3. A particularly dissolute Roman emperor of the third century.

4. Tocqueville to Kergorlay, August 5, 1836, *OC*, 15, 1:389. The same thought is expressed in a rejected passage of *Democracy* (Tocqueville 2010, 3:962).

5. Pierre Manent concludes from examination of some of these passages that Tocqueville cannot be considered a relativist, despite the "two humanities" (1982, 107). The conclusion is correct but somewhat beside the point when discussing the political implications of Tocqueville's views—which were what concerned Tocqueville most.

the other hand, in a democratic society something needs to be done on behalf of the angel, in order to counter the materialism natural to democracy. The fundamental truths of religion may not be altered by time, but the functions of religion, both political and spiritual, do change over time. Religion properly understood in a democratic society is thus understood differently than in an aristocratic society. For example, in democratic societies, religion is needed to limit tendencies that, if left unchecked, will prove detrimental to freedom.

In this negative role as limitation, religion accomplishes a utilitarian function. The limits religion imposes on politics and mores, by restricting the scope of the majority's power, can be politically useful, regardless of a religion's truth or of any value it may have in itself. But religion's role is not limited to the negative one of being a check on the democratic majority, according to Tocqueville. Religion also performs a balancing function. A force in its own right, religion acts as a power independent of the sovereignty of the majority. Religion balances the imperatives and inclinations of human nature in democratic society, above all materialism. It presents an alternative ideal to democratic society, an ideal of a certain kind of human perfection (e.g., the love of God) as a good in itself regardless of its utility.[6]

Tocqueville is thus both a utilitarian, when considering the "checks" performed by religion, and a perfectionist, when discussing the "balances" it offers democratic societies.[7] This dual function of religion, utilitarian and perfectionist, has often been missed by commentators. While "utilitarianism," that is, "the greatest good of the greatest number," is a widely familiar term, "perfectionism" is not. "Perfectionism" was originally invented by Stanley Cavell to describe the ideas of the American essayist Ralph Waldo Emerson, but it has since been widely adopted and given a broader application. The "perfectionist" tradition in Western thought goes back to Plato and Aristotle, and other examples would include canonical thinkers such as Nietzsche and contemporaries such as Alasdair MacIntyre. Perfectionists value human excellences, variously defined, "regardless of how much a person enjoys or wants them" (Hurka 2014, 2). Some perfectionists care about only the perfection of a handful (Nietzsche), or of a minority (Matthew Arnold, Nietzsche in other moods). Some, such as Tocqueville, strive for the perfection of the majority. The ultimate political perfection, for Tocqueville (and for Tocqueville political

6. The role of religion as a check or limit on democracy is found equally in the 1835 and 1840 volumes of *Democracy*. Religion's role as a balance to democracy, its perfectionist side, is found almost exclusively in the 1840 volume. This is certainly not a contradiction of volume 1, but it is a new development.

7. This is why Tocqueville offers "a particular mix of allusion to transcendent norms and appeal to collective self-interest that has always been a challenge to his interpreters" (Welch 2001, 166).

perfection is probably the highest form of perfection), is the attainment and preservation of political freedom.

A person will lack the scope for fully perfecting himself or herself unless he or she possesses political freedom. Political perfection, however, is the peak, as well as often the origin, of a set of other human perfections referred to by Tocqueville, often as human "grandeur" or "greatness" (Cavell 1981; Hurka 1993).[8]

Schematically, therefore, when Tocqueville talks about religion checking democracy's bad tendencies, he adopts a utilitarian perspective on religion, and when he talks about the balance religion offers democratic souls by, for example, encouraging them to pursue "higher" goals, he adopts a perfectionist perspective. We might add that his utilitarian viewpoint represents his recognition that democracy is more just than aristocracy, because it is for the greatest good of the majority. His perfectionist perspective represents the aristocratic aspect of his thought, devoted to the achievement of the noblest aspects of human nature. Religion both moderates or limits inevitable democratic materialism (a check) and provides an alternative to it (a balance). It works to improve both happiness (utility) and greatness (perfection). Tocqueville himself summarizes this dual function neatly: "If religion does not save men in the next world, it is at least very useful to their happiness and to their greatness in this one" (Tocqueville 2010, 3:744). Insofar as it provides a check on materialism, and insofar as it helps to balance materialism with higher pursuits, it helps to perfect human beings.

In practice, Tocqueville frequently commingled utilitarian and perfectionist language and perspective. An example of this can be found in his use of the angel and beast metaphor in *Democracy*: "What makes us superior . . . to animals is that we use our soul to find the material goods toward which their instinct alone leads them. With man, the angel teaches the brute the art of satisfying himself. Man is capable of rising above the good of the body and even of scorning life, an idea animals do not even conceive; he therefore knows how to multiply these very advantages to a degree that they also cannot imagine" (Tocqueville 2010, 3:964). In this passage, the soul or angel is useful, since it helps us satisfy material needs. But it also gives us the capacity to rise

8. However, Tocqueville did not regard political participation as crucial to a woman's freedom. He adhered to a version of the "separate spheres" doctrine and deliberately gendered his view of human greatness: "[The Americans] have not imagined for the woman a greatness similar to that of the man, but they have imagined her as great as the man, and they have made her their equal even when they have kept the necessary right to command her" (Tocqueville 2010, 4:1067). On the other hand, he thought that women should have a strong attachment to freedom and instill patriotism in their menfolk. See Tocqueville to Madame Swetchine, September 10, 1856, in Boesche (1985, 338–39).

above the good of the body and even scorn life, by implication in the name of a spiritual perfection that has nothing to do with utility. An effective religion is both utilitarian and perfectionist:

> Everything that elevates, enlarges, expands the soul, makes it more capable of succeeding at even those enterprises that do not concern it.
>
> Everything that enervates the soul, on the contrary, or lowers it, weakens it for all things, the principal ones as well as the least ones, and threatens to make it almost as powerless for the first as for the second. Thus the soul must remain great and strong, if only to be able, from time to time, to put its strength and its greatness at the service of the body.
>
> If men ever succeed in being content with material goods, it is to be believed that they would little by little lose the art of producing them, and that they would end by enjoying them without discernment and without progress, like animals. (Tocqueville 2010, 3:964)

As the conclusion of this passage indicates, one of the chief functions of religion in democratic societies is to combat materialism. In part, it does this because religious groups are associations, rather than because of anything special about religion as such. While in certain respects religion is unique, Tocqueville derives other attributes of religion from its status as an association rather than from either religious character or particular dogmas. On at least one occasion Tocqueville ascribed the Catholic Church's "instinct to dominate" to a trait common to all strong and successful associations (Tocqueville 1998–2001, 2:257). Of broader import is Tocqueville's description of the voluntary associations Americans form as the functional equivalents of aristocrats, as collective bodies that play some of the roles individual aristocrats had once played (as noted most recently in Drescher 2003, 627). In common with all other associations, religions therefore play an aristocratic role within democratic society. However, the relationship between religion and aristocracy in Tocqueville is stronger than that of the generic civil association and goes to the heart of the role religion plays to provide checks and balances on individualism and materialism.

Tocqueville goes so far as to describe religion in general as "the most precious heritage of aristocratic centuries" (Tocqueville 2010, 3:958). Here religion itself seems to be the product of aristocracy. This is paradoxical on several levels. Viewing religion as an inheritance from aristocratic society is in one sense inevitable, since human society was historically both aristocratic and religious. Yet for Tocqueville human nature has a natural tendency toward belief in God and spirituality, regardless of the social context. Religion is as natural to human beings as hope, because all or almost all people hope for eternal life. Thus, a religious impulse is part of human nature: "Unbelief is an accident; faith alone is the permanent state of humanity" (2:482). Furthermore, Christianity in particular has a special affinity with democracy, rather than aristocracy, because it is based on free will and the equality of all souls before God.

Why then does Tocqueville insist that while religion has universal, that is, democratic, appeal (if it did not, there would be no point in trying to encourage religion in democratic societies), it plays, or ought to play, an aristocratic role in democratic societies? This is because otherwise religion would not be sufficiently different to be either useful or an aid to perfection. Tocqueville, long before the term became fashionable, was searching for a way to establish difference in democratic society, difference that would both limit the majority and provide it with balance (Antoine 2003, 153).[9]

Because Tocqueville sees the role of religion as providing checks and balances, as representing alterity, it is a mistake to see him, as some commentators do, as precociously adopting a Durkheimian vision of religion (cf. Jaume 2011, 113). Emile Durkheim, in *The Elementary Forms of Religious Life* (1912), famously argued that religions are the embodiment of the social structure that produces them. They thus cannot be fundamentally at odds with that social structure. Tocqueville does not present a Durkheimian analysis of religion as the self-worship of society because a Durkheimian religion cannot perform the functions of checks and balances for a society to which it is too close. For Tocqueville, religion cannot just embody society, nor can it simply exalt the favorite attributes of the majority, like Comte's Religion of Humanity. Comte's religion, which was very attractive to Tocqueville's correspondent John Stuart Mill, held no attraction for Tocqueville because it essentially prescribed a kind of self-worship by human beings of what they, as a group, deemed to be their best traits. A religion that does not establish an authority other than that of the majority would be useless to Tocqueville.

Tocqueville does, it is true, insist that democratic societies must have a democratic God, that is, one who regards all souls as equal, because "alongside each religion is found a political opinion that is joined to it by affinity. Allow the human spirit to follow its tendency, and . . . it will seek, if I dare say so, to harmonize earth with heaven" (Tocqueville 2010, 2:467). Religion cannot be too different from the society in which it seeks to exist. But at the

9. This is also a reason why Tocqueville rejects pantheism, which cannot create difference because it sees God everywhere. The discussion of alterity and its functions in Tocqueville would be one way to introduce a discussion of Tocqueville and Hegel that is missing from the literature.

same time, a God who resembles humanity too closely is useless because worship of such a God would not act to check and balance the human soul. Francis I said that the king was the first gentleman, that is, aristocrat,[10] of France. For Tocqueville, God is the first gentleman of the universe, and in a democratic society perhaps the only gentleman left. At least, God is responsible for making sure that something can stand up against democratic society's leveling tendencies, its materialism and mediocrity.

Religion in democratic society must therefore play the aristocratic (perfectionist) role of restoring the possibility of greatness to democratic souls who would otherwise be unable to conceive of it, much less attain it. The democratic soul, precisely because it lives in a democratic society, is subject to unique dangers: "Equality . . . tends to isolate [men] from one another and to lead each one of them to be interested only in himself alone. It opens their souls excessively to love of material enjoyments" (Tocqueville 2010, 3:745). The antidote to this is religion, almost any religion:

> The greatest advantage of religions is to inspire entirely opposite instincts. There is no religion that does not place the object of the desires of men above and beyond the good things of the earth, and that does not naturally elevate his soul toward realms very superior to those of the senses. Nor is there any religion that does not impose on each man some duties toward the human species or in common with it, and that does not in this way drag him, from time to time, out of contemplation of himself. This is found in the most false and most dangerous religions. (Tocqueville 2010, 3:745–46)[11]

Religion thus plays the same role that enlightened self-interest and civil associations do for Tocqueville, but on a spiritual plane. Tocqueville wants a cure for the ills of the democratic soul, for its individualism and its pettiness, and religion provides a cure that self-interest, no matter how well understood, cannot. He wants people to look higher, and he is afraid that in democracies man will not: "It is to be feared that in the end he may lose the use of his most sublime faculties, and that by wanting to improve everything around him, he may in the end degrade himself" (Tocqueville 2010, 3:957). In response, "legislators in democracies and all honest and enlightened men who live in democracies must apply themselves without respite to lifting up souls and keep-

10. In French, *gentilhomme* means not merely a gentleman but a nobleman.

11. See also Tocqueville (2010, 3:924): "Particular necessity for religions in democracy; even dogmatic and not very reasonable religions, for lack of anything better. Show heaven even if it is through the worst instruments."

ing them pointed towards heaven," by spreading "the taste for the infinite, the sentiment for the great and the love for non-material pleasures" (3:957).[12] It is not only religion that plays the role of uplifting the democratic soul; legislators and all the upright are called upon. The religious spirit is by no means identical to human greatness for Tocqueville, and certain views of religion are even antithetical to it. Nevertheless, religion plays a privileged role in the endeavor to make democratic peoples great, because "religious peoples are naturally strong precisely in the places where democratic peoples are weak; this makes very clear how important it is for men to keep their religion while becoming equal" (Tocqueville 2010, 3:746, 957).

However, Tocqueville does acknowledge the role that self-interest itself plays in religious belief. Indeed, he says that all "positive religions" mix self-interest with duty in order to facilitate practice. "In Christianity, for example, we are told that it is necessary to do good *out of love of God* (magnificent expression of the doctrine that I have just explained) and also to gain eternal life" (Tocqueville 2010, 924; see also 927). Tocqueville, however, clearly prefers the love of God to the bribe of Paradise. This is why he has mostly contempt for Pascal's Wager—it is a crass appeal to self-interest. But even an interested religious belief, adopted for the sake of Heaven, ennobles (3:928d). Contrasting the doctrine of enlightened self-interest with interested religion, Tocqueville writes that "there is this great difference between them, that the first places this interest in this world and the others outside of it, which is enough to give actions an infinitely less material and loftier purpose. . . . So although the cause of actions is the same [self-interest], these actions are very different" (3:925). Religion enables people to perform a kind of psychological jiujitsu, in which they think they are acting out of self-interest, that is, the desire to go to Heaven, when they are really motivated by "the most pure, most noble and most disinterested instincts of human nature" (3:925; see also 3:921). Tocqueville finds this to be particularly the case in America (Tocqueville 2010, 3:921, 924, 925, 927, 928d).

Of course, one may wonder whether the love of God or duty will ever motivate more than a minority of people. Tocqueville admits that "interest is the principal means that religions themselves use to lead men, and I do not doubt that it is from this side that they take hold of the crowd and become popular" (Tocqueville 2010, 3:927). But this only makes religion analogous to political freedom, which, according to Tocqueville, "from time to time, gives sublime pleasures to a certain number of citizens" (3:876). Religion thus plays in the spiritual realm the role freedom plays in the political realm. There is a structure

12. Here Tocqueville takes the Rousseauian position that this is a task for legislators to concern themselves with, although he rejects the idea of a state religion.

at work in Tocqueville in which the religious and the secular fulfill parallel but not quite identical functions. In the secular sphere, the doctrine of enlightened self-interest serves to limit the damage that materialism could cause. Indeed, enlightened self-interest turns a vice (the pursuit of self-interest) into a virtue (by harnessing self-interest in the service of the community), or at least changes a potentially harmful attitude into a beneficial one. Similarly, religion limits materialism. In the secular and religious spheres, the art of association serves to balance the democratic evils of individualism and materialism.

In this case, freedom and religion serve a more or less parallel function. They are both aspects of human perfection. As Tocqueville wrote to his friend Kergorlay, both freedom and religion "pursue an ideal of human perfection, a certain perfection of the species whose image raises souls above the contemplation of petty personal interests." Indeed, the highest level of greatness is only attained by a combination of the two: "The real greatness of man is to be found only in the accord of the feeling for freedom and the feeling for religion, working simultaneously to inspire and limit souls. For thirty years my sole political passion has been to assure that accord." Freedom and the love of God are sublime accomplishments for the few, and yet also beneficial for the many.[13]

Unfortunately, in democratic eras the doctrine of enlightened self-interest penetrates religion deeply. "It cannot fail to give the spirit of religion a certain character, and you must expect that, in the soul of the *devout*, it will make the desire to gain heaven predominate over the pure love of God" (Tocqueville, 2010, 3:928e). Nevertheless, like political freedom, religion properly understood at least some of the time has the potential to lift everyone a little ways beyond petty materialistic concerns. It thus contributes to the perfection of democracy (3:928e).

The functions that Tocqueville ascribes to religion are not purely perfectionist and aristocratic, of course. Religion must check and limit as well as balance, it must serve utilitarian as well as perfectionist purposes, and indeed most commentary has focused on these. Tocqueville's view of religion's limiting function in democratic society—the ways in which it limits the scope of the majority's authority by placing mores, or at least some part of them, off-limits to democratic decision making—is relatively easy to establish. In America, according to Tocqueville, the general acceptance of Christianity means that "everything is certain and fixed in the moral world." Whereas anything can happen in American politics, when it comes to morals "the human mind

13. Tocqueville to Kergorlay, October 18, 1847, OC, 13, 2:209, my translation, also available in Boesche (1985, 192); Tocqueville to Corcelle, September 17, 1853, *OC*, 15, 2:81, my translation, also in Boesche (1985, 295).

never sees a limitless field before it; whatever its audacity, it must stop before insurmountable barriers. Before innovating, it is forced to accept certain primary givens, and to subject its boldest conceptions to certain forms that retard and stop it" (Tocqueville 2010, 2:474). We might speculate whether Tocqueville would have thought that gay marriage was evidence that this has changed in contemporary America. Would he see it as proof of the decline of religion, for traditional reasons, or perhaps as evidence of the strength of religion in America, where however radical people's sexual choices might be, they insist on following the conservative custom of marriage? Be that as it may, for Tocqueville it is clear that religion serves to limit democracy's scope for action and prevents democracy's worst excesses: "Until now no one has been found in the United States who has dared to advance this maxim: that everything is allowed in the interest of society. . . . Therefore, at the same time that the law allows the American people to do everything, religion prevents them from conceiving of everything and forbids them to dare everything" (2:475).

These are not the only limits religion imposes on American society, nor the only ways it contributes to the happiness of Americans by limiting some of their options. Tocqueville uses religion to limit the harmful effects of Cartesian doubt and of unlimited personal choice, for example. But, as this territory has been well covered, it does not need to be analyzed further here. Having established that religion's function is to provide checks and balances for democratic souls, it remains to be established which religion(s), according to Tocqueville, are able or best able to fill this function. Or, by analogy with Tocqueville's concept of "self-interest properly understood," which religion is *bien entendu*? Without an answer to this question, the discussion of how religion can promote freedom would remain hopelessly abstract, of no interest to the ever-pragmatic Tocqueville.

Readers might be forgiven for thinking that any religion would do, since Tocqueville wrote that "no matter which religion has put down deep roots within a democracy, be careful about weakening it; but instead protect it carefully" (Tocqueville 2010, 3:958). But while Tocqueville does say that any religion is better than none, and that any religion found among a nation in democratic times must be preserved, he does not think that all religions are capable of checking and balancing democratic souls in the desired manner. Commentators have spilled much ink trying to establish "Tocqueville's favorite religion." Naturally, they have most often concluded that it is their own, or should have been.

The question is not easy to decide and probably has no answer in the abstract. Tocqueville did not write about the truths of religion in the abstract. He was not a theologian, despite claims otherwise (cf. Mitchell 1995, 164, 223). Rather, his discussion of particular religions was always informed by the situation in which he lived. The picture he drew of religion always had democratic society as the background and Catholic France in the foreground of his concerns.

The democratic background imposes a set of characteristics necessary "for religions to be able, humanly speaking, to persist in democratic centuries" (Tocqueville 2010, 3:747). They must be monotheist, "based on the idea of a *unique* being imposing at the *same* time the *same* rules on each man" (3:742). They "must carefully stay within the circle of religious matters," that is, accept the separation of church and state and "carefully draw the circle within which they claim to stop the human mind, and beyond that circle they must leave the mind entirely free" (3:746). They cannot attempt to eliminate the love of material well-being, though they must "purify" and "regulate" it (3:742). They must limit forms and rituals as much as possible, since in democratic times "the trappings of ceremony leave [men] cold, and they are naturally led to attach only a secondary importance to the details of worship" (3:750). They must seek to please the majority "in everything not contrary to faith" and "not unnecessarily . . . go against generally accepted ideas and the permanent interests that rule the mass" (3:751).

This background applies to all religions in democratic societies. In the foreground of Tocqueville's discussion of religion, however, is the relationship between Catholicism and France. Particularly in writings intended for publication, Tocqueville took tactical positions intended to convince his French Catholic readers that freedom and Catholicism could be reconciled, and reciprocally to convince French anticlericals that they were not necessarily enemies.

Sometimes confusing the issue are Tocqueville's personal religious views. Tocqueville held the Gospels in high regard, but he was not a Christian.[14] As we know from his letters to Mme. Swetchine, he held minimal religious beliefs—the existence of God, of free will, of an afterlife, of some form of reward and punishment after death. "But beyond these clear ideas, everything which goes beyond the boundaries of this world seems to me to be surrounded by shadows which terrify me."[15] Outside his correspondence with Swetchine, there is no acknowledgement of this, however, and no argument is made in favor of this credo. Frank Turner was probably correct to conclude that Tocqueville's personal religious views had only a modest effect on his understanding of the role of religion in democratic societies (Turner 2006, 153).

Under these circumstances then, what religion did Tocqueville prefer? We can begin with the also-rans. Pantheism is rejected in the chapter devoted to it in *Democracy*. It cannot fulfill the utilitarian or perfectionist functions

14. On his respect for the Gospels, see his letter to Gobineau, October 2, 1843, OC, 9:57.
15. Tocqueville to Mme. Swetchine, February 26, 1857, OC, 15, 2:315.

Tocqueville assigned to religion, and so "all those who remain enamoured of the true greatness of man must join forces and struggle against it" (Tocqueville 2010, 3:758).[16] Tocqueville also rejected Hinduism, largely (but not exclusively) on the grounds of the fundamental incompatibility of a caste system with democratic society and the inseparability of Hinduism and caste (Kahan 2013).

Islam, on the other hand, is a democratic religion according to Tocqueville, based on the equality of all human beings in the eyes of God. In one important respect it is even more democratic than Christianity, because it has no consecrated priesthood, a fact that impressed Tocqueville greatly (and perhaps indicates some crypto-Protestant tendencies). He nevertheless found Islam inferior to Christianity on a number of grounds, but above all because it lacked any separation between mosque and state. However, unlike pantheism and Hinduism, it is possible to construct an Islam that would potentially serve as a check and balance on democratic souls from a Tocquevillian perspective. Tocqueville himself did not, because he was not writing for Muslims (Kahan 2013). His chief concern was Catholic France, and more generally the historically Christian West. He therefore concentrated on Christianity in his search for a religion that would serve democratic souls.

Democracy in America is of course set in a largely Protestant country, and since the French Revolution a current in French thought had seen Protestantism as the natural religion of free democratic societies. There are echoes of this view in Tocqueville. For example, in a rejected passage from *Democracy*, he wrote, "I do not doubt that Protestantism, which places all religious authority in the universality of the faithful acting by themselves, is very favorable to the establishment of [v: indirectly supports the political dogma of the sovereignty of the people and thus serves] republican government" (Tocqueville 2010, 2:470e).[17] Meanwhile, Catholicism had more affinity for limited monarchy. This is ominous for Catholicism, since in Tocqueville's view constitutional monarchy is only a way station on the road to the republic. It is also in contradiction with Tocqueville's chapter on why Catholicism will succeed in America. The contradiction is in part a result of Tocqueville's tactical need to placate French Catholic readers, but it also points to some of the tensions in Tocqueville's views of Protestantism.

Tocqueville's attitude to Protestantism was complicated. His view that religion was de facto necessary to a free democratic society, and that Catholi-

16. Here and throughout I have substituted "greatness" for "grandeur" as a translation for the French *grandeur*, following Arthur Goldhammer in this instance.

17. The section bracketed at "v" is a variant in the manuscript. See also 3:749–50, where Tocqueville suggests that giving importance to saints and angels does not fit with democracy.

cism was de facto the only possible religion for the great majority of the French, gave him strong incentive not to embrace a Protestant perspective, but writing about a successful Protestant democracy in America made it difficult to avoid.[18]

Tocqueville worried about how to approach Protestantism in *Democracy*, for fear of offending his Catholic audience. In the margin of a reference to the Reformation he wrote, "The Protestant religion (perhaps religions should only be touched as little as possible for fear of burning my fingers)" (Tocqueville 2010, 3:702k). Nevertheless, he drew a connection between Protestantism and democracy. The Reformation's emphasis on personal judgment, for Tocqueville, was a sign that society had already become or was becoming democratic in the sixteenth century. "Who does not see that Luther, Descartes and Voltaire used the same method?" (3:704). But Protestantism was more than a symptom of democracy; it was itself democratic. "The Protestant religion professes higher esteem for the wisdom of man than Catholicism does. It shows a greater confidence in the light of individual reason. Protestantism is a democratic doctrine that precedes and facilitate[s] the establishment of social and political equality. Men have, if I may say so, made democracy pass by heaven before establishing it on earth" (3:1041c). Tocqueville removed this passage from *Democracy*, putting a note in the margin of the manuscript that explains why: "Probably delete this. It is dangerous ground on which I should go only by necessity" (3:1041c). Nevertheless, Tocqueville does not merely connect the Reformation and democracy; he seems to endorse the connection. In a letter to Kergorlay he says that the rehabilitation of the flesh vis-à-vis the spirit began to be "legalized" by the Reformation, and that "everywhere the indirect effect of the Reformation has been to lead men to improve their material condition, without entirely losing the other world from sight as a result." This passage, in the same letter as Tocqueville's discussion of the need to strike a balance between the angel and the beast, the spiritual and the material, can only be considered an endorsement of Protestantism over Catholicism.[19]

But these passages are an endorsement of the Reformation over medieval Catholicism, rather than of Protestantism over Catholicism as Tocqueville found them in nineteenth-century America. Tocqueville was genuinely dubious as to whether the Protestantism of his day could continue to perform its checking and balancing function. From America, he prophesied the decline of Protestantism (Tocqueville 2010, 1:lxviii). Even worse, he reported that al-

18. In unpublished writings Tocqueville also admired the relationship between Anglicanism and English society. See Antoine (2003, 196); Tocqueville to Kergorlay, August 4, 1857, *OC*, 13, 2:328.

19. Tocqueville to Kergorlay, August 5, 1836, *OC*, 13, 1:388.

ready in American Protestant churches "faith is evidently inert . . . you hear them speak of morality, of dogma not a word. . . . This so-called tolerance, which, in my opinion, is nothing but a huge indifference."[20] And indifference was the great threat to religion in democratic societies, as Tocqueville had learned from Lamennais.

Tocqueville was aware of the fervent American Protestant revivalism of his day, but he was no more favorable to it than to Protestant religious indifference. In an essay on American religious sects, written at the same time as *Democracy* but unpublished, Tocqueville described a fervent Methodist preacher and a congregation rolling in the aisles from fear of damnation and longing for salvation. His reaction was to flee, "full of disgust and penetrated by a profound terror. . . . Must man be degraded by fear in order to raise himself up to [God]?" (Tocqueville 2010, 2:368).

Overall there are two kinds of reactions to Protestantism in Tocqueville: (1) suppressed sympathy (suppressed because its expression would brand Tocqueville a heretic in the eyes of the Catholic faithful of France), and (2) rejection, on the grounds that Protestantism in the long run may not be able to offer sufficient checks and balances for the democratic soul. This gives Tocqueville further reason for not attempting to persuade France of the virtue of what might, at best, be a short-term solution to democracy's spiritual problems.

While Tocqueville had reason not to praise Protestantism's democratic features, he had no such reason to avoid praise of Catholic democracy; indeed, the opposite was true. The more he could persuade both French Catholics and anticlericals that Catholicism was the natural religion of democracy, the closer he would be to achieving his political goals. This is the approach he adopts in *Democracy*, although he was not without misgivings. Tocqueville needs Catholicism, he fears for it, and he fears it, all at the same time.

In *Democracy* Tocqueville proclaimed that if only Catholicism could escape from the political hatred born of its entanglement with the French monarchy and crystallized in the French Revolution, "the spirit of the century, which seems so contrary to it, would become very favorable to it, and it would suddenly make great conquests." The same message is conveyed in *The Old Regime*—Tocqueville felt the need to reconcile Catholicism with democracy in France throughout his life. The draft of *Democracy* continues: "and that [Catholicism] would end by being the only religion of all those who would have a religion" (Tocqueville 2010, 3:755, 755e). Catholicism often serves Tocqueville not merely as a particular religion but as the basic pattern of all religions, at least all monotheistic religions, from which deviation is in the long run futile. In this

20. Tocqueville to Kergorlay, OC, 13, 1:227–28, also available in Boesche (1985, 48–50).

chapter of *Democracy* and elsewhere Tocqueville predicts that the world will one day be divided between Catholics and atheists (Tocqueville 2010, 3:756).

Given this choice, it would seem that Tocqueville's preference would be clear. But in private Tocqueville held, at least from the early 1840s, different opinions and different fears. In 1843 he wrote to a friend that while Catholicism had to be supported in France because it was the only form religion could plausibly take there, "Catholicism, I am very afraid, will never adopt the new society" and would hasten to abuse any influence it might attain.[21] Catholicism was, he feared, fundamentally intolerant of other religions.[22]

He was also afraid that Catholicism was fundamentally out of tune with democratic society. In his correspondence he opposed the proclamation of the dogma of the Immaculate Conception of the Virgin in 1854 on these grounds, and he thought that in the modern world there was no place for the temporal power of the Pope.[23] Tocqueville's need for religion in general, and French Catholicism in particular, was strong enough to overcome these fears, at least in public, and he did his best to try to convince his readers that Catholicism and democracy were natural friends. He was not very successful at this, with himself or with others. He was not, in fact, a great admirer of nineteenth-century Catholicism, any more than he was of nineteenth-century Protestantism.

He was, however, always a great admirer of Christianity. Rather than any actual Christian religion, however, Tocqueville admired an idealized version of Christianity that was the perfect source of checks and balances for democratic society, at least in the West. As Turner puts it, he appealed to a "best self of Christianity against its historically institutionalized lesser self" (2006, 155). Tocqueville summed up this best self of Christianity in words borrowed from the Gospel of Matthew: "love God with all your heart and your neigh-

21. This letter was written after a controversy over state recognition of and/or funding for Catholic schools in France, in which Tocqueville had personally suffered for rejecting both the laical and church positions and contending for state recognition of Catholic diplomas without state funding. He was much disappointed by the attitude of the church in the controversy. See Boesche (1983).

22. See the various remarks to this effect in Tocqueville to Kergorlay, vol. 1, June 29, 1831, *OC*, 8, 1:299; Tocqueville to Corcelle, November 15, 1843, *OC*, 15, 1:174; Tocqueville (1998–2001, 2:354).

23. Tocqueville to Corcelle, November 15, 1843, *OC*, 15, 1:174; December 28, 1854, *OC*, 15, 2:129; October 1, 1849, *OC*, 15, 1:438. He was no friendlier to the so-called progressive Catholics of his day, centered around Montalembert. Partly, he found the word "progressive" ugly, but more to the point he thought that a religion must present itself as true or false: "How can it make progress? . . . Progress can only come in the application, not in the doctrine"; otherwise, religion would not give the democratic spirit the respite from doubt it so sorely needed. See Tocqueville to Corcelle, December 31, 1853, *OC*, 15, 2:90.

bor as yourself—this contains the law and the prophets."[24] He attributed to Christianity the origins of all modern morality, no matter how seemingly "advanced" or "secular." Avant-garde moral and economic principles, including socialism, were just variations of Christianity due to the democratic social state.

Tocqueville's ideal Christianity is the most democratic of all religions, because it appeals solely to the free choice of the individual. It is also the most favorable of all religions to equality, and its appeal is the most universal, because it is not limited to a particular country or even to a particular social state, as proved by the fact that it flourished in both aristocratic medieval Europe and ultrademocratic nineteenth-century America. Tocqueville's ideal Christianity, however, must possess one element that no form of historical Christianity has possessed, according to Tocqueville: it must be religiously attached to political freedom. When vaunting to Gobineau the superiority of Christianity, Tocqueville acknowledged one significant weakness: "The duties of men to each other in their capacity as *citizens*, the obligation of the citizen toward the nation, in a word the public virtues seem to me badly defined and fairly neglected in Christian morality" (Tocqueville 2010, 1:49–50).[25] His outlook was summed up in a letter to Swetchine, born of his outrage at church support for Napoleon III: if one of the merits of Christianity was its ability to exist under any form of government, it did not follow from this that "it must be insensible to or indifferent to these evils [that bad governments create], and that Christianity does not impose on everyone the duty to courageously deliver his fellows from them by the legitimate means that the light of his conscience reveals to him." But when he looked at France, or at most of Europe, he saw that the forms of Christianity that actually existed at the time, both Catholic and Protestant, were notably failing to preach this lesson (Tocqueville 2010, 2:468–69, 482u, 3:748f).[26]

An ideal version of Christianity, then, rather than any existing form of Christianity, Protestant or Catholic, is Tocqueville's preferred foundation for democratic freedom. In its absence, many forms of Christianity will do, as is shown by the examples of America, England, and Ireland, even though Tocqueville is disgusted by the Methodists and worried about Pius IX. If one

24. Tocqueville to Gobineau, October 2, 1843, *OC*, 9:58.

25. Tocqueville certainly recognized that the American Puritans were attached to political freedom. But while their religion bolstered their freedom, its origins were English, rather than Christian, according to Tocqueville.

26. Tocqueville to Gobineau, September 5, 1843, *OC*, 9:46; Tocqueville to Mme. Swetchine, October 20, 1856, *OC*, 15, 2:297. Tocqueville repeated this criticism on several occasions. 1:88; Tocqueville to Broglie, July 20, 1856, in Tocqueville (2003, 1178).

must name Tocqueville's favorite religion then, one must say Christianity and stop there, not because of any ecumenism on Tocqueville's part, but rather because all the real versions of Christianity failed to live up to his ideal. The exception is the one that was not necessarily Christian at all, as far as Tocqueville was concerned. Not enough has been made of Tocqueville's encounter with William Ellery Channing and American Unitarianism.

Tocqueville was not quite sure whether Unitarianism was an extreme form of Christianity, the last step before Deism, or else a pure form of Deism—he says both things in different letters.[27] He had never heard of Unitarianism before he came to America, and it both surprised and impressed him. What impressed him most was the speed with which Unitarianism was gaining converts, especially among the upper classes. This led him to prophesy that in the end American Protestantism would one day disappear, and Catholics and Unitarians would be left to battle it out for American souls—not, perhaps, one of Tocqueville's most prescient predictions. This was for far in the future, however. In the meantime, Tocqueville read the works of the leading Unitarian preacher, William Ellery Channing, heard him preach, and visited him.

His conversation with Channing touched on some of Tocqueville's most basic ideas about religion. Tocqueville asked Channing whether, in purging Christianity of its irrational elements, the Unitarians would not also deprive it of its substance, ending up with merely "natural religion."[28] Channing responded, in words that would later become part of Tocqueville's own perspective on religion, that the human spirit needed a positive religion, and why would it wish to abandon Christianity (i.e., Unitarianism), which need fear nothing from rational examination? But Tocqueville did not adopt all of Channing's views. When Tocqueville objected that the majority of human beings would be unable to think through a rational religion and needed a dogmatic religion, Channing responded that the truths of religion were sufficiently simple to be rationally understood by any honest person. Here Tocqueville did not agree, as can be seen in *Democracy* (Tocqueville 2010, 3:744–45).

Tocqueville was impressed with both Channing and Unitarianism, however. Its Deism, after all, was not too far from his own personal beliefs. While he was not willing to imagine Deism/Unitarianism as an adequate replacement for Christianity in a democratic society, one capable of providing the necessary checks and balances to all democratic souls, he was willing, at least when

27. It is Deism in the letter to Kergorlay, June 29, 1831, *OC*, 8, 1:230. It isn't, quite, in the letter to Chabrol, October 26, 1831, in Tocqueville (2003, 247).

28. Tocqueville, *Voyages*, *OC*, 5, 1:100–110. What Tocqueville meant by "natural religion," and to what extent this concept was borrowed from Rousseau, is a subject for which there is insufficient space here. Suffice it to say that Tocqueville owed much to the Savoyard Vicar.

still under Channing's spell, to consider it for an elite: "Can deism ever be suitable for all classes of a nation? Above all those which have the most need of the bridle of religion? This is what I can't persuade myself. I confess that what I see here inclines me more than I was previously to believe that what is called natural religion, can be enough for the upper classes of society, provided that belief in the two or three great truths it teaches is real and some kind of exterior worship is included in it."[29] But before the masses will be able to see in this more than atheism, and thus avoid falling into mere self-interest, they would have to become different from any mass the world had ever seen, according to Tocqueville. Tocqueville regrets this. It is proof of the "misery of our nature," he says, that a religion that preaches reason and toleration is "an inert thing, without power and almost lifeless," while another religion (Christianity? Catholicism?) that preaches fanaticism and intolerance and divides the living human race into the saved and the damned, rather than leaving judgment to God, gives rise to real belief and devotion.[30]

Would Tocqueville have preferred Unitarianism even to an ideal Christianity? Perhaps not, given his view of the need for dogma: "The longer I live, the less I can see peoples doing without a positive religion; this makes me less severe . . . towards the problems that all religions present, even the best."[31] In any case, Unitarianism is not a practical solution to the problem of providing checks and balances for the democratic soul, at least not for the masses, and Tocqueville drops the subject. Nevertheless, it is perhaps relevant to an appreciation of the role religion might play in America and elsewhere in the West in the twenty-first century. Would it be too bold to suggest that it is the dominant religion of some parts of Europe today?

Tocqueville wants religion to provide a system of spiritual checks and balances that would give both utilitarian and perfectionist counsel to the democratic soul. In this way religion will indirectly strengthen freedom in democratic societies. His preferred religion for this task is an ideal Christianity, since Unitarianism can work only for the elite, but in practice French political considerations led him to emphasize the suitability of Catholicism for the role,

29. Tocqueville to Kergorlay, June 29, 1831, *OC*, 13, 1:230–31. Note that in this passage Tocqueville seems to equate Unitarianism with natural religion, unlike in his conversation with Channing, perhaps because Channing, despite denying the Trinity and the notion of redemption for original sin, persisted in describing Unitarianism as a form of Christianity. See the letter to Chabrol, October 26, 1831, in Tocqueville (2003, 247).

30. Tocqueville to Kergorlay, June 29, 1831, *OC*, 13, 1:231. Interestingly, on this point Tocqueville's judgment echoes that of Pascal: "A purely intellectual religion would be more appropriate to the clever, but would be no good at all for the people" (Pensee no. 219, *Pensées*, 99). Pascal also concludes that only Christianity will do for both.

31. Tocqueville to Gobineau, October 2, 1843, *OC*, 9:58.

despite some misgivings. If we share Tocqueville's concerns, if we do not think that enlightened self-interest is enough to maintain freedom in the long run, then we must learn to understand religions, our own or those of others, in terms of the checks and balances they provide democratic souls. Only in that way, Tocqueville would tell us, can either the soul or the nation remain free.

REFERENCES

Antoine, Agnès. 2003. *L'Impensé de la démocratie. Tocqueville, la citoyenneté, et la religion*. Paris: Fayard.

Boesche, Roger. 1983. "Tocqueville and Le Commerce: A Newspaper Expressing His Unusual Liberalism." *Journal of the History of Ideas* 44:277–92.

———. 1985. *Alexis de Tocqueville: Selected Letters on Politics and Society*. Berkeley: University of California Press.

Cavell, Stanley. 1981. *Conditions Handsome and Unhandsome: The Constitution of Emersonian Perfectionism*. Chicago: University of Chicago Press.

Drescher, Seymour. 2003. "Who Needs *Ancienneté*? Tocqueville on Aristocracy and Modernity." *History of Political Thought* 24:624–46.

Hurka, Thomas. 1993. *Perfectionism*. Oxford: Oxford University Press.

———. 2014. "Nietzsche, Perfectionist." http://thomashurka.files.wordpress.com/2014/02/nietzsche-perfectionist.pdf.

Jaume, Lucien. 2011. *Tocqueville*. Paris: Fayard.

Kahan, Alan S. 2013. "Beyond the Frontiers of Christendom: Tocqueville, Islam, and Hinduism." In *Tocqueville beyond the Frontiers*, ed. Ewa Atanassow and Richard Boyd, 89–110. Cambridge: Cambridge University Press.

Manent, Pierre. 1982. *Tocqueville et la nature de la démocratie*. Paris: Fayard.

Mitchell, Joshua. 1995. *The Fragility of Freedom: Tocqueville on Religion, Democracy and the American Future*. Chicago: University of Chicago Press.

Pascal, Blaise. 1966. *Pensées*. Trans. A. J. Krailsheimer. New York: Penguin.

Schleifer, James T. 2000. *The Making of Tocqueville's Democracy in America*. Indianapolis: Liberty Fund.

Tocqueville, Alexis de. 1951–. *Oeuvres complètes*. Paris: Gallimard.

———. 1998–2001. *The Old Regime and the Revolution*. Chicago: University of Chicago Press.

———. 2003. *Lettres Choisies*. Paris: Gallimard.

———. 2010. *Democracy in America*. Ed. Eduardo Nolla, trans. James T. Schleifer. Indianapolis: Liberty Fund.

Turner, Frank. 2006. "Alexis de Tocqueville and John Stuart Mill on Religion." *Tocqueville Review* 27:149–72.

Welch, Cheryl. 2001. *De Tocqueville*. Oxford: Oxford University Press.

Tocqueville on Religion and Liberty

HARVEY C. MANSFIELD

ABSTRACT

Tocqueville declares himself to be a "new kind" of liberal, and the most striking feature of his reform is to propose, and to find in America, an alliance, rather than hostility, between religion and liberty. As opposed to an overt foundation in the state of nature, he sets the actual practice of religion in America, which brings moderation and limitation to liberty. Religion also supplies the notion of soul, which validates the prideful free agency of humans as against the determinism and materialism of the state of nature. It helps to secure modern democracy against the evils Tocqueville discerned and so notably described of individualism and mild despotism. And it provides the basis for the art of the legislator, a classical function revived by Tocqueville to use both nature and convention in cooperation, instead of distinct and at odds.

> I stop the first American I meet . . . and I ask him if he believes religion to be useful to the stability of laws and to the good order of society; without hesitation he answers that a civilized society, but above all a free society, cannot subsist without religion. . . . Even those least versed in the science of government know that much. (Tocqueville 2011, 3.2, 140)

Alexis de Tocqueville was a liberal, but, as he once said, a "new kind of liberal."[1] "One of the noblest enterprises of our time," he added, would be to show that "morality, religion and order" do not need to be opposed to "liberty and the equality of men before the law." For us today, no feature of his new liberalism is more remarkable than the alliance between religion and liberty that he sees in America and proposes to be imitated, wherever it can, in every free society. That alliance is part of his attempt to make liberalism political. For in his view the early, original theory of liberalism, by beginning

Harvey C. Mansfield is Senior Fellow at the Hoover Institution, Stanford University, and Kenan Professor of Government, Harvard University, 1737 Cambridge Street, #417, Cambridge, MA 02138 (h_mansfield@harvard.edu).

1. "*un liberal d'une espèce nouvelle*"; Letter to Eugène Stoeffels, July 24, 1836, in Tocqueville (2003, 352–55).

from outside politics through a concept of the state of nature, rather than from the practice of politics, was never able to find politics, or return to it, once its practice was left behind.

The reason for abstracting from politics was its potentiality for religious conflict, as revealed in the actual wars of the seventeenth century that convulsed Europe but not America. Tocqueville goes on to say that even though there is no country where the boldest political doctrines of the eighteenth-century *philosophes* were applied more than in America, the antireligious doctrines for which they were best known never appeared there. We learn from his writings that the wisdom of ordinary Americans, in this regard and in general, not only illustrates the science of government but indeed, through the self-government Americans practice, provides the source of that science. "That great science of government," apparently the same as the "new political science" said to be needed in the introduction to *Democracy in America*, is never elaborated by Tocqueville but rather left to be discerned by his readers. They will find it "only in the play (*jeu*) of free institutions," that is, in America, not in theories or in the Old Regime of France (Tocqueville 2000, introduction, 7; Tocqueville 2011, 3.1, 132).

In liberalism today, there is a debate over the question whether liberal theory needs or should avoid a "foundation."[2] Tocqueville is not surely on either side of this debate. He may seem to take the foundational side, as he uses the words "first foundation" (*premier fondement*) to say what an individual needs to "build the edifice" of his own thoughts. This foundation is not chosen by his will; rather, the "inflexible law of his condition" constrains him to it. This law for "man separately" is not explained. A society, any society, needs "dogmatic" beliefs, for without common ideas there could be no common action. Neither of these is an intelligible "foundation" in reason of the kind foundational liberals desire and supply. Neither mentions "nature."

Tocqueville never mentions the "state of nature," the standard foundation of seventeenth-century liberalism, and in *Democracy in America* he omits any reference to the Declaration of Independence with its ringing foundational assertion that "all men are created equal" (Winthrop 1991, 415–16). Yet, if he avoids laying a foundation in reason, he also thinks that religion is essential to political liberty because of certain "very fixed ideas" or "ready-made beliefs" that it offers to ground the practice of self-government (Tocqueville 2000, 2.1.5, 417; 2.1.2, 408; Tocqueville 2011, 3.2, 132). These are doctrines of faith, since for Tocqueville "religion" means revealed religion, not a rational

2. In the following remarks on foundations, I borrow from a companion article (Mansfield 2014, 202–5).

or natural religion, such as "deism," which other liberals in the seventeenth and eighteenth centuries had proposed to replace revealed religion.[3]

If these doctrines of faith are not natural religion, they yet rest on "an immovable foundation in [human] nature," for the human soul has needs—a "taste of the infinite" and "a love of what is immortal"—that must be satisfied (Tocqueville 2000, 2.2.12, 510–11).[4] This foundation in nature leads directly away from the liberal state of nature that reveals the need to satisfy man's bodily self-preservation. It reveals the need for the supernatural—an "edifice" of faith that eclipses even while it satisfies man's natural desire for the spiritual as opposed to the material. Faith is in accord with human nature yet not rationally constructed upon it, as is liberal society according to the early liberals. There are, to be sure, articles of reason encompassed in religious faith. Tocqueville was a strong opponent of divine right and a strong proponent of the separation of church and state. Although he praised the Puritans highly as being the "point of departure" for democracy in America, he criticized its theocratic character (Tocqueville 2000, 1.1.2, 32–35; 1.2.9, 266–67; 2.1.19, 468; n. V, 680–83; n. VI, 688–89). Personally, he seems to have suffered a crisis early in life when, as he recounts it, he came upon the books of eighteenth-century materialists in his father's library and promptly lost his faith, as far as we know never recaptured. The loss was not confined to religion but extended to "all the truths" that supported his beliefs and his actions.[5]

Questions arise that are still with us: What does Tocqueville hold against the introduction of foundational philosophical principles in democratic politics, and how can they be kept out? What is the relationship between philosophy and religion, given the hostility of modern philosophers (particularly the French *philosophes*) to religion and his desire to make an alliance between the two? Just what essential support does religion supply to political liberty—the essential liberty according to Tocqueville—so that, despite the separation of church and state necessary to political liberty, he can say that religion "should be considered the first of [the Americans'] political institutions" (Tocqueville 2000, 1.2.9, 280)?

3. Tocqueville said in a letter to Louis de Kergorlay (June 29, 1831, in Tocqueville 2003, 197) that deism, or what is called "natural religion," might suffice for the upper classes of a society but that the people would see in it the absence of belief in the other world and would tumble directly into the sole doctrine of self-interest.

4. For "foundation" rooted in "nature," see also Tocqueville (2000, 1.2.10, 328; 2.3.12, 573; 2.4.7, 673). "Foundation" occurs 19 times in *Democracy in America*.

5. Letter to Sophie Swetchine, February 26, 1857, in Tocqueville (2003, 1242–45). See also Letter to Arthur de Gobineau, October 2, 1843, where he says, "I am not a believer (which I am far from saying in order to boast)" (Tocqueville 2003, 525). On the incident of his youth, see Goldstein (1975, chap. 1), who treats the loss of faith as only in religion; see also Welch (2000, 178–80) and Bégin (2011, 170–72).

MORES AND RELIGION

To see how Tocqueville understands religion, one must look to his view of mores, for in *Democracy in America*—his main discussion of religion—he first treats religion as the most important of mores. Mores (*moeurs*), defined as "the whole moral and intellectual state of a people," comprise both morals and customs (Tocqueville 2000, 1.2.9, 275). The definition comes from "the ancients" and is related to the ancient emphasis on virtue in human affairs, but it is virtue understood as typical, ordinary, or average, so that modern thinkers who seek laws or rules of social behavior could find the concept useful and congenial. Tocqueville could have found important discussion of mores in two of his favorite philosophers, Montesquieu and Rousseau—for whatever his doubts, he read broadly and deeply in philosophy.[6] In the nineteenth century the concept of mores was picked up by the founders of sociology and became fundamental for that new discipline because, contrary to the ancients, it separated society from politics, implying that politics was not essential to the identity of society. In our time the concept of mores is used as value-neutral, replacing "morals," to try to describe without judging, which was emphatically not Tocqueville's practice.

In Tocqueville's thought, mores are connected to another, newer concept of the "social state" (*état social*), the product of fact and laws, or the two united, which then, in turn, one can consider the "first cause" of most of a society's laws, customs, and ideas (Tocqueville 2000, 1.1.3, 45; see also Manent 1998, 65–77). Mores and the social state comprise what is chosen by a society and what is not chosen, the two elements confused together. The consequence is to blur the clear view of the social contract liberals that politics is best understood as primarily a human choice, one made to escape the state of nature, not chosen by us.

We see too that the difference between politics and the social state is similarly confused, as the social state would seem to come first if it is the first cause. But then we note that there are two social states called "aristocratic" and "democratic," political designations implying that politics exists already in the social state and could not be caused by it. If politics comes first, and is the first cause, we are reminded of Aristotle, for whom the regime (*politeia*) is the main cause of a society and its *nomos* (his equivalent of social state; Aristotle 2013, 3.3, 6). If politics comes after society, we are reminded of the

6. "Broadly" might be conceded by Tocqueville scholars, but "deeply" will be contested. Tocqueville tends to sum up philosophy in its political effect, as will be seen, but not because philosophy is mere shallow rationalization of deeper interests or urges. See Tocqueville's *Discourse to the Academy of Moral and Political Sciences* (1852), in Tocqueville (1991, 1:1215–26).

liberal social contract theorists of the seventeenth century, for whom political rule is subsequent to the state of nature. As Tocqueville has it, the social state replaces Aristotle's regime as the first cause and ignores the state of nature as a pre-political condition that antedates both politics and society. Now the regime and the social contract are both taken to be chosen, though differently, by the philosophers who conceived them and by peoples who apply them. The regime is a choice of the kind of rule establishing and maintaining a certain way of life, and the social contract is the choice of an instrument necessary to all free choices of how to live. Tocqueville's conception blurs the view shared by Aristotle and the early liberals that politics is best understood as a human choice. It also blurs the distinction between Aristotle and the early liberals as to whether politics decides the way of life or merely makes it possible while leaving it open to the choice of society or the individual.

Exploring the reason for this, we note that Tocqueville declares in the introduction to *Democracy in America* that democracy is a "providential fact." It is a trend that began 700 years ago and that only in his time has come to be noticed as providential in the one country, America, that has adopted it and applied it fully and successfully. To call it providential means to deny that it is a human choice or discovery, for example, that of John Locke, the philosopher who inspired the Declaration of Independence. Instead of Locke and the Declaration, Tocqueville begins with the Puritans, whom he calls the "point of departure" for America. The Puritans indeed came to America with an idea, for "they wanted to make an *idea* triumph," but it was a religious and Christian idea, for which they called themselves pilgrims, and in which they were "obey[ing] a purely intellectual need." Yet the religious doctrine was blended with "the most absolute democratic and republican theories," not merely of equality but also of self-government and public education, both of which were first put into practice by the Puritans (Tocqueville 2000, 1.1.2, 32).[7] In a later letter Tocqueville speaks of the "religious passion" that drove the Puritans into the "political passion" of wanting to govern themselves.[8] The religious passion was not the same as the political passion, for the Puritans had received their political education in the "rough school" of English township government, but their particular religion confirmed it (Tocqueville 2000, 1.1.2, 29).

In place of liberalism and its deistic or atheistic foundation in the state of nature Tocqueville sets the Puritans—their religious idea together with their practices. It was they who first brought democracy into "broad daylight," not as a foundation but active and complete as a way of life. They did not merely

7. In regard to public education, Tocqueville notes that in America it is religion (i.e., not philosophy) that has brought enlightenment (Tocqueville 2000, 1.1.2, 42).

8. Letter to Louis de Kergorlay, October 18, 1847, in Tocqueville (2003, 586–90).

offer an idea but also were able to live by it, transforming it into the mores of a social state that could be considered the "first cause" of American democracy.

This much said on behalf of the Puritans, however, Tocqueville goes on to criticize them gently and without Puritan severity, but profoundly. They were, after all, "puritanical," as we use the term, in their "ardor for regulation" and their "narrow spirit of sect" to legislate against sin with abundant resort to penalties of death. Their excesses had to be corrected, and they were corrected in what James Ceaser has called "Tocqueville's second founding" (2011, chap. 2, 23–43) at the time of the American Revolution, when many states abandoned the establishment of religion in favor of the separation of church and state. Yet, since the correction of Puritanism was established by the sovereignty of the people that the Puritans created and exemplified, one could also say, with Pierre Manent, that these were two phases of the same process. The ardent faith of the Puritans gave way to the "grave but superficial respect" for religion of their descendants (Manent 1996, 94).[9]

The point of departure needed to be departed from, and it is replaced by the principle or dogma of the sovereignty of the people, established at the time of the American Revolution. Not wishing to offend religion or praise its enemies, Tocqueville mentions the abolition of aristocratic entail at this time but not the disestablishment of religion. He only says that according to this sovereignty, "the people reign over the American political world as God does over the universe"—as if somehow the people who are like God had replaced God (Tocqueville 2000, 1.1.4, 55).[10] In the implication of this declaration the first cause of America—now the people—becomes more visible than in Puritan democracy, or visible as God is not. The Puritan usage of ancestral religion in their names and modes of speech disappears, and we are directed to conclude that in America, religion in the form of theocracy was the cradle of liberty, but that liberty grew up and out of its cradle. Or one could say that the true theocracy is democracy that has transformed its undemocratic sectarian beginning into religion for all—by command of the people. For all Tocqueville says in support of the alliance between religion and liberty in the United States, the people have no authority above themselves. They set an authority above themselves when they establish the Constitution, and they could hardly retain

9. Tocqueville himself does not speak of a second founding, and he seems to understand the first one as a kind of birth, a "point of departure," rather than as a founding (Tocqueville 2000, 1.1.2, 28, 39–45).

10. This statement apparently exaggerates the power of the people, for if God reigns over the universe, and the universe includes the people and the American political world, then He reigns over both of these too. The people are like God but replace God, so that the principle of the whole—all things—is human, not divine. The statement declares an assumption of human responsibility for the whole.

the power to unseat God as they do the Constitution. Yet they would seem to be able to unseat what they can seat. Tocqueville asks, "What makes a people master of itself if it has not submitted to God?" (Tocqueville 2000, 1.2.9, 282). A people, like an individual person, makes itself more powerful with self-restraint, not less—but self-restraint may be self-excused.

The people sustain that alliance in their mores in a way that improves on Puritan theocracy. In discussing what sustains a democratic republic in the United States, Tocqueville brings up three "principal causes," which are "accidental and providential causes," namely, its situation far from Europe, its laws, and its mores (Tocqueville 2000, 1.2.9, 265). The laws have more force than the situation, the mores more than the laws, and among mores the first in importance is religion. We note that "religion considered as a political institution" has more influence than providence as an accidental cause, by not working through politics. If the people are sovereign, the religion over them is by their choice, shown in the way in which each religion seeks to "harmonize earth with Heaven" (Tocqueville 2000, 1.2.9, 275).[11]

Since religion has its influence in America through mores, it works more indirectly than directly. The *philosophes* believed that religion would lose its force as freedom and enlightenment advanced; America proves that they were wrong. The fact they overlooked is that, even when considering religion "from a purely human point of view," it has an unfailing source of strength in human nature: "the desire for immortality that torments the hearts of all men equally" (Tocqueville 2000, 1.2.9, 284). Here is *eros*, the yearning part of the soul in Plato's presentation. When founded on this desire, religions can aim at universality, but when they become united with government, they apply only to certain peoples and temporarily. Religion should avoid attaching itself to earthly authority and forswear all reliance on divine right, using mores to regulate democracy rather than relying on laws as much as did the Puritans. Religion is more powerful if it is pure, and it is pure only if it avoids earthly attachments. The purity of religion arises from human nature: "among all the beings, man shows a natural disgust for existence and an immense desire to exist" (Tocqueville 2000, 1.2.9, 284) Now we recognize the *thumos* that Plato discerned as the other part of the soul that simultaneously defends one's existence and risks it. *Thumos* risks the self in the very act of defending it by claiming a selfless rationality beyond individual existence. In self-defense one

11. Note "earth with heaven" rather than the reverse. Surely the harmonizing works both ways, and perhaps in reverse more than as it is said. But Tocqueville emphasizes the noble. One could agree with Sheldon Wolin that for Tocqueville religion is an earthly method of "social control," and even that it has a "repressive role," if it were equally stressed that it is self-imposed by the people (Wolin 2001, 324–25).

suddenly becomes willing to die for a cause that is both one's own and beyond one's own: God's cause (Plato 1968, 375a–e, 439e–441c). Applying the point to Tocqueville, we see that religion is paradoxically more powerful politically if it stays out of politics, if it does not appear as an authority in its own regard but under cover of the mores that the people practice and hold to. Its universality can then remain pure, surely an advantage to religion, and at the same time be adapted to the democracy of the American people.

This paradox suggests two points of advantage for Tocqueville's conception of the alliance of religion and liberty: First, it is a qualified advantage to religion enabling it to sustain its otherworldliness without renouncing its influence on earthly affairs. This is a particular advantage to the Christian religion because it lacks or forswears a political doctrine and a law, such as the law of Judaism or Islam, either of which would compel it to enter into earthly politics. Tocqueville has harsh words for the conquering nature of Islam, and in a letter he says that after studying the Koran, he came out with the conviction that "few religions are as dire [*funeste*] to men as that of Mohammed."[12] He seems to take it for granted, and as given by Providence, that the religion of liberty is Christianity, which itself provides the distinction between church and state that he accepts and develops in the interest of both religion and liberty. His argument opposes the worldly ambition of both the church and its enemy, the *philosophes*, because he wants to benefit the pride and ambition of democracy. The qualification to this advantage is that the church must accept the necessity of accommodating its ambition to that of democracy.

The second point of his paradox is a theoretical advantage to the democratic idea itself. Always chary of making theoretical arguments, he does not make this second point himself, but it can be made on his behalf. It is a serious failing of the democratic theory he ignores that it never proves that all men are created equal. Hobbes says that men are naturally equal, or equal in the state of nature, but this turns out to mean that each man, satisfied with his own share of prudence, and eager to place his own interest first, considers or presumes himself equal to others—if only by denying that anyone else is better than he (Hobbes 1996, chap. 13).[13] Each man's vanity is foiled when he sees the same vanity in others, but that forced recognition does not raise tamed

12. Letter to Arthur de Gobineau, October 22, 1843, in Tocqueville (2003, 533–36); see also Tocqueville (2000, 2.1.5, 419–20); see the comments in his writings on Algeria in Tocqueville (2001, 27–35, 140–42) and Goldstein (1975, 110–12).

13. Hobbes in effect admits that societies of men have no direct access to or unmixed perception of human nature; their opinions are always present, always in the way. By never mentioning the "state of nature," Tocqueville calls it into question, and by replacing it with the "social state," he indicates that democracy is based on opinion, but on justifiable human pride rather than indefensible vanity (Mansfield 2010, 19–20, 48–49; Mansfield 2014, 225).

vanity to the level of truth. Similarly, Locke says that all men are equal in having the faculty of reason, but he never states clearly why this similarity in possessing the faculty is more important than the great inequalities in degree of possession. Tocqueville too, explaining the "equality of conditions" he found in America, says that all men there consider themselves similar (*semblables*) if not precisely equal to others: a poor man there can approach a rich man on an equal level without abasing himself. Here again, in his account of Americans' beliefs, one finds no convincing proof for the belief (Tocqueville 2000, 1.1.3, 51; 2.3.13–14).

The difficulty is that any quality or set of qualities that might define a human being is held very unequally by one human being vis-à-vis another, and only by a very few in full. That which humans share by contrast to all other beings—which would have to be reason or some quality mixed with reason—is also the basis of very great contrast among humans. But when the basis of equality is religion, and all men are held to be equal in the sight of God, equal in the immortal souls they possess, then the argument transcends the human point of view, and democratic theory is excused from its embarrassment at having no sufficient proof for its most fundamental assertion. Tocqueville says at this point, as noted above, that he is "considering religions from a purely human point of view," but precisely from that point of view, no human being is satisfied with the human point of view. In this way the usefulness of religion arises from human nature and does not abstract from its truth but raises the question of its truth.

Tocqueville speaks of "what ought to be, in our day, *the natural state* of man in the matter of religion" (Tocqueville 2000, 1.2.9, 286–87; italics in original). This is the state of religion in America, not in some abstract state, where religion is not as powerful as it might be for short periods but more lasting because its strength is reduced to what inspires it in human nature (see Manent 1996, chap. 8). Nature, for him, is a kind of foundation, but it is divided into the material, the source of self-interest, and the spiritual, which wants to rise above the material in the form of religion. Thus, "nature" is not a simple, clarifying notion to which humans have direct access and by which they can guide their lives with certainty, as in the early liberal "state of nature." Americans go to religion rather than nature because nature is divided against itself, its influence overwhelmed by the conventions of democratic opinion. In the statement quoted above the "natural state" is said to arise out of "our time," the democratic age that gives rise to democratic conventions. By these conventions Americans see religion as useful for democracy, even for their self-interest ("self-interest well understood"). But their religion must lack purity to the extent that it is maintained because it is useful. If it is useful for democracy, it suffers from the same connection with politics that weakened the church in France under the Old Regime. From this one could infer that Americans, because they are firmly and publicly religious, are also hypocrites who find it useful to be religious (Tocqueville 2000, 1.2.9, 281). Yet clearly religion will not be useful unless it is believed to be true. There is no upper class of aristocrats in America to look down on the religious delusions of the multitude. Americans must therefore identify the useful with the true. The result is terrific pressure on society, *from society*, to believe that religion is true, all the while reducing religion to what is useful. As Manent (1996, 92) puts it, the truth that religion is useful because it forbids belief in the unlimited power of society is itself imposed by the unlimited power of society, the sovereignty of the people, in America. Religion is, after all, a part of politics, "the first of [the Americans'] political institutions."

These are Tocqueville's formulations, yet ever careful as he is to deprecate the role of philosophy and of the philosopher, he presents them as opinions of Americans, not of his own. The paradox of greater power for religion in politics with less involvement is the perception, he reports, of American priests. Not that they have much choice: they perceive that the majority wants them to stay out of politics (Tocqueville 2000, 1.2.9, 280, 286; 2.1.5, 423; Garsten 2009, 361–64). There is another power with whom American clergy share their indirect influence, and that is American women. Religion, he says, does little to restrain the American man from his ardor for self-enrichment, but it "reigns as a sovereign over the soul of woman, and it is woman who makes mores" (Tocqueville 2000, 1.2.9, 278; see also Zuckert 1981, 264–66; Manent 1996, 83–87; Wolin 2001, 330). It was a commonplace of the *philosophes* that credulous women were willing victims of the manipulation of superstition by the clergy, but when we consult the five chapters on women in the third part (on mores) of *Democracy in America*, we find a contrary statement. Tocqueville says that Americans give girls an education in reason as well as religion, and that they resort to religion for defense of their virtue only when "they have reached the last limits of human force" (Tocqueville 2000, 2.3.9, 565; 2.3.12, 573–76).

Here, as with the clergy, one may suspect that Tocqueville's description is idealized, and that it masks a recommendation he would prefer not to give outright. He is as modest and as manly as the American women he pictures. These women, treated as equals, are content with the separation of roles that used to mark them as unequal. Tocqueville's treatment nicely illustrates his refusal to ground his thought on a foundational nature. He asks whether democracy would not act on "the great inequality of man and woman . . . which seemed to have its eternal foundations in nature." In American democracy women's natural inferiority is being overcome, he says, but the difference between the sexes, whether natural or not he does not say, is retained in order that women may have authority to moderate democratic mores. This they could not do if they were not wives apart from the business of men. American women exercise their sovereignty over mores by freely accepting the bonds of marriage as equals, submitting by their own choice and not by nature's dictates. They moderate democracy not only without violating democracy but even while vindicating the power of democracy to govern itself. Yet Tocqueville would not have been surprised that women in our time, joining the onward march of democracy, have chosen to imitate men and abandoned the defense and enforcement if not quite the practice of modesty.

RELIGION AGAINST MATERIALISM

In the second volume of *Democracy in America*, Tocqueville turns to the question of the truth of religion as opposed to, or in addition to, its usefulness. His approach to the question is still through the usefulness of religion, but now we get a better view of just how it is useful and why American democracy has a stake in its truth. We also see better why he distrusts ideas and why philosophy needs to be concealed under religion.[14] In the end we receive his best estimate, or report, of the general truth that God offers to mankind, which proves to support the alliance he sees from the first between religion and liberty.

Religion is useful mainly because it hinders the taste for material enjoyments that is endemic to American democracy, indeed in modern democracy as such. It is of course a brake on licentious liberty and on the sovereignty of the democratic majority. It opposes the "maxim that everything is permitted in the interest of society," an impious maxim, Tocqueville says, "that seems to have been invented in the century of freedom to legitimate all the tyrants to come" (Tocqueville 2000, 1.2.9, 280). As we have seen, the maxim is enforced by the power of the democratic society it is designed to limit. Yet the true danger is not in the occasional viciousness of democracy, but in the mediocrity of soul it teaches to law-abiding citizens through the taste for material pleasures. This taste, though surely bourgeois, in his view comes from democracy, not from what we call capitalism. "Capitalism," or in his phrase "the passion for material well-being," he believed to come from democracy.[15]

Tocqueville's reasoning is that when all are equal, no one has natural authority over anyone else, and that when a democratic citizen looks for a guide to life, he finds no superior in whom to trust and ends his search by settling on

14. On philosophy and religion in Tocqueville, see Lamberti (1989, 155–65), Lawler (1993, chap. 8), and Mansfield (2014).

15. The objection that capitalism antedates the appearance of democracy is countered by Tocqueville's view that democracy incubated for centuries in the bosom of monarchies that brought it to birth, to their surprise, without meaning to (Tocqueville 2000, introduction).

himself. To this person, on the basis of no authority but his own, there is no distant goal in life to which he can devote himself, for everything beyond the immediate is vague and beyond his ken. The only evident goods to him are palpable and available—material goods—and he devotes himself to goods that he and everyone like him (his *semblables*) can appreciate. This is why those living under democracy, trusting in their own reason above all, conclude that "everything in the world is explicable" and have "an almost invincible distaste for the supernatural" (Tocqueville 2000, 2.1.1, 404). In America, however, this distaste, natural to democracy, is counteracted if not defeated by the taste for the infinite in human nature.

Religion is a "form of hope" in human nature. Its most important practical teaching is that man has an immortal soul, which is therefore divine, and man's natural hope is that he will live forever (Tocqueville 2000, 1.2.9, 284; 2.2.12, 510; 2.2.15, 520–21). To have an immortal soul is a possession of inestimable value to the perfection of which one can devote one's life, yet it is also universal and equal, hence democratic, its perfection not a goal of aristocratic honor that sets one above others. As a form of hope, religion is not primarily a form of fear (except insofar as one fears that one's hope for salvation may be dashed), as the early liberal theorists, particularly Thomas Hobbes, supposed. The fear of invisible spirits (in Hobbes) and the uneasiness of the self (in Locke) turn one's attention to the present; hope appeals to the future. In the future lies accomplishment in which one can take pride. The early liberals set their hopes on human enlightenment that they promised would eventually replace religious fears and in the meanwhile keep them in check. Their enlightenment would rest on the premise that man must first of all consult his fear for his own self-preservation.

For this reason the early liberals believed human pride to be the source of trouble, especially from the prideful notion that human beings are special in the universe because of their immortal souls. To them this claim, which is so easy to make and so hard to specify, leads easily to the tyranny of religion and then to the miseries of civil war. They thought that religion feeds pride and pride feeds partisanship. But for Tocqueville, the reliance on worldly passions such as fear and material gain produces abject souls more fit for despotism than liberty: the weaknesses of democracy are rather stability and stagnation than anarchy and rebelliousness. Thus, the early liberals were defending against the lesser danger and inviting the greater one. So for him religion promotes liberty by teaching men that they are special and that they deserve to take pride in their accomplishments. His most significant apparent departure from Christianity is from Christian humility. It is in regard to pride that he says with apparently conflicting import that religion is "the most precious inheritance from aristocratic centuries," and yet that religion warms itself at the hearth of patriotism in America (Tocqueville 2000, 1.1.2, 43–44; 1.1.5, 89; 1.2.6, 225; 1.2.9, 281; 2.2.15, 519).

The pride constituting the specialness of man emerges in Tocqueville's insistence on the greatness of man. He seeks to rally the "true friends of liberty and human greatness," and the two go together because liberty in mediocrity leads to the new sort of despotism he identifies at the end of *Democracy in America*, mild despotism (Tocqueville 2000, 2.4.7, 670; 2.4.6). Mediocre souls trapped in material enjoyments will readily trade their political liberty for peace and security in those enjoyments. Such people suffer from the new democratic ill he identifies as "individualism," a new sentiment conceived by Tocqueville, which occurs when democratic citizens believe and feel themselves to be passive victims of large, impersonal, historical forces they cannot control or influence. In reaction, they withdraw from the public, forgetting they are citizens, and concentrate their lives on family, friends, and themselves. Losing sight of the public, they become oblivious to any distant goal and welcome the benevolent aid of big government, "the immense being" that acts on their behalf with their passive consent because it knows better and offers to take over responsibility for the "trouble of thinking and the pain of living," Tocqueville says sarcastically (Tocqueville 2000, 2.2.2; 2.4.3, 644; 2.4.6, 663).

Thus, the only true liberty is political liberty, in which the goal and the result may sometimes be greatness but the activity of which always exercises the soul. He remarks on the Americans' veneration for Plymouth Rock, a piece of matter that matters to them: "Does this not show very clearly that the power and greatness of man are wholly in his soul?" (Tocqueville 2000, 1.1.2, 34n8). Religion provides a confirmation that men are not mere pawns of fate or of chance forces hostile or indifferent to them; it is a guarantee of greatness in human spirituality as it connects men to God. Religion combats the shortsightedness and fecklessness of democracy and gives it something to be proud of, above the mediocrity of material enjoyments.

When this mediocrity appears as the main enemy of democracy through the erosion of political liberty, we come upon the baleful influence of democratic ideas. We begin to appreciate the reason why Tocqueville is so suspicious of philosophy. What he often simply calls "doubt" as characteristic of democratic ages is philosophic doubt of religion that issues in the suspense of belief—or in practice, when suspense is no longer possible, in denial of belief, in materialism. The doubt in question amounts to a denial of the human soul and, in consequence, of human agency (as we say today). The spiritual, not the material, is what is doubted—though in modern mathematical physics it turns out not to be so easy to define or grasp what matter is.

In the early liberalism Tocqueville opposes or rejects, men are liberated from prejudice and superstition only to be enthralled to the worldly passions of fear and gain; they are conquered or bullied into promising obedience (in Hobbes's theory; Hobbes 1996, chaps. 21 and 25; cf. the milder "perform" in chaps. 14 and 15), or "quickly driven into society" (in Locke's words; Locke 1960, 2:127) rather than freely choosing to do so. The model for liberty is the abstract, pre-political state of nature, which is posited and may or may not exist, rather than the model of political liberty existing in practice that Tocqueville finds in the township of New England. Early liberalism is apolitical; it supports politics with nonpolitical motives and contradicts the goal of liberty with the passive and slavish means it specifies for achieving liberty. This is not liberalism with soul, like Tocqueville's, because it degrades souls by overwhelming them with fear and seducing them with incentives for material gain. It is not a liberalism that can sustain liberty. Liberalism needs motives for liberty that can be prompted by pride. If pride is evaded by the appeal to interest, deflected out of politics into moneymaking, or suppressed by denying the worth of honor, liberty becomes a gift of fortune or nature and man a mere agent in larger motions.

In the second volume of *Democracy in America*, Tocqueville specifies two schools of idea-mongers he deplores, pantheists and democratic historians. Pantheism had its origin in Spinoza and in Tocqueville's time had its influence through German philosophy and French literature. It appeals to the democratic mind by its desire for generality and unity. It seeks to enclose God and the universe within a single whole that destroys human individuality, for if God can be enclosed, so, a fortiori, can man: "all who remain enamored of the genuine greatness of man should unite and do combat against [pantheism]" (Tocqueville 2000, 2.1.7, 426; see Manent 1996, 102–3). By denying the special status of human beings within nature, it reveals itself as a democratic convention that falsely simplifies nature. Democratic historians he contrasts to aristocratic historians who look to the wills and humors of certain men as the causes of events; the former attribute no influence to the individual, almost as though society advanced by itself. They look for general causes that provide excuses both for mediocre politicians, whose faults are lost in the impersonal trends of history, and for mediocre historians, who shirk the difficult task of discovering individual influences within those trends (Tocqueville 2000, 2.1.8, 469–72). Both pantheists and democratic historians have lazy minds; like the democratic peoples they think for, they are satisfied with, or insist on, generalities to simplify the understanding of things.

Such thinkers deny to citizens the power to influence their own fate, and subject them to inflexible providence or blind fatality. They encourage the tendency toward the "individualism" Tocqueville conceived. As opposed to old-fashioned selfishness, a universal human vice, democratic individualism is "reflective and peaceable" rather than depraved; it is based on the "erroneous judgment" encouraged by democratic thinkers that individuals are impotent in the face of general causes and impersonal forces. It is caused or encouraged by democratic ideas of many sorts, all of which feed the appetite of democratic peoples for "general ideas" (Tocqueville 2000, 2.1.3, 411; 2.2.2, 482; see Schleifer 2000, chap. 18).

General ideas formulated in disregard of relevant differences are hostile to forms of thinking and behavior that are established with the intent to preserve those differences. Democratic peoples are hostile to forms; they demand informality in everything—in thought, mores, and politics. In thought, they prefer unity to articulation, species to individuals, surface to depth and height; in mores, they want access over distance, inclusiveness over exclusiveness, friendliness over reserve; in politics, they seek direct action over due process, decision over deliberation, sensation over reflection. Respecting the forms and formalities in all human activity is fundamentally aristocratic rather than democratic, but Tocqueville thinks that it is vital to the orderliness and good sense of democratic life, as well as to the protection of liberties, especially of the weak against the strong. With their impatience, often represented as a "can-do" attitude, "democratic peoples naturally have more need of forms than other peoples, and they naturally respect them less" (Tocqueville 2000, 2.4.7, 669; cf. 1.1.4, 55; 1.2.6, 220; 2.1.1, 404; 2.1.5, 421). Hostile to forms, democratic peoples are particularly receptive to materialism, a group of ideas that tends to reduce difference of form to sameness of matter.

It may seem contrived or superficial to claim a connection between the philosophic doctrine of materialism and the popular taste for material well-being, but Tocqueville does just that. The ancient materialists were hardly partisans of democracy, as they made a distinction among kinds or forms of pleasure, the pleasures of philosophy for the few above bodily pleasures for the many. Still, the connection between the reduction of form to matter and of the good to pleasure is clear, and modern materialists who abandon the soul for the self might seem more consistent than Lucretius with his soul atoms tenuously held distinct from other atoms. And with both the ancient and the modern materialists, politics and public-spiritedness are dismissed as troublesome, inconvenient, and irrational. Tocqueville sees democracy, especially when carried to an extreme in democratic ideas, as fundamentally anti- or apolitical, hence fundamentally indisposed to liberty—not hostile to liberty, often even tolerant or welcoming of it, but definitely subordinating it to equality and private ease. Equality and private ease are best found in despotism, in mild, democratic despotism. That is why materialism is to him the main enemy in our democratic age. It is not that souls are so corrupted that men sink into criminality, but that honest as opposed to criminal materialism "softens them and in the end quietly loosens all their tensions" (Tocqueville 2000,

2.2.11, 509). Democracy does not carry men away into forbidden pleasures, as one sees in the criticisms of it in Plato and Aristotle, so much as it absorbs men in the relaxed enjoyment of permitted pleasures. Tensions within the soul are required for elevating the soul, for its striving toward greatness (Tocqueville 2000, 2.4.6, 665). Tocqueville's criticism is directed at the enervation of the soul rather than its lack of harmony, and he argues for greatness rather than goodness as its aim.

Materialism teaches democratic peoples that they have nothing special in them to be proud of, and that, in the form of scientific determinism—powerful in Tocqueville's time as well as ours—they are incapable of avoiding the fate that chance decrees and science uncovers. But since pride is in human nature, materialists are unable to avoid taking pride in themselves. Their system might be useful if it gave them and taught others to take a modest idea of oneself—all of us, including Nobel Prize winners, being matter of little account—but they do not in fact draw or expound this lesson. When they believe they have proved that men are no better than brutes, Tocqueville says, they are "as proud as if they had demonstrated they were gods" (Tocqueville 2000, 2.2.15, 519–20).[16] The scientific materialism that deprives citizens of their belief in the possibility of self-government is used to justify instead the rational control of citizens by experts with knowledge of that science.

The danger of materialist ideas in our democratic age induces Tocqueville's leery distrust of philosophical ideas and his selective trust in religious ideas. The religious ideas he presents have more to do with philosophy than with revelation. He approves of certain philosophical ideas, those advancing spiritualism, but without much discrimination. He would rather you believe that your soul can migrate to the body of a pig than that you have no soul.[17] He reserves his approval for whatever spiritual doctrine emerges from philosophy and criticizes the usual effects of philosophical inquiry in democracy. Philosophical inquiry begins with doubt, but in a democracy doubt of superior authority spreads from the few who think carefully to the many who are reckless, leading to the assumption of authority by the doubters. Instead of truly doubting, people taught to doubt systematically by a dismissive method merely doubt the authority of others, and then, since authority there must be, they turn to themselves and their own authority. That is why Tocqueville

16. See also Letter to Henry Reeve, February 3, 1840, in Tocqueville (2003, 457), which speaks of "realists" rather than materialists.

17. Tocqueville implies that the Aristotelian notion that brutes have souls is some protection against the reduction of men to matter, which in fact results in merely reducing men to brutes. Materialists do not go as far or as deep as they promise; in fact, their reductionism only reaches the level of brutes with some appearance of commonality with humans (e.g., the greediness of a pig).

treats Descartes, the philosopher of doubt, as, in effect, and perhaps despite himself, a teacher of democracy (Tocqueville 2000, 2.1.1, 405).[18] This is a perceptive estimation one will not find in textbooks.

When Cartesian doubt is generalized and transferred from philosopher to citizen, the result is the democratic dogma that each individual has sufficient reason to run his own life. So Descartes's thought is most perfectly realized in America, where nobody has read him because nobody needs to read him in a society where doubt of dogmatic authority has become the dogmatic authority of doubt.[19] Socrates and Plato, by contrast, enjoy their reputation from their spiritual doctrine of the immortality of the soul, which with its anchor in human nature, with its "sublime spark," keeps them attractive at all times (Tocqueville 2000, 2.2.15, 520).[20] In the modern age the democratic propensity for material well-being, with its mediocrity, its individualism, and its mild despotism, renders philosophical materialism dangerous and all philosophy suspect because in that age philosophy is likely to be materialist. Tocqueville wants to make "spiritualist opinions" reign, particularly in times of democracy, but to do so through religion, not the opinions of Plato—which would be included in the truths he first doubted as a youth. It is a mistake to consider him a spiritualist or idealist, for he can see truth in both spiritualism and materialism, as in both aristocracy and democracy. In aristocratic times, love of material enjoyments is a corruption expressed in brilliant vices not so harmful as honest mediocrity in democracy (Tocqueville 2000, 2.2.11, 508).[21]

It is a more fundamental mistake to overlook the importance of Tocqueville's hostility to materialism in his thought on religion.[22] He had no use for

18. See Letter to Charles Stoeffels, October 22, 1831, in Tocqueville (2003, 238–41): "I consider doubt as one of the greatest miseries of our nature"; see also Letter to Louis Bouchitté, January 8, 1858, in Tocqueville (2003, 1278–80). J. Judd Owen notes nicely that Tocqueville says that Descartes is "best followed" in America, but not "most faithfully" (Owen 2015, 116).

19. The displacement of doubt by the assumption of authority is not the only instance of pride inconsistent with the democratic principle to be found in democratic peoples. See Tocqueville (2000, 2.1.21), the chapter entitled "On Parliamentary Eloquence in the United States," in which one learns that democratic representatives, typically obscure figures, try their best to make themselves and their constituents feel important.

20. Socrates and his school settle on the sole belief "that the soul has nothing in common with the body and that it survives it." This differs from immortality joined with the "opinion in favor of rewards and punishments," which is religious and Christian, though Tocqueville does not say so.

21. It might be better to say that spiritualism aims at religion than that religion aims at spiritualism (cf. Bégin 2011, 193).

22. In two recent articles, Schleifer (2014) and Noll (2014), both writers make extensive use of Tocqueville's abundant marginalia and working papers for *Democracy in America*, and Schleifer (2014, 270) remarks that Tocqueville sometimes "simply dropped" material he could (and, it is implied, should) have used in his text, which represents "only part" of his

the "secularization thesis," widespread since Max Weber, which alleges that modern society became secular, as it were, unwittingly and inevitably through the corruption of dissenting Protestantism. The love of material enjoyments did not come out of the dissenting sects of the Protestant religion, resulting from its encounter with worldly temptations, but against it and with a willing surrender to such temptations. Though always reluctant to discuss philosophy, Tocqueville makes it clear that the modern philosophy of doubt in Descartes and of pantheism in Spinoza expresses the materialism of democracy. He does indeed mention Luther as an innovator, a man who "comes to conceive in a single stroke a system of ideas" and who submits to individual reason "dogmas of the ancient faith," using "the same method" as Descartes and Voltaire (Tocqueville 2000, 2.1.1, 405; 2.3.21, 613). It is an odd description of Luther, one better suited to Machiavelli, almost as if, *per impossible*, Tocqueville had made a typographical error in his text and then repeated it.[23]

RELIGION IN PLACE OF PHILOSOPHY

The alliance between religion and liberty that Tocqueville adopts from the political lives of Americans to supply the basis for his liberalism arises from the new relationship between religion and philosophy that he also finds among them. The latter is a working relationship that he wishes to fashion into another alliance connected to the first. As to philosophy, Tocqueville says, "Americans have not needed to draw their philosophic method from books; they have found it in themselves." And as to religion, he says, "Men . . . have an immense interest in making very fixed ideas for themselves about God, their souls, their general duties" (Tocqueville 2000, 2.1.1, 404; 2.1.5, 417). The "very fixed ideas" do not arise from practice but precede and guide practice, and they must come from religion rather than philosophy.

In a letter written just before *Democracy in America* was published, Tocqueville calls it "the philosophico-political work" (*l'ouvrage philosophico-politique*) he was preparing. But he does not say that in his book. In a later letter to a writer of books on metaphysics, he allows, "I would have had a passionate taste for the philosophic studies that have occupied all your life if I could have drawn more profit from them." But whether it was the defect of his mind, or

---

thought on religion. But this is to determine his thought by what he chose not to say. It is one thing to infer what he might have thought from what he said, as is often necessary and legitimate, and quite another to give rejected words equal or preferred standing to chosen words.

23. See Mansfield and Winthrop (2014, 91) for a different speculation.

lack of courage in pursuing his design, or "the particular character of the material," he always found that the sciences never led him further than, and sometimes not as far as, "a few very simple ideas" that all men have more or less grasped. These ideas easily lead one to belief in a "first cause that is at the same time evident and inconceivable," the fixed laws one can see in the physical world and must suppose in the moral world. The most refined metaphysics, he adds, do not give him clearer notions than "the grossest good sense" (*le plus gros bon sens*). Then Tocqueville, using the word, refers to "what I have called the foundation that I cannot reach" (*le fonds que je ne peux pas toucher*), which is the plan of this "singular being" we call man. Having come to the bottom of his sheet, he closes his letter by joking that "the end of my paper warns me to finish my philosophy." Here is a man who prizes philosophy but keeps it under wraps or in its place.[24]

Those who try to rely on philosophy for the fixed ideas they need in their ordinary lives, Tocqueville says, do not find them but come to grief in doubt.[25] "Doubt takes hold of the highest portions of the intellect and half paralyses all the others." Each person becomes accustomed to hearing confused and changing opinions on matters of most interest to himself and people like him—vaguely troubling issues of the day in which it is hard to follow the arguments. We throw up our hands, feeling defeated, and in cowardly fashion refuse to think. If people will not think, doubt "cannot fail to enervate souls," thereby threatening the maintenance of liberty because enervated souls will not take the trouble to exercise liberty or defend it. Thus, in one of his memorable phrases, he professes, "I am brought to think that if [a man] has no faith, he must serve, and if he is free, he must believe" (Tocqueville 2000, 2.1.5, 417–18).

Here is a liberal rejecting liberal foundations in philosophy yet requiring them in religion. He seems to reject philosophy because it is not sufficiently or successfully dogmatic and to welcome religion because its dogmas support, or can support, human liberty. He turns to the practice of self-government in America—taking the antitheoretical path of today's antifoundationalism—yet claims to find precisely there the "philosophical method" that he avoids considering directly. His statement against doubt blames it for preventing people from thinking, that is, from thinking practically and usefully. Philosophical thinking leads to paralysis of practical thinking, in which overmatched would-be philosophers are led ultimately to passive acceptance of things as they

24. Letter to Gustave de Beaumont, December 3, 1836, in Tocqueville (1967, 8:176); Letter to Louis Blouchitté, January 8, 1858, in Tocqueville (2003, 1278–80); Letter to Arthur de Gobineau, October 22, 1843, in Tocqueville (2003, 533–35). Tocqueville disparages philosophy when writing to those he thinks are abusing it.

25. Here I am borrowing from Mansfield (2014, 204–7).

are. Philosophy may begin from the questioning of authority, but when it appears that all the questioning leads to no answers, it stops and finds rest in the conclusion that nothing can be done. Faith, then, is a substitute not for reasoning simply but for philosophical reasoning; it is actually the basis for reasoning about one's closest interests.

Tocqueville says that religion imposes a "salutary yoke" on the intellect by preventing the use of individual reason to raise doubt and by establishing "general ideas" about God and human nature that permit men to recognize "an authority" (Tocqueville 2000, 2.1.5, 418).[26] Such ideas, or dogmas, are necessary even to the practice of the sciences, where specialists must trust other specialists, and whose remote ideas are even more inaccessible to the majority. Tocqueville's objection to philosophy or metaphysics, unlike our postmodern antifoundationalism, is not intended as an attack on reason, but as an aid to reason. It does for reason what reason cannot do for itself, which is to establish an authority for itself by which reason can operate in daily life without having to become exhausted from chasing down solutions to unanswerable questions. The problem is that reason as philosophy gets in the way of reason as practice because the one attacks authority and the other requires it. Now what is the solution? Is it merely to declare that the two aspects of reason are antithetical and that, practice being more important than philosophy, the need for active practice must dominate the pleasure, if it is a pleasure, of speculating, and dogma must silence philosophy?

Tocqueville does not adopt that solution, though he may appear to do so because sometimes he seems to criticize all philosophy, philosophy itself. But in fact, or in practice, he particularly criticizes what one might call, though he does not, modern or liberal philosophy. He uses the word "foundation" when he notes that Americans adopt the "philosophic method" of Descartes as their "foundation" because just by living in a democratic social state they already know what he writes without having read his works (Tocqueville 2000, 2.1.1, 403). For them their social state makes it unnecessary to read Descartes; without his help it does the work of his method, his foundation, which is to bring doubt to an end. The end is not the fundamental truth found by philosophy, but the fundamental truth that philosophy cannot supply a fundamental truth on which to ground practice. Yet Tocqueville shows appreciation for the contemplative life of the philosopher, praising the "ardent, haughty, and disinterested love of the true" one finds in Pascal and the lofty contempt for practice as "vile, low, and mercenary" in Archimedes, while distinguishing the science of the "most theoretical principles," which may flourish in aris-

26. Cf. "salutary servitude" leading to the "good use of . . . freedom" (Tocqueville 2000, 2.1.2, 408).

tocracy, from "general truths . . . [that] lead by a direct, short path to practice," which are characteristic of democracy. It is a weakness of democracy that it does not encourage "the contemplation of first causes." This is true even from the standpoint of applications of science, for when practice loses sight of the principles of science, it becomes decayed and uninventive (Tocqueville 2000, 2.1.10, 433–38). Tocqueville himself does not renounce philosophy. At the beginning of *Democracy in America* he warns his readers that he feels "obliged to push each of his ideas to all its theoretical consequences," and later in the book he does not hesitate to speak of "first causes."[27]

Religion, then, does not replace philosophy or science, but it serves as their public face and supplies the fixed ideas that men need not merely to live by but to live in freedom. Servility of soul is not the consequence of religion, as the *philosophes* asserted, but of antireligious materialism, which denies the soul by demeaning man into matter or abases the soul by endorsing the democratic propensity to a life of material well-being. At the end of *Democracy in America* Tocqueville discloses something of the character of the religion he recommends. It is not just any religion, as he seemed to imply earlier when speaking of religion as part of democratic mores, but a reasonable religion that confirms the intelligibility of nature and of the world. In this it is unlike the religion recommended by the liberals he departs from, for whom a reasonable religion is one that compensates for the unintelligibility of nature and of the world and not incidentally confirms that they are nothing but matter, while providing refuge for the weak.[28]

THE MIND OF GOD

In this climactic passage Tocqueville goes beyond the view of religion he took earlier as a "salutary yoke on the intellect," and beyond "the purely human point of view." At the end of the first volume, he had, in his own name, striven to achieve a "clear idea of the whole" of America like the voyager who climbs a hill outside a vast city to survey it. Now, at the end of the second volume, in his own name he strives, one may suppose like a philosopher, a youthful

27. Tocqueville (2000, introduction, 15). On first causes, see especially Tocqueville (2000, 1.1.2, 28–29; 1.1.3, 45); Letter to Louis Bouchitté, January 8, 1858, in Tocqueville (2003, 1278–80); and Mansfield (2014, 219).

28. Thus, for Hobbes, a reasonable religion corrects the fear of invisible spirits, not by reassuring humans that there are reasonable spirits but by appealing to the fear of the visible power of the sovereign's sword. Locke prescribes an appeal to heaven when parties conflict, which is to a more powerful judge, not to a just order. Rousseau's Savoyard Vicar counsels reliance on reason, which is "my reason," not God's. My reason criticizes revealed religion instead of finding it orderly.

Pascal but with a view of the intelligible, to enter into the inclusive "point of view of God" (Tocqueville 2000, 2.1.5, 418–19; 1.2.10, 391; 2.4.8, 675). He had said at the beginning of the second volume that God does not have to use the "general ideas" that men, and particularly democratic men, find convenient for simplifying the perceptions of their weak intellects (Tocqueville 2000, 2.1.3, 411–13). In accord with democratic simplification, democratic poets prefer to appeal to the vastness of God, presiding over the destiny of humanity, rather than to flatter separate peoples or individuals (Tocqueville 2000, 2.1.17, 461–62; see also Kessler 1994, 44–48). But for Tocqueville, God is approachable to man through His mind, and His point of view encompasses democracy and aristocracy, the permanent, ruling distinction among mankind that apparently declares the existence of "as it were (*comme*), two humanities." Here he justifies the comparisons he has made continuously throughout the book by referring them to one superhuman whole in which they are joined. "God" is apparently a person, and clearly distinct from His Creation. Tocqueville does not insist on the difference between revealed and natural or rational religion, and earlier he had remarked that "it was necessary that Jesus Christ come to earth to make it understood that all members of the human species are naturally alike and equal" (Tocqueville 2000, 2.1.3, 413). Revealed truth is distinct from the truth of nature, but revelation makes nature apparent to us in a way that unassisted human reason cannot (cf. Tessitore 2015, 85). Thus, one could call religion "natural" because it fulfills yearnings of human nature, matching God's mind to human need, and one could also call it "civil" because it is part of self-government. But as religion it is revealed, and as the true or best religion, it is Christian. Philosophy is then under a duty not to overlook but also neither to broadcast the difference between itself and Christian revelation nor to present itself as hostile to it. The order that Tocqueville sees in or imputes to God's mind leaves untouched the statements in scripture of God's hidden character without contradicting them.

Earlier, in the chapter on the tyranny of the majority in the first volume, Tocqueville had said that "only God . . . can be omnipotent without danger, because his wisdom and justice are always equal to his power" (Tocqueville 2000, 1.2.7, 241). This is not the case of any human authority, which always needs to be prevented from acting without control and dominating without meeting obstacles. Thus, the perfect rule of God stands above all actual human rule as a necessary and desirable reproach and limitation rather than as inspiration to do God's work on earth. It is because we cannot successfully imitate God that we must serve Him. The mystery of His perfection encompasses His bodiless superiority to humanity, which prevents Him from holding partisan attachments but also reminds us of our limitations. Tocqueville remains a liberal, if of a "new kind," because at least in a democratic age he wants to obstruct human tyranny as much as he wants to instruct it; hence, in the first place he describes democracy as it is in America rather than discourses in political philosophy. Yet it is also true that liberty needs to be explained and defended as well as secured—or in order to be secured. So in the first volume he has to instruct democrats that they are limited and partisan and do not possess God's wisdom and justice, but in the second volume he has to instruct them that, contrary to democratic theories, they are capable of acting freely. Religion hinders democrats from tyrannizing others by majority tyranny and also from being tyrannized by democratic doctrines, when majorities tyrannize themselves. For the first task, liberals must use religion to limit human authority, and for the second, liberals must use it to empower human authority: both negative liberty and positive liberty are required.

To support positive liberty, religion must be understood as the order of God's mind, which Tocqueville now, at the end of his book, makes available to his readers. So understood, it repels "false and cowardly doctrines" that "men necessarily obey I do not know which insurmountable and unintelligent force born of previous events, such as the race, the soil, or the climate." Tocqueville renames this force "Providence" and describes it differently so that it leaves men leeway: "Providence has not created the human race either entirely independent or perfectly slave." Here are two extremes, implying two doctrines. The first, that man is entirely independent, appears in the aristocratic criticism of democracy as anarchic; the second, that man is perfectly slave, is the democratic idea to be found in pantheism and the democratic historians that peoples "necessarily obey . . . [an] insurmountable and unintelligent force born of previous events" (Tocqueville 2000, 2.4.8, 676).[29] Both extremes may be found in the early liberal, social contract theories, the first in the state of nature, in which men are anarchic and at war with one another, and the second in the means for escaping the state of nature, which play on fear and subject men to "insurmountable and unintelligent force" consisting variously of laws of subrational motivation discovered by history and social science. Under Tocqueville's analysis, the state of nature in which men are independent of one another and the subjection of men in civil society combine in the apolitical individualism he finds in modern democracy. Under his program, as opposed to this danger, religion can cement its alliances with liberty and with reason, all three together in the politics of democracy.

The two contraries of entirely independent and perfectly slave stand for the two aspects of chance, unpredictability and subjection—chance fate—to which

29. On the alternative of perfectly free and perfectly slave, see Tocqueville's remarkable chapter on the three races, in which the Indian represents perfect freedom and the black, perfect slavery (Tocqueville 2000, 1.2.10).

religion is opposed. The most fundamental democratic idea, as we learn from Aristotle, is that of the lottery. It is a system in which a decision is arrived at without a choice, in which every one, without discrimination, has an equal chance. No reason is exercised in making the decision, and none is found in the result. No freedom exists, as one simply receives what befalls him. No virtue is required, and none is rewarded or expected. Opposite to a lottery is voting, which requires making a choice and is aristocratic because one chooses for what one thinks is best, still according to Aristotle (Aristotle 2013, 4:16). We moderns think that voting is the clearest sign of democracy, but we forget the aristocracy necessarily mixed in democracy. Even to institute a lottery requires choice, thought, and freedom—all items opposed to lottery, which is democracy in its raw, basic sense of mere chance. Religion as Tocqueville portrays it tries to make our life predictable, but not so predictable that we can succeed without trying. And it sets limits to our intellect, our freedom, and our choice—but not such narrow limits that we can never succeed no matter how hard we try (Tocqueville 2000, 2.2.17, 524). The task of politics, which Tocqueville sometimes calls, in the manner of Plato and Aristotle, the task of the legislator, is to cooperate with religion and to guide our lives so that our virtue is rewarded and our freedom preserved.

"The legislator" in the singular has an art or science or theories or genius that is above democracy.[30] It rescues democracy from the grip of chance by vindicating the contribution of intelligence to the common good.[31] Like God's

30. For art, see Tocqueville (2000, 2.2.15, 518); science, Tocqueville (2000, 1.2.6, 222); theories, Tocqueville (2000, 1.1.2, 41); genius, Tocqueville (2000, 1.1.8, 129, 154). "The legislator" for Tocqueville is not "an extraordinary man in the state" apart from the "principles of political right," as for Rousseau, but an abstract person who combines the science of politics with the wisdom to apply it in circumstances (Rousseau, *The Social Contract*; 2014, 2.7). He stands for political science in practice, and one could assemble a survey of "political science" in *Democracy in America* by gathering the many (about 40) references to "the legislator." One of them, comparing him to a pilot, has a special classical redolence: "The legislator resembles a man who plots his course in the middle of the sea. Thus he can direct the vessel that carries him, but he cannot change its structure, create winds, or prevent the ocean from rising under his feet" (Tocqueville 2000, 1.1.8, 155). Generally, "the legislators" means particular legislators, e.g., "the American legislators," but once Tocqueville speaks of "the American legislator" (1.1.7, 102), and four times of "the legislator" as the majority (1.2.7, 237–38, 243). Deviating from wisdom, "the legislator" can keep blacks in slavery (1.2.10, 340, 343) and forget the principles of religious liberty (1.1.2, 39). See also the discussion of political science in Tocqueville (2011, 3:1–3, 127–51) and Tocqueville's address of 1852 to the Academy of Moral and Political Sciences, in which he distinguishes political science from the "art of governing" (Tocqueville 1991, 1:1217).

31. Unlike the democratic intellectual, the legislator is aware of his own inequality: "When the unequal is interpreted as random or arbitrary, as having no basis accessible to human understanding, then the natural can be understood only as the equal" (Hancock 1998, 375). See also Owen (2015, 138).

mind, and like Tocqueville himself, it sees both the similarities and the differences of human beings while recognizing that either democracy or aristocracy must be chosen as a whole, each distinct from the other, a visible political whole that is partial in respect to the unseen whole of God's mind, where they are brought together. Thus, the legislator combines the ("as it were") two distinct humanities that Tocqueville makes available to his readers through his frequent, and always illuminating, contrasts of democracy to aristocracy. His political science is necessarily left scattered and uncollected because it cannot be set forth separately from its context in American politics in the form of a model without becoming excessively schematic, thus doing violence to its basis in practice. A schematic political science risks forgetting its basis in practice and claiming a false impartiality above practice—like our "democratic theory" today, which loses sight of the fact that democracy is not the whole of politics but a partial and partisan whole within the whole of politics. Our democratic theory is both less detailed and more parochial than Tocqueville's understanding.

Although being a democratic citizen is quite different from being "the legislator," Tocqueville's political science gives us an awareness of the connection between the two. To the task of the legislator our religion contributes "certain fixed ideas," which, though fixed, are not arbitrary, not unreasonable, not merely posited because we need them. The power that men must obey is not chance, or does not have to be chance. It permits "peoples . . . [to be] masters of themselves" if they take the legislator's wisdom to heart. Thereby the democratic dogma that each has sufficient reason to guide himself would be justified as the democratic principle: the intelligence of the legislator meeting the intelligibility of God's Creation and communicated to the democratic citizen. It is then the task of citizens to make their accomplishments worthy of reasonable pride. Tocqueville does not have the legislator make up a religion (like Rousseau) or even propose that he revise an existing one (like Hobbes and Locke). The legislator works through the "American legislators," who accommodate the existing religion that Providence has supplied. By his multicultural analysis the best religion for the protection and fostering of democratic liberty is Christianity, but with apparent conditions—that it stay out of politics and that it compromise Christian humility.

Tocqueville presents himself initially as impressed with the strength of religion in America, but as he proceeds, we see that he was exaggerating: religion is not strong enough and needs to be strengthened by the legislator (Owen 2015, 142). That is why his book was written "under the pressure of a sort of religious terror in the author's soul" (Tocqueville 2000, introduction, 6), realizing as he did that religion is more friendly to human greatness than is philosophy.

REFERENCES

Aristotle. 2013. *Politics*. 2nd ed. Trans. and ed. Carnes Lord. Chicago: University of Chicago Press.

Bégin, Christian. 2011. "Tocqueville et la Fracture Religieuse." *Tocqueville Review* 32:167–99.

Ceaser, James W. 2011. *Designing a Polity: America's Constitution in Theory and Practice*. Lanham, MD: Rowman & Littlefield.

Garsten, Bryan. 2009. "Seeing 'Not Differently, but Further, than the Parties.'" In *The Arts of Rule*, ed. Sharon R. Krause and Mary Ann McGrail. Lanham, MD: Rowman & Littlefield.

Goldstein, Doris S. 1975. *Trial of Faith*. New York: Elsevier.

Hancock, Ralph C. 1998. "The Uses and Hazards of Christianity in Tocqueville's Attempt to Save Democratic Souls." In *Interpreting Tocqueville's "Democracy in America,"* ed. K. Masugi. Savage, MD: Rowman & Littlefield.

Hobbes, Thomas. 1996. *Leviathan*. Ed. R. Tuck. Cambridge: Cambridge University Press.

Kessler, Sanford. 1994. *Tocqueville's Civil Religion*. Albany, NY: SUNY Press.

Lamberti, Jean-Claude. 1989. *Tocqueville and The Two Democracies*. Trans. A. Goldhammer. Cambridge, MA: Harvard University Press.

Lawler, Peter A. 1993. *The Restless Mind*. Lanham, MD: Rowman & Littlefield.

Locke, John. 1960. *Two Treatises of Government*. Ed. P. Laslett. Cambridge: Cambridge University Press.

Manent, Pierre. 1996. *Tocqueville and the Nature of Democracy*. Trans. J. Waggoner. Lanham, MD: Rowman & Littlefield.

———. 1998. *Modern Liberty and Its Discontents*. Trans. D. Mahoney and P. Seaton. Lanham, MD: Rowman & Littlefield.

Mansfield, Harvey C. 2010. *Tocqueville: A Very Short Introduction*. Oxford: Oxford University Press.

———. 2014. "Intimations of Philosophy in Tocqueville's *Democracy in America*." In *Tocqueville's Voyages: The Evolution of His Ideas and Their Journey beyond His Time*, ed. Christine Dunn Henderson. Indianapolis: Liberty Fund.

Mansfield, Harvey C., and Delba Winthrop. 2014. "Tocqueville's Machiavellianism." *Perspectives in Political Science* 43:87–92.

Noll, Mark. 2014. "Tocqueville's *America*, Beaumont's *Slavery*, and the United States in 1831–32." *American Political Thought* 3:273–302.

Owen, J. Judd. 2015. *Making Religion Safe for Democracy*. Cambridge: Cambridge University Press.

Plato, 1968. *Republic*. Trans. and ed. Allan Bloom. New York: Basic.

Rousseau, Jean-Jacques. 2014. *The Major Political Writings of Jean-Jacques Rousseau*. Trans. John T. Scott. Chicago: University of Chicago Press.

Schleifer, James T. 2000. *The Making of Tocqueville's Democracy in America*. 2nd ed. Indianapolis: Liberty Fund.

———. 2014. "Tocqueville, Religion and *Democracy in America*: Some Essential Questions." *American Political Thought* 3:254–72.

Tessitore, Aristide. 2015. "Tocqueville's American Thesis and the New Science of Politics." *American Political Thought* 4:72–99.

Tocqueville, Alexis de. 1967. *Oeuvres Complètes*. Ed. A. Jardin. 18 vols. Paris: Gallimard.

———. 1991. *Oeuvres*. 3 vols. Paris: Gallimard.

———. 2000. *Democracy in America*. Trans. and ed. Harvey C. Mansfield and Delba Winthrop. Chicago: University of Chicago Press.

———. 2001. *Writings on Empire and Slavery*. Trans. and ed. Jennifer Pitts. Baltimore: Johns Hopkins University Press.

———. 2003. *Tocqueville: Lettres Choisies, Souvenirs*. Ed. Françoise Mélonio and Laurence Guellec. Paris: Gallimard.

———. 2011. *The Ancien Régime and the Revolution*. Trans. A. Goldhammer. Cambridge: Cambridge University Press.

Welch, Cheryl. 2000. *De Tocqueville*. New York: Oxford University Press.

Winthrop, Delba. 1991. "Rights: A Point of Honor." In *Interpreting Tocqueville's "Democracy in America,"* ed. K. Masugi. Savage, MD: Rowman & Littlefield.

Wolin, Sheldon. 2001. *Tocqueville between Two Worlds*. Princeton, NJ: Princeton University Press.

Zuckert, Catherine. 1981. "Not By Preaching: Tocqueville on the Role of Religion in American Democracy." *Review of Politics* 43:264–86.

Religion, Civic Education, and Conformity

DANA VILLA

If, in the first stage of the Revolution, the French were animated by the desire to "abolish their entire past" by creating an artificial caesura—a destructive and impossible task, as Hegel had pointed out—the Americans had no such need. Theirs had been, from the start, the "land of the future." The corporate society of old Europe had simply been left behind with the crossing of the Atlantic by the Pilgrims.

Not for nothing did Tocqueville single this moment out as the *point de départ* of American democracy (Tocqueville 1992, 29–31, 34–36; 2004, 31–34, 38–41). Along with the rest of their Puritan brethren, the Pilgrims shared "more notions of rights and more principles of true liberty, than most any other European people" (Tocqueville 1992, 34–36; 2004, 36–38). From New England these ideas penetrated, first, the entire confederation of the colonies and, later, the entire continent of North America (Tocqueville 1992, 34; 2004, 36). If, in principle, all the European colonies in the New World "contained at least the germ, if not the mature form, of a complete democracy," it was only in New England that this germ took root, flowered, and then spread across the land. This was, in Tocqueville's estimation, in large part due to the peculiar interpenetration of religious and political ideas of equality in the minds of the Puritans (Tocqueville 1992, 40; 2004, 41). Indeed, as he famously observed, Puritanism was "almost as much a political theory as a religious doctrine," one that coincided "in several respects" with "the most absolute democratic and republican theories" (Tocqueville 1992, 35, 38; 2004, 39, 37).[1]

Leaving aside, for the moment, the originally theocratic structure and legislation of the Massachusetts colony (and Tocqueville's rather blithe assurance that "a real and active, wholly democratic and republican political life flourished within every community" in New England by 1650), the Puritan empha-

Dana Villa is Packey J. Dee Professor of Political Science, Department of Political Science, University of Notre Dame, 219 O'Shaughnessy Hall, Notre Dame, IN 46556 (dvilla1@nd.edu).

1. For a contemporary historical appraisal of just how false this claim is, see Gaskill (2014, 64).

sis on equality had a potential downside (Tocqueville 1992, 44; 2004, 45). Were it not for the shared faith, language, and habits of self-government born of a specifically English political heritage, the Puritan—and, more broadly, Congregationalist—emphasis on covenants and binding promises would have placed them in uncomfortable proximity to the teachings of the social contract tradition.[2] For Tocqueville and other proponents of the *société en poussière* thesis such as Edmund Burke and Pierre Royer-Collard, such proximity hardly counted as a recommendation.

Virtually all of the teachings in the social contract tradition—with the possible exception of Hobbes's version—emphasized the importance of a "horizontal" pact of association among equal, free, and rationally self-interested individuals.[3] Social contract theories were, in their basic structure and intent, studiously indifferent—and even hostile—to the kind of cultural and religious presuppositions thematized in the early modern republican tradition. The chief aim of the modern natural-law tradition was to identify a minimal morality that all rational human beings could agree to, regardless of cultural—and even religious—differences.[4] Thus, without the addition of mores, habits, ideas, and attitudes to the mix, we find ourselves—at least in Tocqueville's view—back on the terrain of the very "atomism" that Hegel had so savagely

2. For a good corrective to Tocqueville's biased and Puritan-centric account, see Gooch (1959). The Levelers and Independents play absolutely no role in Tocqueville's genealogy of American democratic ideas and practices. This is the result of not only a certain degree of willful ignorance but also outright bias in favor of the more moralistic and creed-centered sources (e.g., the Puritans, whose attachment to democracy and republicanism is greatly exaggerated by Tocqueville).

3. Hobbes must be excepted because his version of the "social contract" emphasized (*a*) the impossibility of persons acting together prior to the creation of political society and the sovereign power that defined it, and (*b*) the fact that "society" is only created through the simultaneous submission of a mass of individual wills to a sovereign "representative." This act of submission—rather than any form of agreement between "the people" and its rulers or governors—is the act that first constitutes a society, with a will of its own (namely, the sovereign's, who "impersonates" each individual of newly born association, deciding for them what laws and actions are conducive to order and the public good). Rousseau's version attempts to split the difference between modern natural-law teaching and the republican–Montesquieuian focus on mores, customs, and civic formation. The result is a curious attempt to frame an ethos or morality of the common good in the individualist idiom of modern natural-law teachings.

4. See Richard Tuck's discussion in Tuck (1989, 51–64). In this context I should note that Tocqueville shared Burke's contempt for the kinds of theoretical abstraction built into such a project, viewing it as the perennial temptation of thinkers and *littérateurs* who had little concrete experience in politics. The desire to "substitute basic and simple principles, derived from reason and natural law, for the complicated and traditional customs which ruled the society of their times" (Tocqueville 1998, 196) was the characteristic *idée fixe* of the theoretical mind. This desire was harmless enough when confined to intellectual circles, but—in Tocqueville's view (and Hegel's as well)—it exerted an "extraordinary and terrible influence" when it "descend[ed] to the crowd" during the French Revolution.

critiqued. We find ourselves, in other words, in the presence of a "political" association whose only purpose (and adhesive force) is found in the prudential self-interest of each of its members.

Yet even though the New England Puritans had a "thick" consensus and sense of community to back up their otherwise individualist notions of right and conscience, this particular *Sittlichkeit* could hardly be expected to extend to the whole of the "confederation," let alone the entire continent. As Tocqueville was well aware, there were more than Puritans in seventeenth-century America, to say nothing of later times. No matter how important the *point de départ* may be, it is, by its very nature, just that: a point of departure. The dispersion of ideas, habits, attitudes, and practices is, as a result, also the process of their gradual thinning out, their progressive "universalization" and formalization.

For those skeptical that Puritanism exemplified quite the close fit of "the spirit of religion" with the "spirit of liberty" that Tocqueville imagined, this process of formalization and transformation appears as absolutely necessary and largely benign. Without it, it is almost impossible to conceive of a liberal democracy evolving from such an unpromising starting point, namely, an intolerant theocracy, one predicated on the most extreme forms of moral and religious discipline and homogeneity. For Tocqueville, on the other hand, the thinning out of such a "concrete" ethical life (to use Hegel's terminology) signaled, potentially, the beginning of the end—not only of the integrity of a moral-religious community but of "democratic and republican" political life altogether. Formalization dissolves the most important of the ties that bind a community together, namely, its mores, habits, customs, and opinions. And this raises the specter of a triumphant (and, from Tocqueville's perspective, disastrous) "individualism."

Had this been the case, *Democracy in America* would have ended before it had barely begun. Or, rather, the story it tells would have been the familiar republican one of original virtue followed by inevitable corruption and decline, with Puritan moral uprightness substituting for neo-Roman civic virtue. The Anglo-Americans were saved from this fate, according to Tocqueville, because of their enduring religiosity and the fact that the Puritans had transplanted the all-important English habit of local government, "that prolific seed of free institutions," to American soil. Thus, while a democratic *condition sociale* presented fertile ground for atomization and the spread of individualism qua privatism, the habit of local self-government and political liberty generated strong and overwhelmingly positive associational energies. Or, as Tocqueville put it in volume 2 of *Democracy in America*, "the Americans have used [political] liberty to combat the individualism born of equality, and they have defeated it" (Tocqueville 1992, 617; 2004, 591).

In Tocqueville's estimation, American "free institutions" and political rights—made concrete in the shared business of local (township) administration—were "constant reminders to each and every citizen that he lives in society" and that he is, in myriad ways, dependent on his fellow citizens and the institutions they share (Tocqueville 1992, 620; 2004, 593). The employment of this most elementary form of the art of association thus provides, in Tocqueville's view, one of the most effective antidotes to the "natural" tendency toward dissociation that threatens any democratic society. The point I want to stress here is that Tocqueville saw this antidote as more or less imprinted on our cultural and political DNA, thanks to the Puritans. And, indeed, "every people bears the mark of its origins." However, Tocqueville follows up this reasonable and innocuous statement with an assertion that is breathtaking in both its monocausal inclusiveness and its pseudopredictive hubris. "There is not a single opinion, habit, or law," he writes, "I might almost say not a single event, which the point of departure cannot readily explain" (Tocqueville 1992, 31; 2004, 33). Hegel is often accused of some form of the genetic fallacy owing to his evident contention that the end is, somehow, contained in the beginning. Tocqueville, as this passage and others attest, is, if anything, even guiltier on this score.[5]

Tocqueville's version of the genetic fallacy is noteworthy because it lays the groundwork of so much that is to come in *Democracy in America.* Anyone who claims that the Puritan communities admirably united the "spirit of religion" with the "spirit of liberty," thereby uniquely facilitating the American transition to a robust democratic society, one that is able to keep *individualisme* in check, is, at the very least, guilty of radically simplifying what was, in fact, a far more complex story.

To begin with, the New England townships may well have provided the original "small schools of democracy" in America. Thankfully, by the start of the eighteenth century these were more generically Congregationalist than Puritan in character. Moreover, the townships were home to growing num-

5. Tocqueville's rhetoric is, on this score, over the top, as the following passage from volume 1, chapter 2 of *Democracy in America* attests: "Go back in time. Examine the babe when still in its mother's arms. See the external world reflected for the first time in the still dark mirror of his intelligence. Contemplate the first models that make an impression on him. Listen to the words that first awaken his dormant powers of thought. Take note, finally of the first battles he is obliged to fight. Only then will you understand where the prejudices, habits, and passions that will dominate his life come from. In a manner of speaking, the whole man already lies swaddled in his cradle. Something analogous happens with nations. . . . If we could trace societies back to their elements and examine the earliest records of their history, I have no doubt that we would discover the first cause of their prejudices, habits, and dominant passions, indeed, of every aspect of what has been called the national character" (Tocqueville 2004, 31).

bers of literate men and women whose reading extended well beyond the confines of the Old Testament, where the heart of covenant theology was located (see Miller 1939, 375–77). Many of these readers were familiar with the protoliberal vocabulary of Locke, the Independent and democratic ideas of the Levelers, and a republican idiom derived from Sydney, Harrington, and Montesquieu. Indeed, in their minds, these theories and ideas could be mixed more or less promiscuously, with little sense of contradiction and little need for scriptural backup.[6] They did not see themselves as, first and foremost, engaged in a perpetual struggle against Satan, a struggle that demanded the strictest possible forms of spiritual and social discipline and that took political form as a militant Calvinism organized along hierarchical lines.[7] Finally, it is important to remember that these men and women were just as influenced by Enlightenment philosophy, and just as immersed in the histories of the ancient republics, as were the French—perhaps more so.[8] They were people for whom the world Hawthorne would resurrect in *The Scarlet Letter* was a distant and somewhat primitive memory (see Brooks 1985, 12).

Tocqueville's yearning to uncover religious, and not just republican, roots for political liberty is understandable, given the stringent anticlericalism of the French Revolution. He sought to demonstrate to his incredulous countrymen that religion and new political and social order stood in need of each other (see Tocqueville 1998, 195–208). This is the context for his idealization of the Puritan settlements, an idealization that culminates in his comparison of these communities to the open and democratic order of ancient Athens (Tocqueville 1992, 44; 2004, 46).

As a piece of rhetoric, this is effective and flattering. As a piece of history, however, it is false and misleading. It ignores the fundamental transformations affected by the end of theocratic government and the widening deployment of nonbiblical, and often decidedly secular, influences of the sort I have just mentioned. Indeed, aside from the township structure itself (an English rather than

6. As Gordon Wood has pointed out, they had little or no sense of tension or contradiction between the claims of reason and the claims of English tradition, between Locke's "natural rights" to life, liberty, and property and the customary rights of "free-born Englishmen." See Wood (1998). For the genesis of the Atlantic Republican tradition and the Sydney–Harrington connection, see Pocock (1975).

7. As George Armstrong Kelly notes, by 1787 the men who would become the founders had "dismissed the theological doctrines of depravity, conversion, and election; at least they denied them any part in the concerns of the profane order. They remained prudent about the millennium, as was appropriate to their preservative politics, a politics that was Lockean and anti-Augustinian" (Kelly 1984, 75). See also Walzer (1965, 160–71).

8. Bailyn (1993), incorporating both the Federalist and Anti-Federalist papers, has numerous references to both ancient Rome and Athens, and none to the Puritans, Cotton Mather, or John Calvin. The Quakers are considered insofar as they had been the object of discrimination and persecution. See also Bailyn (1992, chaps. 2 and 3).

a specifically Puritan inheritance), it seems more plausible to argue that the genesis of American democracy depended less on a continuity with its Puritan religious past than on its at least partial overcoming.[9]

* * *

If we place Tocqueville's dubious claims about the influence of the American *point de départ* to one side, we are free to concentrate on his far more interesting ideas about the nature of *individualisme* and about the nature, extent, and effects of the "art of association." It is here that his religious and aristocratic prejudices take a back seat and that many of his enduring contributions to modern political theory are to be found.

Tocqueville saw individualism as a more or less inevitable consequence of a democratic *condition sociale.* Such privatization and withdrawal into the little world of home, friends, and business associates spelled doom for a robust public sphere and the practice of self-government. Indeed, would-be tyrants would like nothing more than that a given populace turn in on itself and pursue only its narrow social and economic concerns. This had happened in France, first under Napoleon and then again, more starkly, under his nephew Napoleon III (a true "democratic despot"; see Corley 1961). The same narrowing of the individual citizen's moral horizon could be observed in 1830s America as well, but—as we have seen—Tocqueville thought that the Americans had successfully combated this structural tendency toward dissociation through their perfection and employment of "free institutions" (*institutions libres*).

What does Tocqueville mean by "free institutions," and why did he think that these were the primary vehicles of the "art of association"?

The first of these questions is easily and uncontroversially answered. By "free institutions" Tocqueville meant the public-political realm of contemporary American democracy. Within this realm, the government of public affairs was divided into federal, state, county, municipal, and township levels, each with its appropriate sphere of jurisdiction and administration. Such a decentered democratic structure did not restrict popular political participation to the election of a national congress, parliament, or convention (the French model). Rather, fully aware of the potential dissociative effects of democratic equality, Amer-

9. If Tocqueville really was concerned simply with delineating a key influence on the later course of American history (as Beaumont claimed in a letter home), my critique would be off base. Yet the rhetoric of *Democracy in America* is unmistakable in its desire to place this influence in a unique and privileged position. The supposed continuity of development of American political culture from its Puritan origins signals Tocqueville's desire, once again, to rely on a certain "providential" reasoning, one distinct from teleology yet just as keen to efface the specter of overdetermination and contingency—hence the radical simplification of the story.

ican lawgivers "thought it appropriate to foster political life in each portion of the territory so as to create endless opportunities for citizens to act together to remind them daily of their dependence upon one another." "In this," Tocqueville concludes, "they acted wisely" (Tocqueville 1992, 617–18; 2004, 591).

Such a decentered, multilevel political realm obviously contributes to keeping the bogey of governmental centralization and usurpation of authority at bay. Yet for Tocqueville, this liberal or constitutional function is not its chief importance. The positive contribution of such a multileveled arrangement is that it draws average citizens into the consideration and management of public affairs. And it is precisely such consideration and management that leads the average citizen to expand his moral horizon beyond household and business. By acting together with his fellow citizens in public, he comes to see what Tocqueville calls "the close connection [*le lien étroit*] that exists between the particular interest and the general interest" (Tocqueville 1992, 618; 2004, 592).

Two points need to be emphasized here. The first is Tocqueville's almost Rousseauian faith in the moralizing effects of political participation. The second concerns his focus on local affairs. For it is here, in the debate, deliberation, and management of township affairs, that citizens are most effectively drawn out of their private sphere, becoming genuinely interested in "the public good."[10] What seems, at first glance, to be a mixture of sociological insight with common sense actually masks a profound theoretical innovation. For what Tocqueville is doing is showing how the Rousseauian–republican concern with *la chose publique* is best approached, not through active popular sovereignty at the national level, but rather through hands-on administration of local affairs. This departure from the French republican tradition points to another. For it is not by juxtaposing our "particular" or individual will to a more general and abstract "will of the people" that we attain civic consciousness and (possibly) come to practice civic virtue. Rather, it is by expanding outward from the narrow circle of our family and business concerns to the broader circles of association represented by the township that we come to

10. Perhaps unsurprisingly, it is this aspect of Tocqueville that Sheldon Wolin sees as genuinely political, as opposed to his more "culturalist" fixation on *moeurs*—the "habits, opinions, usages, and beliefs" of a people (Tocqueville 2004, 336). See Wolin (2001, 207–17). In general, I am in concurrence with Wolin on this point. However, as will be seen below, I disagree with his conclusion that while the township was the locus of genuine political education and action in volume 1 of *Democracy in America*, Tocqueville substituted a largely "apolitical" conception of civil society to take its place in volume 2 (see Wolin 2001, 378). Wolin seems to me guilty of projecting the apolitical bent of today's neo-Tocquevillians back onto Tocqueville himself.

see not the abyss between particular and general interest, but the "close connection" between them.

It would be easy to suggest that Tocqueville is here primarily concerned with making the public-political world once again safe for the expression and pursuit of private interests. But that would be a mistake. While, like any good liberal—and, indeed, like Hegel—Tocqueville thinks that the pursuit of private interest is an ineradicable feature of the modern world, he does not think that the point of the public-political world is simply to preserve and protect this pursuit. Tocqueville directed his most withering contempt toward such a bourgeois attitude, a classic feature of the *individualisme* he so feared. The general interest is not a mere aggregation of private interests or preferences (as the utilitarians liked to think), but neither is it something essentially defined by its separation from, if not opposition to, those interests (the classic republican stance).

Like Hegel, Tocqueville thinks that the reconciliation of the universal and the particular is a critical goal of political life. Such reconciliation cannot come about, however, if one side of the equation is reduced to the other—if we are condemned, in other words, to the choice between Adam Smith and Jean-Jacques Rousseau. Both Hegel and Tocqueville believed that the moral-political *Bildung* of modern citizens is achieved through expanding circles of associational ties and interests. These circles lead us from family and business narrowly construed to broader community interests and (ultimately) to concern with national affairs.[11] The idea in both Hegel and Tocqueville is that as we progress through ever-expanding circles of associational life, we come to an ever-fuller—and more correct—appreciation of the "close connection" between public and the private. This progress occurs because our very conception of what is legitimate private or public interest has itself matured in the course of our associational life. An "educated" citizen rejects both unmediated forms of self-interest and empty abstractions like *la volonté générale*. Greed and "antique" virtue are antisocial extremes that impede any and all possibility of the reconciliation of universal and particular, public and private (see Tocqueville 1995, 5 and passim).

It is, of course, on the matter of just how the citizen is "educated" by these associational experiences that Tocqueville and Hegel most sharply diverge. For Hegel, it is a question of everyday experience and proper socialization as one moves through these progressively larger circles—from family, to trade or profession, to corporations more broadly, and finally to the state itself.

11. Or, as Hegel would put it, from the sphere of particular altruism (the family) to the sphere of universal egoism (civil society) and, finally, to the sphere of universal altruism or community concern (the state).

They must be supplemented, of course, by proper interpretation of this experience and socialization. It is precisely the latter service that philosophy (now supported by state-sponsored universities) is able to provide. The educated citizen grasps his proper place in the political and social through a process of deciphering and understanding what Hegel called the "hieroglyph of reason." The uneducated one, though deprived of such conceptual understanding, absorbs the laws of the land and an ethos of "my station and its duties."[12] It is through this ethos that the more abstract dimensions of *Sittlichkeit* and the "concrete universal" are brought down to earth.

For Tocqueville, on the other hand, the apparent abyss between private and public interest is bridged not so much by thought as by practice. In the New England townships, the jury system, and the broad associational realm of "civil society," Tocqueville saw democratic self-education in action.[13] Learning by doing (rather than learning though an appropriately structured socialization process as family member, burgher, and citizen) is thus the central American contribution to the problem of democratic political education. This problem—the paradoxical problem of an education to autonomy or self-government—is, of course, one that plagues modern political theory the moment popular sovereignty (no matter how virtual in form) becomes the underlying principle of all legitimate government. It is in local free institutions, the jury system, and civil and political associations that Tocqueville detected the "large free schools"—the *grandes écoles gratuites*—of democratic civic education (Tocqueville 1992, 631; 2004, 606). Here the people taught themselves the administration of public affairs, the law and its application, and—last but by no means least—the all-important art of association.

Did Tocqueville then stumble on the solution to the problem of democratic education in the process of demonstrating how general and particular interests might be reconciled? In one respect, the answer is yes. Impelled, as was Hegel, to somehow bridge the dichotomies between particular and universal, *homme*

12. My adaptation of Bradley's famous phrase is deliberate. See Bradley (1927, 160–206).

13. With regard to local institutions and the townships, Tocqueville writes, "It is at the local level that the strength of a free people lies. Local institutions are to liberty what elementary schools are to knowledge; they bring it within reach of the people, allow them to savor its peaceful use, and accustom them to rely on it. Without local institutions, a nation may give itself free government, but it will not have free spirit" (2004, 68). With regard to participation of ordinary citizens on juries, he notes that "the jury is incredibly useful in shaping the people's judgment and augmenting their natural enlightenment. It should be seen as a free school, and one that is always open, to which each juror comes to learn about his rights, and where he enters into daily contact with the best educated, most enlightened members of the upper classes and receives practical instruction in the law" (316). I deal with the "learn by doing" aspects of associational life below.

and *citoyen*, Tocqueville highlighted the institutional sites and associational forms that enlisted regular and (for the most part) enthusiastic participation. By entering into the public sphere and by acting in accordance with institutional (local) forms, the Americans did not simply learn how democracy works; they also learned just what sort of civic virtues are necessary to keep it going. These included an "enlightened" view of interests, public spirit, civic responsibility, and a respect for the rights of others. It is hardly an exaggeration to state that Tocqueville values the latter virtues of political participation—its moralizing dimension—over the more "technical" knowledge of the workings of democratic institutions. And, perhaps most importantly, this whole civic education apparently takes place from the bottom up rather than the top down. The Rousseauian paradox is solved.

Or is it? The American way of doing things apparently obviated the need for a "great legislator" to form and teach the people. And it made them a far more active agent of their own government and political education than anything either Rousseau or Hegel could conceive. Yet it hinged, perhaps fatally, on a unique constellation of cultural factors and historical contingencies that could hardly be expected to crop up elsewhere. First and foremost among these factors was a high degree of social equality—the absence, or so Tocqueville and Beaumont thought, of anything approximating a class society—as well as a high degree of literacy and general "enlightenment." It is thus no surprise to find Tocqueville's and Beaumont's letters home full of doubts as to whether the American example of a "regulated" democracy could or should be applied anywhere else in the world. In France, poverty, the absence of collaboration between the classes, and lack of general education seemed to make the self-education of the demos impossible. Add to this the absence of what Tocqueville called "free *moeurs*" in France (the habits, ideas, and opinions of a free and self-reliant people), and one might well despair of teaching American political lessons to the volatile yet subservient French.

Yet, as the very act of writing *Democracy in America* attests, Tocqueville ultimately thought there were lessons to be learned, hence the unmistakably didactic tone of both volumes of the work—a "textbook" if ever there was one. From Tocqueville's warning in the preface to the first volume that democratic equality is the wave of the future to his concluding insistence that it need not result in a centralized, administrative state, the emphasis is on what can be done, not on what has to be suffered. The multiple threats to be faced—*individualisme* and privatism, administrative despotism, political extremism, recurrent revolutions, and popular unrest—are all dangers that can be avoided, if only certain institutions, practices, and attitudes are introduced to the French.

Who will introduce them? The answer is clear: statesmen and political elites who have read and been persuaded by Tocqueville's analysis of the inevitability of a democratic social condition and its attendant dangers.[14] Oddly enough, the "bottom-up" model of political (self-)education is to be introduced from the top down. Constitutional reform, undertaken by the lawmakers of France, could reintroduce citizens to the habit of local self-government, thereby jump-starting the needed change in habits, attitudes, and opinions. "In America," Tocqueville writes, "free habits have created free institutions, in France it's for free institutions to create the habits" (quoted in Pierson 1996, 414). Where the majority of the public is poor and "unenlightened," political elites abdicate their reforming and pedagogic responsibilities by supporting politics as usual (the stringent limitation of the electorate to a small fraction of the population under Guizot and Thiers is an instance of the latter).[15] The result of such abdication, Tocqueville warns, will be renewed revolution and accelerated centralization.

Here we have the reintroduction of Rousseau's paradox, this time written in small rather than capital letters.[16] The "more enlightened classes" must lead, and not through mere persuasion or dispersion of ideas. The political situation was too dire, and the imperative of action too immediate. The cause of reform required public-spirited and enlightened men, men capable of "great" actions for the cause of liberty in France. Both Tocqueville and Beaumont dreamed, in their youth, of being among this select group and of gaining real political power. In this hope they were to be, for the most part, sadly disappointed, not to say disillusioned. Tocqueville's own brief opportunity at actual

14. As Françoise Mélonio notes, "Tocqueville did not believe measured evolution toward democracy possible except under the direction of the enlightened classes. The 'public,' coextensive in theory with the community of the French people, in fact was limited to the elites. If a new political science was needed for a brand-new world, it was for use by 'the more powerful, the most intelligent, and the most moral classes of the nation,' by those 'virtuous and peaceful individuals whose pure morality, quiet habits, opulence, and talents fit them to be the leaders of their fellow men'" (1998, 25). Both of the cited characterizations are taken from Tocqueville's introduction to volume 1 of *Democracy in America*.

15. One should never forget the fact that the electorate under the July Monarchy comprised a mere 241,000 voters of demonstrated means out of a population of over 30 million. Rarely, if ever, was a more narrow class rule of the bourgeoisie achieved.

16. Indeed, in volume 1 of *Democracy in America* Tocqueville more or less repeats the problem of an "enlightened" people as articulated by Rousseau in book 2, chapter 6 of *The Social Contract*, while giving it his own "aristocratic liberal" twist: "Hence it is as difficult to conceive of a society in which everyone is highly enlightened as of a state in which every citizen is wealthy; the two difficulties are related. I am perfectly willing to concede that most citizens very sincerely want what is good for their country. Taking this one step further, I would go so far as to add that in general the lower classes of society seem to me less likely than the upper classes to adulterate this desire with considerations of personal interest. What the lower classes invariably lack to one degree or another, however, is the art of judging the means to the end they sincerely wish to achieve" (Tocqueville 2004, 226). As Rousseau would say, "The people by itself always wills the good, but it does not always see it. The general will is always right, but the judgment which guides it is not always enlightened."

constitutional reform (in 1848) was not conspicuous in its success. And, as any reader of the *Souvenirs* knows, he came to have nothing but contempt for the very elites upon whom all hopes for reform rested (Tocqueville 1995, 5–11). The young and hopeful Tocqueville, yearning to meaningfully unite theory and practice in the cause of top-down reform, gives way to the Cassandra-like Tocqueville of his later years (roughly 1848 onward).[17] American lessons had failed to be learned, not because of differences in culture and circumstances, but because the political class had turned out to be craven and self-deluded.

* * *

Like most of his predecessors in the tradition of Western political thought, Tocqueville could not conceive a stable political society that did not reside on the firm basis of shared habits, attitudes, ideas, and beliefs.[18] It is on the latter that institutions and laws rested, not the other way around. True, Tocqueville

17. See in this regard Tocqueville's famous speech to the Chamber of Deputies on January 29, 1848, in which he decries the "degradation of public mores" that will lead to revolution and pleads to his fellow deputies to change not laws, but "the spirit of the government, for . . . it is the spirit that is leading you to the abyss" (Tocqueville 1995, 14–15). The excerpt from this speech that Tocqueville reprints in his *Recollections*, together with the damning characterization of the "spirit of the middle classes" that had become the "spirit of the government" preceding it, confronts us with the problem of how to institute a reform program from the top down when the very political elites on whom we rely are themselves notoriously lacking in genuine public spirit. Did Tocqueville really expect a chamber full of deputies animated by place mongering and the inner workings of parliamentary politics to change their own spirit and that of the government on the force of his dire words alone? How can "public mores" be reformed when elite mores are, if anything, even lower in tone? This is a problem that confronts all political thinkers and actors who see "mores, habits, attitudes, and ideas" as more important, ultimately, than institutional, legal, and procedural reforms. Tocqueville's mature despair over conditions in France is a function of his complete and utter disillusion with the political class and his own increasing tendency to take on the mantle of the last virtuous public man in the realm.

18. It is only quite recently, with the publication of Rawls (1993), that this assumption has been questioned directly and in a worked-out manner. By starting with what he calls the "fact of pluralism"—that is, the presence of a wide array of "reasonable though incompatible religious, philosophical and moral doctrines in our stable liberal democracy"—Rawls proceeds to ask, "How is it possible that deeply opposed though reasonable comprehensive doctrines may live together and all affirm the political conception of a constitutional regime? What is the structure and content of a political conception that can gain the support of such an overlapping consensus?" (1993, xviii). The idea of a relatively autonomous "domain of the political" that Rawls draws on to construct his answer is one that would have made absolutely no sense to Plato, Aristotle, Machiavelli, Rousseau, or Hegel, all of whom presuppose an underlying moral consensus as the *conditio sine qua non* of political stability. Even Locke and Kant would have had severe problems with Rawls's approach, since both thought there was a clear and singular moral law that had to be acknowledged before a polity based on consent could claim to be genuinely legitimate (and, thereby, achieve a degree of stability most real-world polities lacked).

allowed for a good deal of pluralism of associations and interests in his portrait of the (stable) American regime, as well as a fair degree of religious pluralism (albeit all within the ambit of Christianity). But the idea of anything approximating real moral pluralism—the presence of multiple and incompatible religious, philosophical, and moral doctrines within a single society—would have seemed to him a recipe for (at best) institutional impotence or (at worst) anarchy and revolution.

Tocqueville's insistence on the primacy of mores, customs, and attitudes implies, then, a high degree of moral homogeneity. Without such homogeneity, mores and beliefs could hardly play the fundamental stabilizing role he assigns them. However, this broad sociological perspective—shared, as we have seen, by both Rousseau and Hegel—pales in comparison to the importance Tocqueville attributes to religion and the basic tenets of the Christian faith. These are seen as absolutely necessary supports of the "ordered liberty" Tocqueville thinks the Americans have achieved.

The priority of religion as a "cause which tends to maintain democracy" in America against an unlimited exercise of popular sovereignty and majority rule is made perfectly clear by the penultimate chapter of the first volume of *Democracy in America*. Here Tocqueville surveys the respective contributions of America's peculiar circumstances (geography, lack of powerful neighbors, abundant natural resources), its laws, and "the manners and customs of the people." Unsurprisingly, it is the last topic that garners the lion's share of Tocqueville's attention in this chapter, effectively providing the conclusion of the book and containing some of Tocqueville's more heavy-handed didactic points.[19]

There are, Tocqueville notes, countless religious sects in America. They may have different rituals and theological bases, but "they all agree about man's duties to his fellow man. . . . Each worships God in its own way, but all preach *the same morality* in God's name" (Tocqueville 1992, 335–36; 2004, 335). This is, of course, the Christian morality, broadly construed. This well-nigh universal

19. As many have noted, the chapter that follows the one entitled "On the Principal Causes That Tend to Maintain the Democratic Republic in the United States" has a somewhat peculiar relation to the rest of volume 1. This chapter—"Some Considerations concerning the Present State and Probable Future of the Three Races That Inhabit the Territory of the United States"—contains some of Tocqueville's most moving prose. His depiction of the condition and probable fate of the Native Americans, as well as the profound difficulties the United States will have in overcoming the legacy of slavery, is more than penetrating. Yet, structurally speaking, the chapter has the feel of an extended appendix. This makes the prior chapter, "On the Principal Causes," the effective planned conclusion to the work. That Tocqueville chooses to end his work with an extended consideration of the role religion plays in stabilizing American political life is clearly significant, revealing how intertwined he saw the "spirit of religion" and the "spirit of liberty"—a clearly debatable viewpoint.

subscription to the basic tenets and moral teachings of Christianity plays, in Tocqueville's view, an absolutely critical role in stabilizing and preserving the "democratic republic." As Tocqueville explains,

> Some Anglo-Americans profess Christian dogmas because they believe them, others because they are afraid lest they seem not to believe them. Christianity therefore reigns without impediment, by universal consent. As I said earlier, the consequence of this is that everything in the moral world is *certain and settled*, though the political world seems given over to controversy and experiment. Thus boundless opportunity is never what the human spirit sees before it: for all its audacity, it sometimes runs up against seemingly insurmountable barriers. Before it can innovate, it is forced to accept certain basic assumptions and to mold its boldest conceptions to certain forms, and in the process it is slowed down or even brought to a halt. (Tocqueville 1992, 337; 2004, 337; emphasis added)

The hegemony of the Christian religion in the United States teaches all citizens "habits of restraint" that conduce to the "tranquility of the American people." Without the fixed and immovable points provided by Christian morality, the political world of the Americans would be dangerously untethered, prone to revolutions and the idea that "everything is permitted in the interest of society" (Tocqueville 1992, 337; 2004, 337). Not for nothing does Tocqueville call religion—meaning, in this case, Christianity—"the first of America's political institutions" (*la première de leurs institutions politiques*). He adds, "For even if religion does not give Americans their taste for liberty, it does notably facilitate their use of that liberty" (Tocqueville 1992, 338; 2004, 338).

Anchored in a world of shared fundamental religious beliefs and morality, American political life is more or less immune to the spread of revolutionary social or political ideas. Faith-based morality is the antidote to all forms of political radicalism. The lesson Tocqueville wants his French readers to draw could not be clearer. The revolutionary turn away from France's Christian-Catholic roots has been a disaster, opening the floodgates to all manner of radical secular ideologies, ideologies that will not permit France to escape from a seemingly never-ending cycle of revolution and counterrevolution. When Tocqueville states, in volume 2 of *Democracy in America*, that "lawmakers in democracies and all decent and enlightened men who live in them must apply themselves unstintingly to the task of uplifting souls and keeping them intent on heaven," he is not simply arguing for a counterbalance to the material life (Tocqueville 1992, 657; 2004, 635). He is arguing that religious belief must be present if there is to be any chance of achieving (and maintaining) "ordered liberty." If man "has no faith, he must serve." And if man is to be free, "he must believe" (*S'il n'a pas de foi, il faut qu'il serve, et, s'il est libre, qu'il croie*; Tocqueville 1992, 532; 2004, 503).

For the religiously minded, this might seem anodyne and commonsensical enough. Who could complain if Tocqueville's sociological analysis revealed religion to be a key factor in the social and political stability of early nineteenth-century America? Moreover, hadn't he argued that "definite and fixed" ideas about morality, God, and human nature serve as an important bulwark against majority tyranny? Religion is not the problem; rather, it is an essential part of the solution to this most characteristic of democratic dilemmas.[20]

To this the more skeptical reader of Tocqueville on religion might respond as follows. Let us assume, for the sake of argument, that widespread religious belief and a shared Christian morality did indeed contribute to the stability of the early years of the republic. Let us also assume—again, for the sake of argument—that this fact teaches us something about the nature and sources of social stability more generally (a cherished idea of many contemporary civil society enthusiasts).[21] Is it plausible to argue that this historical stability and its theoretically generalized cousin do not come at a substantial cost to liberty itself?

Those who think that the answer to this question is an unqualified yes would do well to ponder Tocqueville's approving description of how a judge in Chester County, New York, refused to swear in a witness who had stated "that he did not believe in the existence of God or the immortality of the soul" (Tocqueville 1992, 338–39; 2004, 338). Compare this supposedly edifying testament to the faith and morality of the Americans with Mill's anger and indignation at the fact that, in 1857 at the Old Bailey in London, "two persons, on two separate occasions, were rejected as jurymen, and one of them grossly insulted by the judge and one by the counsel, because they honestly declared they had no theological belief" (Mill 1977, 239). Unquestioned and widespread belief may provide certain "fixed points" and a kind of stability. This stability comes, however, at the price of effectively disenfranchising religious, political, and cultural dissidents.

Like many in America today, Tocqueville did not think that this was too steep a price to pay. On the contrary, he thought that unbelievers and those whom he calls "materialists" were dangerous to the moral health of society

20. In his stimulating book, Joshua Mitchell (1995) goes much further, arguing that Tocqueville viewed religion and shared belief not only as a precondition for social stability but also as a necessary and permanent feature of any democracy that wishes to be an "ordered" one. The underlying argument is Augustinian in character, and Mitchell detects much Augustinianism in Tocqueville.

21. See the essays collected in Eberly (2000), esp. Berger and Neuhaus (2000).

and therefore should be denied any positive (legal, cultural, or political) recognition. "If you encounter among the opinions of a democratic people," Tocqueville writes, "any of those wicked theories that intimate that everything perishes with the body, you must regard those who profess such theories as natural enemies of the people" (Tocqueville 1992, 657; 2004, 635). Why? Because philosophies, political theories, or scientific ideas that promote disbelief in God and the immortality of the soul are dangerous and demoralizing for society at large.

Such had been the case in France, according to Tocqueville. The *philosophes* of the Enlightenment were read by the upper classes. As a result, "unbelief established itself first in the minds of the very people who had the most personal and pressing interest in keeping the state in order and the masses obedient." And not only did "enlightened" aristocrats and bourgeois welcome unbelief, but "in their blindness they spread it downward" (Tocqueville 1998, 207). From there it was but a few steps to the impious violence of the revolutionary mob. The French Revolution may have been "prepared" by "the most civilized classes of the nation." However, it was carried out by "the most coarse and ignorant," who no longer had the fear of God to restrain them (243). The result, in Tocqueville's opinion, was a catastrophe of world-historical proportions.

Given his strong opinions about such "wicked" (*malfaisantes*) ideas and theories, it is not surprising to find Tocqueville (in *The Old Regime and the Revolution*) wishing that the church and the monarchy had carried out a full-scale repression of the anti-Christian writers of the Enlightenment. Instead, "authors were persecuted only enough to make them complain, not enough to make them afraid" (Tocqueville 1998, 205). Intolerance could not be halfhearted. Given the stakes—the demoralization of society and the possibly violent overthrow of the *ancien régime*—effective censorship was not only called for but imperative. The "dangerous literature" spawned by Diderot, Helvétius, d'Holbach, and the rest should have been burned, not read.[22]

22. One should remember, in this regard, that the publication of Rousseau's *The Social Contract* and *Emile* in spring of 1762 was followed swiftly by official condemnation by the Parlement of Paris and the Genevan authorities. Both bodies issued arrest warrants for Rousseau, and copies of *The Social Contract* were burned in Geneva. The Archbishop of Paris, Christophe de Beaumont, went so far as to issue a pastoral letter condemning *Emile* in August of 1762, eliciting a famous response from Rousseau himself in March of 1763, the lengthy *Letter to Beaumont*. Tocqueville no doubt thought that Rousseau was unjustly persecuted. After all, Jean-Jacques was just as hostile to the mainstream Enlightenment as Tocqueville later came to be. The real danger lay elsewhere, with the materialists, of whom d'Holbach and Hélvetius are representative. They, Tocqueville thought, not Rousseau, should have been suppressed.

These are, of course, Burkean ideas, even though Tocqueville has clothed them in Catholic vestments. They reveal just how fragile Tocqueville thought mores, habits, opinions, and customs were, at least in Europe. They also reveal Tocqueville's antipathy toward the skeptical authors whom he had read at the age of 16, in his father's library in the prefecture of Metz. It was these writers who infected him, for the first time, with doubt. And doubt, for Tocqueville, was to prove a personal enemy of long standing. Writing to his friend Charles Stoffels in October 1831, Tocqueville recalls the dissipation of his religious certainty in the library at Metz:

> When I first began to reflect, I believed that the world was full of demonstrated truths; that it was only a matter of looking carefully in order to see them. But when I sought to apply myself to considering these objects, I perceived nothing but inextricable doubts. I cannot express to you, my dear Charles, the horrible state into which this discovery threw me. That was the unhappiest time of my life; I can only compare myself to a man who, seized by dizziness, believes he feels the floor tremble under his feet and sees the walls that surround him move; even today, I recall that period with a feeling of horror. I can say that then I fought with doubt hand to hand, and that it is rare to do so with more despair. . . . I consider this doubt to be one of the greatest miseries of our nature; I place it immediately after illness and death. (Tocqueville 1985, 63–64)

That doubt is a Pascalian worm that never leaves once established is testified to by Tocqueville's letter, some 26 years later (2 years short of his death in 1859), to Sophie Swetchine, in which he recalls the episode at Metz in virtually identical terms: "My life until then had developed in a setting full of faith, which hadn't even allowed doubt to touch my soul. Then doubt entered or rather thrust itself in with unheard of violence, not merely doubt of this or that, but universal doubt. I experienced suddenly the sensation described by those who have witnessed an earthquake, when the earth was trembling beneath them, the walls all around them, the ceiling above their heads, the furniture around them. . . . I was seized by the blackest melancholy" (quoted in Siedentop 1994, 135). And, again in a letter to Mme. de Swetchine, Tocqueville confessed that "from time to time these impressions of my early youth . . . take possession of me again; I then see the intellectual world spinning and I am left lost in the universal movement which overturns or shakes all the truths on which I have built my beliefs and my actions" (135).

These letters enable us to understand more deeply Tocqueville's view of dogmatic opinions as salutary, rather than deadening (as Mill was to view them). The personal shaking of faith, combined with the very real "earthquake" of the French Revolution, produced in Tocqueville a yearning for certainty and a deeply sentimental view of religion generally. Like Tocqueville himself, France had lost her faith, thanks to the Enlightenment and to the shortsightedness of the literate classes.[23] If only one could somehow go back to a world uninfected by doubt. Paradoxically, Tocqueville thought he found such a world in America, the "land of the future" (Tocqueville 1992, 341; 2004, 340). The religiosity of the Americans, combined with the stability of their republic, confirmed Tocqueville in the opinion that a shared general faith is crucial to social stability, and that only by learning the lessons religion teaches could France ever hope to escape the periodic aftershocks of the Revolution. To paraphrase Françoise Mélonio, if the first volume of *Democracy in America* sought to elucidate the institutional prerequisites of an ordered democracy, the second volume sought a "religious pedagogy of the spirit of liberty" (Mélonio 1998, 65).

When we add these various elements together—Tocqueville's view of the social role of religion, his insistence that the presence of a certain number of "dogmatic beliefs" was a good thing, his critique of the Enlightenment, and his own personal struggle with what he saw as the corrosive effects of doubt—it is hard to escape the conclusion that Tocqueville proposed to fight the political form of the "tyranny of the majority" with a social form of the "tyranny of the mind." The conformism implicit in the typical American's view that no civilized society can subsist without religion, and that "respect for religion" is "the greatest guarantee of the stability of the state and the security of the individual," yields a kind of herd mentality, albeit one with which Tocqueville is totally comfortable (Tocqueville 1998, 206). American middle-class mores, faith, and ideas are, in their very narrowness and uniformity, one of the most potent guarantees of social stability.[24]

We see, then, how a faith-based concern with the "demoralization of society" ultimately came to overshadow Tocqueville's more attractive concern

23. The causal connection is, of course, dubious in the extreme. See Cobban (1968) and Chartier (1991). Conservatives such as Gertrude Himmelfarb continue to be deeply invested in the ideas (*a*) that, compared to the moderate and reasonable English and American Enlightenments, the French version was bug-eyed and ideological in the extreme; and (*b*) that the French Enlightenment led directly to a demoralization of society, which in turn led directly to the radicalism of the Revolution. See Himmelfarb (2004, 149–87). In this view—contradicted by the moderate constitutionalism of the Revolution up until the insurrection of August 10, 1792, and the formation of a hard-line Jacobin government—she explicitly follows Tocqueville, who, at least, saw the difference between the men of 1789 and those of 1792.

24. See, in this regard, the following passage from volume 2, chapter 21 of *Democracy in America*: "Hence no matter how the powers of a democratic society are organized, and no matter what weight is assigned to each of them, it will always be very difficult to believe what the masses reject and to profess what they condemn. *This does wonders for the stability of belief*" (Tocqueville 2004, 758).

with a "manly" form of political liberty, one not afraid of dissent or of going against the grain. This evolution, in which the fear of doubt trumps the call for independence of both mind and action, is understandable within Tocqueville's overall frame of sociological analysis (the concern with atomization). But it is almost predictable given Tocqueville's having personally suffered the radically isolating experience of doubt. This experience gave rise to a sentimental view of religion in general and the Christian faith in particular.

Such sentimentalism about religion is utterly absent from both Hegel and Mill, even though Hegel would agree with Tocqueville that (on the whole) a consensus on the basic norms, customs, and attitudes is and must be one of the defining characteristics of *Sittlichkeit*. The contrast with Mill is, however, the more striking. These two "aristocratic liberals," so often viewed as peas in a pod, are separated by a fairly wide gap on the question whether shared belief supports or undercuts liberty. This gap widens into an abyss over the question whether dogmatic belief (together with custom and convention) is something to proudly uphold in the face of science, skepticism, and "materialist" theories of politics and society, or whether it is something that threatens to turn life into a "stagnant pool" devoid of real mental energy and real individual liberty.[25]

The clash between those who, like Tocqueville, see *individualisme* and dissociation as our fundamental problem and those who, like Mill, worry about conformity and the diminishment of doubt, mental energy, and genuine individuality is a real and inescapable one. It is the clash between social conservatives (whether of the Right or the Left) and Socratic moral individualists who, like Mill, are well aware of the social and cultural dimensions of the self. The former think that an atomized society is in need of more "social glue" and, like Tocqueville, see religion as supplying it. The latter see mass culture and public opinion as exerting a greater and greater gravitational pull toward conformity, even—and especially—when that conformity takes the form of an array of consumer demographics and prepackaged lifestyle choices. In the end, the question comes down to whether one thinks, like Tocqueville, that we suffer from too little integration in the "manners and mores" of our society, or, like Socrates and Mill, from too much. It will come as no surprise that I think that the latter diagnosis is more profound and on target, now and for the foreseeable future.

25. Mill himself identified this problem in his 1845 review of the second volume of *Democracy in America*. See Mill (1977, 196–200).

REFERENCES

Bailyn, Bernard. 1992. *The Ideological Origins of the American Revolution.* Cambridge, MA: Harvard University Press.

———, ed. 1993. *The Debate on the Constitution.* New York: Library of America.

Berger, Peter L., and Richard John Neuhaus. 2000. "To Empower People: From State to Civil Society." In *The Essential Civil Society Reader*, ed. Don Eberly, 143–81. Lanham, MD: Rowman & Littlefield.

Bradley, F. H. 1927. "My Station and Its Duties." In *Ethical Studies*, 160–206. Oxford: Oxford University Press.

Brooks, Van Wyck. 1985. *The Flowering of New England, 1815–1865.* Philadelphia: Franklin Library.

Chartier, Roger. 1991. "Enlightenment and Revolution; Revolution and Enlightenment." In *The Cultural Origins of the French Revolution*, trans. Lydia G. Cochrane, 3–19. Durham, NC: Duke University Press.

Cobban, Alfred. 1968. "The Enlightenment and the French Revolution." In *Aspects of the French Revolution*, 18–28. London: Jonathan Cape.

Corley, T. A. B. 1961. *Democratic Despot: A Life of Napoleon III.* New York: Potter.

Eberly, Don, ed. 2000. *The Essential Civil Society Reader.* Lanham, MD: Rowman & Littlefield.

Gaskill, Malcolm. 2014. *Between Two Worlds: How the English Became Americans.* New York: Basic.

Gooch, G. P. 1959. *English Democratic Ideas in the 17th Century.* New York: Harper & Row.

Himmelfarb, Gertrude. 2004. *The Roads to Modernity: The British, French, and American Enlightenments.* New York: Knopf.

Kelly, George Armstrong. 1984. *Politics and Religious Consciousness in America.* New Brunswick, NJ: Transaction.

Mélonio, Françoise. 1998. *Tocqueville and the French.* Trans. Beth G. Raps. Charlottesville: University of Virginia Press.

Mill, John Stuart. 1977. *Collected Works of John Stuart Mill.* Vol. 18, *Essays on Politics and Society.* Ed. J. M. Robson. Toronto: University of Toronto Press.

Miller, Perry. 1939. *The New England Mind: The Seventeenth Century.* Cambridge, MA: Harvard University Press.

Mitchell, Joshua. 1995. *The Fragility of Freedom: Tocqueville on Religion, Democracy, and the American Future.* Chicago: University of Chicago Press.

Pierson, George Wilson. 1996. *Tocqueville in America.* Baltimore: Johns Hopkins University Press.

Pocock, J. G. A. 1975. *The Machiavellian Moment.* Princeton, NJ: Princeton University Press.

Rawls, John. 1993. *Political Liberalism.* New York: Columbia University Press.

Siedentop, Larry. 1994. *Tocqueville.* Oxford: Oxford University Press.

Tocqueville, Alexis de. 1985. *Selected Letters on Politics and Society.* Ed. Roger Boesche. Berkeley: University of California Press.

———. 1992. *La démocratie en Amérique.* In *Œuvres*, vol. 2, ed. André Jardin, Jean-Claude Lamberti, and James T. Schleifer. Paris: Gallimard.

———. 1995. *Recollections: The French Revolution of 1848.* Ed. J. P. Mayer and A. P. Kerr. New Brunswick, NJ: Transaction.

———. 1998. *The Old Regime and the Revolution*. Vol. 1. Ed. François Furet and Françoise Mélonio. Trans. Alan S. Kahan. Chicago: University of Chicago Press.

———. 2004. *Democracy in America*. Trans. Arthur Goldhammer. New York: Library of America.

Tuck, Richard. 1989. *Hobbes*. Oxford: Oxford University Press.

Walzer, Michael. 1965. *The Revolution of the Saints*. Cambridge, MA: Harvard University Press.

Wolin, Sheldon S. 2001. *Tocqueville between Two Worlds: The Making of a Political and Theoretical Life*. Princeton, NJ: Princeton University Press.

Wood, Gordon S. 1998. *The Creation of the American Republic, 1776–1787*. Chapel Hill: University of North Carolina Press.

Part IV

THE TOCQUEVILLE THESIS IN THE TWENTY-FIRST CENTURY

The Saving Minimum? Tocqueville on the Role of Religion in America—Then and Now

CATHERINE ZUCKERT

ABSTRACT
This article seeks to determine exactly what Tocqueville claimed the role of religion was in preserving liberty in America, and to investigate the extent to which the increased diversity of the American population, the "revolution" in sexual mores, and changes in American law have affected that role. Despite recent movements back and forth, left and right, between less and more, liberal and conservative religiosity, the broad outlines of Tocqueville's analysis of the role of religion in America seem to hold true today.

In *Democracy in America* Alexis de Tocqueville famously argues that the religious "mores" of Americans—their beliefs, customs, and sentiments—are so important in preserving their liberty that "religion, which . . . never directly takes part in the government of society, must be considered as the first of their political institutions" (Tocqueville 2010, 475). But the reasons he gives for his coming to this conclusion are troubling. In Europe, where marriages are arranged on the basis of family and property rather than personal inclination, he observes, people find little happiness at home, so they seek satisfaction of their erotic desires in extramarital affairs and excitement in revolutionary public projects. Americans who choose their mates take their marriage vows seriously and find happiness in their domestic family life. "When, coming from the agitation of the political world, the American returns to the bosom of his family, he immediately encounters the image of order and peace. . . . And as he achieves happiness by the regularity of life, he easily gets used to regulating his opinions as well as his tastes." As a result, "in the United States, religion regu-

Catherine Zuckert is Nancy Reeves Dreux Professor of Political Science, Department of Political Science, University of Notre Dame, 350 Decio Faculty Hall, Notre Dame, IN 46556 (czuckert@nd.edu).

[American Political Thought, vol. 5, issue 3, Summer 2016]

lates not only mores; it extends its dominion even to the mind." To be sure, "some profess Christian dogmas because they believe them; others, because they fear not appearing to believe them." But as a consequence of the uniformity of publicly expressed beliefs, "Christianity rules without obstacles. . . . Thus the human mind never sees a limitless field before it. . . . Before innovating, it is forced to accept certain primary givens, and to subject its boldest conceptions of certain forms that retard and stop it" (474).

If Tocqueville's observations were correct, early nineteenth-century Americans enjoyed their political liberty at the price of their intellectual freedom! The generally Protestant Christian beliefs to which Tocqueville saw that Americans had to adhere, for example, if they wished to testify in court, were not usually enforced by law or any other form of external coercion (Tocqueville 2010, 1.2.9, 476). On the contrary, the widespread adherence to these beliefs in the United States constituted an example par excellence of the tyranny of the majority he observed there—a tyranny that was not imposed by law, over which the majority had final and complete control, so much as by the pressure to conform to the opinions and practices of the other members of the community or find oneself completely isolated (1.2.7, 402–20). Although he was unalterably opposed to tyranny and passionately attached to human liberty, Tocqueville suggested that this particular example of the exercise of the tyrannical power of majority opinion was beneficial because it imposed a powerful form of self-restraint on the majority: "Until now no one has been found in the United States who has dared to advance this maxim: that everything is allowed in the interest of society. Impious maxim, that seems to have been invented in a century of liberty in order to legitimate all the tyrants to come" (475).

In the foreword to volume 2 of *Democracy in America*, published 5 years after volume 1, Tocqueville explained that in the first volume he had attempted to show how a democratic social state naturally led the Americans to adopt certain laws and political mores. He had not shown that all their institutions and habits of thought could be traced to the equality of condition prevailing there. On the contrary, he could easily have proven "that the nature of the country, the origin of the inhabitants, the religion of the first founders, their acquired enlightenment, their previous habits, exercise and still exercise, independently of democracy, an immense influence on their way of thinking and feeling" (Tocqueville 2010, 692). Nor had he intended to suggest that American laws and customs were necessarily the best. He had sought the people among whom the social revolution he saw taking place in Europe had reached its "most complete and most peaceful development, in order to discern clearly its natural consequences and, if possible, to see the means to make it profitable to men" (29). When he returned to examine the relation between religion and the maintenance of political liberty under democratic social conditions outside of America in volume 2, he thus altered his approach somewhat by generalizing it. Instead of looking at the effect America's distinctively puritanical origins had on her subsequent political development, he asked simply why maintaining religious beliefs would be necessary in order to preserve the freedom of people living under democratic conditions, how such beliefs could be preserved, and what these beliefs at an absolute minimum were. As Tocqueville indicated most clearly in his concluding discussion of the "type of despotism democratic nations have to fear," he had changed his mind somewhat in the 5 years separating the publication of the two volumes (4.6–7, 1245–77). He no longer thought that the sort of despotism democratic nations had to fear in the future would arise from the political omnipotence of the majority or the tyranny informally exercised over thought. It would arise from the inability of every "equal" individual under democratic conditions to do much for himself, which would require them all to seek ever more services from the central government and so to become ever more dependent on it.[1] In examining the relation between the religious beliefs of citizens and the preservation of their liberty under democratic social conditions in volume 2 of his study, Tocqueville thus emphasized the effects maintaining certain religious beliefs had not only on the politics of the society as a whole but also on the ability of each individual to act on his own behalf.

No society can exist without common beliefs, Tocqueville reminded his readers. "Without common beliefs, there is no common action, and, without common action, there are still men, but not a social body. So for society to exist, and . . . for this society to prosper, all the minds of the citizens must always be brought and held together by some principal ideas; and that cannot happen without each one of them coming at times to draw his opinions from the same source and consenting to receive a certain number of ready-made beliefs" (Tocqueville 2010, 713). Dogmatic beliefs are, moreover, no less indispensable for individuals than they are for societies. "If man were forced to prove to himself all the truths that he uses every day, he would never finish . . . ; as he has neither the time, because of the short span of his life, nor the ability, because of the limitations of his mind, to act in this way, he is reduced to holding as certain a host of facts and opinions that he has neither the leisure nor the power to examine and to verify by himself, but that those more clever have found or that the crowd adopts" (714). Tocqueville ac-

1. This is the "place" or respect in which John Stuart Mill and Tocqueville came to disagree.

knowledged that "every man who receives an opinion on the word of others puts his mind into slavery." But when such received opinions are religious, he suggested, "it is a salutary servitude that allows making a good use of liberty. . . . Religion, by providing the mind with a clear and precise solution to a great number of metaphysical and moral questions as important as they are difficult to resolve, leaves the mind the strength and the leisure to proceed with calmness and with energy in the whole area that religion abandons to it" (716).

In democratic times, Tocqueville again argued, the opinions most people hold will be those of the majority. People who believe that they are the equals of all others do not readily accept the dictates of authority. They take pride in thinking for themselves on the basis of their own experience. When confronted by issues that not even the greatest philosophers have been able to resolve unanimously or with certainty, such people reason that if all human beings are equal, all of their opinions deserve equal respect. Unless I know for certain that things are otherwise, I should therefore adhere to what most people think. As conditions became more equal in Europe, Tocqueville thus predicted, the tyranny of majority opinion would become as great there as it was in America.

What, then, he asked, would or should the content of that opinion be? In the United States the generally Protestant Christian beliefs of its inhabitants had been preserved because there had been no democratic revolution to shake them as all past beliefs had been shaken in Europe. Because democratic peoples resist forms and rituals as signs, if not impositions of authority, it would not be possible to introduce new sets of religious beliefs. The only way to maintain belief in the immortality of the soul, which Tocqueville regarded as the absolutely essential minimum necessary to support a general belief in the dignity and rights of all individuals, would be to separate church and state, so that no person would regard it as an article of faith imposed by a human authority. As he had argued in volume 1, there was a natural "seed" of such a conviction in the attachment human beings had to their own lives, which they easily extended in the form of a hope for an afterlife, that would grow and blossom, if and only if left to develop freely on its own. What he added in volume 2 was the observation that this belief was not, strictly speaking, Christian or even religious. Its function could be supplied by the ridiculous doctrine of metempsychosis, as well as by Platonic philosophy (Tocqueville 2010, 4.958–60). The "religious" foundation Tocqueville thought necessary in order to preserve liberty under democratic conditions thus appeared to be minimal!

More than 175 years later, observers of politics on both sides of the Atlantic have begun to inquire about the extent to which Tocqueville's analysis of the relation between religious belief and the preservation of liberty under egalitarian social conditions holds true.[2] The increasingly secular beliefs of the citizens of northern European democracies have led observers to ask whether religious beliefs are necessary in order to maintain political liberty under egalitarian social conditions. And if they are, what must the content and form of these beliefs and practices be?

Americans appear to remain significantly more religious than the citizens of northern European social democracies such as France, Germany, and the United Kingdom. Yet the number of Americans who identify with particular religious denominations continues to drop, as does the strength and content of their specifically religious convictions. Those who think that respect for the dignity and rights of all individuals requires a transcendental foundation rather than what may be merely the momentary agreement of a majority of the people involved have reason to be concerned.

In this article, I first examine Tocqueville's argument concerning the importance of religion in maintaining the political freedom of Americans in volume 1 of *Democracy in America*. I then examine the way in which he modified his analysis when he applied it to France in volume 2. Finally, I look at some of the current findings concerning the decreasing religiosity of the American public and ask briefly what these findings may or may not mean for the future of democracy in America.

TOCQUEVILLE'S ANALYSIS IN VOLUME 1

In volume 1 of his classic study of democracy in America Tocqueville suggested that religion had a preeminent role in maintaining a democratic republic in the United States. But, he emphasized, that role was not merely primarily but necessarily indirect.

In a chapter entitled "Religion Considered as a Political Institution, How It Serves Powerfully to Maintain the Democratic Republic among the Americans," Tocqueville took note of what has since come to be called "American Civil Religion" (e.g., Rickey and Jones 1974; Bellah 1975).[3] In contrast to France in his time, he observed, no religious group publicly and directly opposed the liberal egalitarian political principles of the regime, not even the Catholic Church.[4] On the contrary, in America both Catholic priests and Protestant

2. For an argument concerning the contemporary applicability and importance of Tocqueville's analysis, see Rahe (2009).

3. By denominating publicly expressed beliefs as "civil," however, such commentators make religion more explicitly a political institution than Tocqueville himself did.

4. As Schleifer and Nolla point out in their roles, respectively, as editor and translator of the bilingual critical edition of *Democracy in America*, Tocqueville suppressed some of

ministers explicitly and frequently prayed to God not merely to support democracy at home but to spread its principles and institutions abroad.

Nevertheless, Tocqueville insisted, the "indirect influence exercised by religious beliefs on political society in the United States" was much greater than the direct effects of such explicit preaching. It was, indeed, "when religion is not speaking about liberty that it best teaches the Americans the art of being free" (Tocqueville 2010, 472).

As many political theorists have argued, the preservation of independence or free government has a moral prerequisite (e.g., Macedo 1990; Galston 1991). Those who are not able to control themselves will inevitably find themselves controlled by others. No one can be independent or self-governed who is not self-controlled. Religion importantly contributed to the development of self-control in America, but Tocqueville thought that the kind of self-control or restraint that religion had fostered in America was severely limited. In both volumes 1 and 2 of *Democracy* he insisted that no set of beliefs could check or oppose the materialistic desires of human beings living under democratic conditions. At most, he suggested, religious beliefs could be combined with extremely worldly, economic concerns to produce two politically desirable results.

First, religion contributed powerfully to the development of the stringent, if not literally "Puritanic," views of individual morality, especially with regard to sexual relations, characteristic of nineteenth-century America:

> I do not doubt for an instant that the great severity of mores that is noticed in the United States has its primary source in beliefs. Religion there is often powerless to restrain the man amid the innumerable temptations presented by fortune. It cannot moderate in him the ardor to grow rich that comes to goad everyone, but it rules with sovereign power over the soul of the woman, and it is the woman who shapes the mores. America is assuredly the country in the world in which the marriage bond is most respected, and in which the highest and most sound idea of conjugal happiness has been conceived. (Tocqueville 2010, 473–74)

Tocqueville did not think that their religious beliefs made Americans more generous, more high-minded, less calculating, and less self-seeking in their

---

the evidence he found of Catholics' lack of sympathy with American egalitarian political principles. As he indicates in his introduction (Tocqueville 2010, 24–27), Tocqueville wanted to convince his French readers that religion and democracy were not necessarily opposed and that they could and should become complementary forces in protecting liberty in the modern world.

public affairs than they might otherwise have been. On the contrary, the respect for the marriage tie inculcated by religion fostered the tendency Americans had on economic grounds to attend more to their own private affairs than to public concerns. Europeans sought to divert, if not to satisfy, their strongest passions through political action, Tocqueville suggested, because they were unhappy at home. "When, coming from the agitation of the political world, the American returns to the bosom of his family," on the other hand, "he immediately encounters the image of order and peace. There, all his pleasures are simple and natural, his joys innocent and tranquil; and as he achieves happiness by the regularity of life, he easily gets used to regulating his opinions as well as his tastes" (Tocqueville 2010, 474).

The second indirect beneficial effect nineteenth-century American religious beliefs had on political "mores" was to restrain not only Americans' engagement in political action but also their expectations with regard to the possible results of that action:

> Nature and circumstances had made out of the inhabitant of the United States an audacious man; it is easy to judge so when you see how he pursues fortune. If the mind of the Americans were free of all hindrances, you would soon find among them the boldest innovators and the most implacable logicians in the world. But the revolutionaries of America are obliged to profess publicly a certain respect for Christian morality and equity that does not allow them to violate laws easily when the laws are opposed to the execution of their designs; and if they could rise above their scruples, they would still feel checked by the scruples of their partisans. Until now no one has been found in the United States who has dared to profess this maxim: that everything is allowed in the interest of society. Impious maxim, that seems to have been invented in a century of liberty in order to legitimate all the tyrants to come. (Tocqueville 2010, 475)

Like their respect for marriage vows, Tocqueville indicated, American resistance to revolutionary political ideas and innovations was not simply or strictly religious in origin. Their practical experience, in both political and economic endeavors, also made Americans much more skeptical about the basis and validity of abstract theories and generalizations than less experienced Frenchmen.

The combined effect on American political "mores" was, nevertheless, of decisive importance. Having read the Constitution, Tocqueville recognized that in the United States a sufficiently large majority could legally do whatever it wanted. The much-vaunted protections of freedom of speech, religion, and assembly in the First Amendment could themselves be destroyed by amendment. "Therefore," he concluded, "at the same time that the law allows the American people to do everything, religion prevents them from conceiving of everything and forbids them to dare everything." Individual liberty can be preserved only where government is limited, and government would remain limited under egalitarian conditions, only so long as the vast majority of the people thought that it should be limited. Insofar as their religion convinced Americans that human aspirations and achievements should be restricted, religion constituted the fundamental support or foundation for the preservation of constitutional democracy. "So, religion, which among the Americans never directly takes part in the government of society, must be considered as the first of their political institutions; for if it does not give them the taste for liberty, it singularly facilitates their use of it" (Tocqueville 2010, 475).

Tocqueville devoted the remainder of his discussion of the role of religion in preserving free government in volume 1 to convincing his French readers that religion retained the influence it did in American politics, ironically enough, precisely because it kept itself and its practitioners strictly separate from the state. Eighteenth-century French rationalists had predicted that religious zeal would disappear with the spread of enlightenment and freedom, but America was living disproof of their claims.[5] Religion was alive and well in America, Tocqueville argued, because religion had a natural source. By leaving Americans free to follow their natural inclinations, rather than trying to impose a set of beliefs by law, the separation of church and state in America allowed religious convictions to arise and be preserved.

Acting purely on the basis of their natural inclinations, human beings would both imagine and desire an afterlife: "Never will the short space of sixty years enclose all of the imagination of man; the incomplete joys of this world will never be enough for his heart. Among all beings, man alone shows a natural distaste for existence and an immense desire to exist; he scorns life and fears nothingness. These different instincts constantly push his soul toward contemplation of another world, and it is religion that leads him there. So, religion is only a particular form of hope, and it is as natural to the human heart as hope itself." Human beings could detach themselves from religious beliefs only "by a type of intellectual aberration and with the help of a kind of moral violence exercised over their own nature" (Tocqueville 2010, 482).

5. A similar prediction about the decline of religion was made in the 1950s by advocates of the "secularization" thesis, e.g., Peter Berger, who argued that as the world became more democratic and industrialized, it would become less religious. Although northern European countries have become increasingly secular, the rest of the world has witnessed a marked increase in religiosity. See Philpott et al. (2010).

If religions founded their influence solely on the longing for immortality native to all human beings, there would be no way to deny or stifle the appeal. When religions sought to increase their influence by exercising temporal power, however, they brought the purity of their concern for the afterlife into question and aroused opposition on grounds of political interest as opposed to questions of faith. The price to be paid for linking church and state might not have been evident when monarchies appeared to be permanent. But as human beings became more equal, governments would change more frequently and ecclesiastical officials who identified their own concerns too closely with temporal authorities would undermine the credibility of their claims to be concerned primarily, if not solely, with the eternal. By allying themselves with a particular political party, churchmen would also provoke hostility on purely secular grounds. But if Europeans followed the American example and established a strict separation of church and state, Tocqueville urged, they could preserve the natural seeds and manifestations of religious sentiments among their populace and enjoy the beneficial political effects.

THE CHANGE IN VOLUME 2

By the time he wrote volume 2, however, Tocqueville no longer believed that it would be possible to preserve Christian beliefs in Europe as they had been maintained in America. The intellectual habits of people living under equal conditions did not favor religion, he observed. People who thought they were equal to all others did not easily accede to authority. They believed that they ought to be able to decide matters on the basis of their own experience. Finding that they were able to solve the minor problems that arose in daily life, they tended to conclude that everything in the world was explicable. They had "little faith in the extraordinary and an almost invincible distaste for the supernatural" (Tocqueville 2010, 701). It would, therefore, be virtually impossible to establish a new religion in democratic times; it would be difficult merely to preserve inherited beliefs.

Religion had persisted in the United States despite rather than because of the egalitarian conditions that prevailed there as a result of two historical circumstances peculiar to that nation. First, because the colonies had originally been established in America to secure religious liberty, religion had become associated in the minds of Americans with the founding of their nation and so had become part of their patriotic sentiments. Second, the Christian beliefs that the immigrants brought with them to the New World had survived unchallenged because America had not experienced a democratic revolution.

"There are no revolutions that do not turn ancient beliefs upside down, enervate authority and cloud common ideas" (Tocqueville 2010, 708). In a nation like France, where equality had been established only after a prolonged and violent struggle among the classes, religious faith could not be preserved as it had been in America merely through separation of church and state. Because of the past association of the church with an aristocratic order, partisans of democracy were apt to be hostile to Christianity, unless they could be convinced that its preservation would serve their own secular ends. The Christian religion would also have to take a distinctly democratic form.

In volume 2 Tocqueville concentrated, therefore, on persuading his democratic countrymen of the utility of preserving a few simple but nevertheless fundamental religious tenets. First, he pointed out, no individual or people could actually live solely on the basis of critically examined, empirically "verified" truths. In order to get through an ordinary day, people had to take a host of propositions on faith. If they tried to act only on the basis of what they knew without a doubt, they would be paralyzed. This was particularly true in the case of the most fundamental, but also most perplexing, questions concerning the existence of God, the immortality of the soul, and the obligations human beings owed others. If the greatest human intellects had addressed these questions for centuries without coming to satisfactory answers, much less agreeing on them, ordinary people certainly could not. It was thus highly desirable to have a widespread, though nonenforced, consensus on the answers to these fundamental questions (Tocqueville 2010, 2.1.2, 711–25).

A consensus on fundamental principles or basic articles of faith is necessary to maintaining any society, Tocqueville observed. But widespread religious beliefs have special advantages for democracies. They counter the two tendencies of human beings living under equal conditions that most threaten to destroy their liberty: their tendency to become isolated from others and think only of themselves, and their tendency to become inordinately fond of material pleasure.

Precisely because religion generally works to counter the strongest tendencies of people living in democratic times, however, religion itself will be destroyed if it remains simply in opposition to its environment. Religious faith might have a natural source in the human desire for immortality, but that desire is not strong enough to counter the more immediate attraction of physical pleasure and material gain. In democratic times religion can be preserved and exercise a salutary effect on morals—both individual and social—only by combining with economic calculation in public opinion as it does in America.

Although past religious beliefs had, like all others, been thrown into question by the revolution, it would be possible to foster a consensus on a few religious principles. Democratic circumstances are not antagonistic to all tenets of faith. On the contrary, "men similar and equal easily understand the notion of a single God, imposing on each one of them the same rules and granting them future happiness at the same cost" (Tocqueville 2010, 747). They also feel the desire for immortality, from which religious sentiments naturally develop. Although human beings who think they are equal to all others believe they ought to be able to decide all questions for themselves on the basis of their own experience, they find, particularly in the case of the most fundamental questions, that they cannot. Unwilling to admit the superior insight or knowledge of a few, democratic people reason that if all are equal, the greatest number must be right. Once formed, Tocqueville thus concluded, public consensus in democratic times will have more influence on individual belief than any tyrant's decree had in the past.

If religious beliefs were to be propagated and preserved by such a public consensus, however, both the doctrinaire and formal aspects antagonistic to democratic tastes would have to be minimized. It would not suffice merely to separate church and state. The content and form of religious services had to be adapted to democratic conditions. Religious leaders would also have to work at achieving a synthesis of secular and sacred beliefs. Rather than stressing the ways in which concern for their eternal salvation stands in opposition to the material interests of their congregations, preachers need to recognize the dominance of public opinion and explicitly align themselves with it in an emphatically nonpartisan way.

The public consensus Tocqueville urged his French readers to foster was not largely or even fundamentally religious. On the contrary, he suggested, the only effective way to counter the isolating tendencies of the primarily materialistic drives and interests of people living under egalitarian conditions was to appeal to those materialistic drives and interests themselves. Americans did not do justice to their own generous impulses when they attributed all their charitable deeds to "interest well understood." Nevertheless, he insisted, the American notion that individuals serve their greater, long-term interest by postponing some present pleasures and contributing some of their present gains to cooperative social endeavors provides the most effective basis for both individual and political morality under democratic conditions. This doctrine serves, indeed, precisely the two functions for which Tocqueville had praised religion. Although it does not destroy the materialist desires of democratic people, "interest well understood" does make them pursue those interests honestly. It also works to overcome the "individualism" or isolation that economic pursuits tended to foster.

Convincing people that it is in their long-term interest to discipline their immediate desires not only could make them act in a more "socially conscious" manner, Tocqueville argued; it could also make them more religious. "If the doctrine of interest well understood had only this world in view, it would be far from enough; for a great number of sacrifices can find their reward only in the other; and whatever intellectual effort you make to feel the usefulness of virtue, it will always be difficult to make a man live well who does not want to die. So it is necessary to know if this doctrine of interest well understood can be easily reconciled with religious beliefs" (Tocqueville 2010, 926). Fortunately, he concluded, it could be:

> The philosophers who teach this doctrine say to men that, to be happy in life, you must watch over your passions and carefully repress their excesses; that you cannot gain lasting happiness except by denying yourself a thousand passing enjoyments, and that finally you must triumph over yourself constantly in order to serve yourself better.
>
> The founders of nearly all religions adhered more or less to the same language. Without pointing out another path to men, they only placed the goal further away; instead of placing in this world the prize for the sacrifices that they impose, they put it in the other. (926–27)

Even if people in democratic times were not entirely convinced that there was a God, an immortal soul, or an afterlife, Tocqueville thought, they could be persuaded to act as if they were. If the doctrinal and formal requirements of religion were minimized, people would not have to act much differently on grounds of faith than they would or should act on grounds of interest. They were used to calculating the relation between short-term sacrifice and long-term advantage. As Pascal suggested, the immediate cost of professing belief or even, perhaps, attending church services was small compared to the possible long-term gain.[6]

If religion survived in modern egalitarian societies, Tocqueville concluded, it would be as a result of such self-interested calculations made generally effective through the force of public opinion. The specifically religious content of "interest well understood" was minimal, but irreplaceable. To convince individuals to risk their lives for the sake of the common good, beliefs in God and in judgment in the afterlife are extremely helpful, if not indispensable. The necessary beliefs are few, simple, and, we should note, not distinctively Christian. Indeed, when he turned to discuss the basis of individual morality, Tocqueville suggested that even belief in divine retribution or punishment was not essential.[7] "Most religions are only general, simple and practical means to teach

6. Lawler (1992) and Rahe (2009) have emphasized the influence of Pascal on Tocqueville's political thought as a whole.

7. Tocqueville thus minimizes the necessary content of a "civil religion" even more than Jean Jacques Rousseau did in *Social Contract* (Rousseau 2012, 4.5–9).

men the immortality of the soul" (Tocqueville 2010, 958). And, he observed, that function could and had been performed by a belief in reincarnation.[8] What was essential was for people to see that there was more to human life than the goods of the body, to maintain a more elevated view of the potential of human life, and hence to set themselves higher and more distant goals.[9]

Although he himself was most concerned about maintaining the spiritual qualities that distinguish human beings from animals, Tocqueville thought that materialistic concerns would remain dominant under democratic conditions.[10] Rather than appeal to higher but rarer human inclinations and desires, he thus consistently couched his analysis in terms of interest. So he concluded his comments on the importance of maintaining religious beliefs in democratic times by observing that without an elevated conception of human potential and correspondingly distant goals, human industry and hence prosperity would themselves eventually suffer (Tocqueville 2010, 2.2.15–17).

"If it is easy to see that, particularly in times of democracy, it is important to make spiritual opinions reign, it is not easy to say what those who govern democratic peoples must do to make them prevail" (Tocqueville 2010, 961). Because democratic peoples resist authority and judge on the basis of their own experience, no attempt to prescribe a public creed is apt to succeed. "The only effective means that governments can use to honor the dogma of the immortality of the soul," he concluded, "is to act each day as if they believed it themselves" (962). What cannot be taught by precept can be fostered by example.

Because people in democratic times trust their own experience much more than anything they are told, the best way to shape their opinions is to affect their experience. And the primary way of shaping the experience of people

8. In this respect, Tocqueville follows Montesquieu, who characterized Stoicism as a religion. Like Montesquieu, Tocqueville also had serious doubts about the compatibility of Islam with human liberty, if for no other reason than that it does not allow for the necessary separation of church and state.

9. This is the place or respect in which Tocqueville foreshadows Nietzsche most closely. Unlike Nietzsche, however, Tocqueville looked for sources of elevation compatible with democratic social conditions and found such a source of virtue in individuals and greatness in a people only in the idea of rights (Tocqueville 2010, 1.2.6, 389–91). He did not, like Nietzsche (e.g., in *Beyond Good and Evil*, pt. 9, "What Is Noble?"), seek to found a new aristocracy, because he thought that "it is impossible to imagine anything more contrary to the nature and to the secret instincts of the human heart than a subjugation of this type" (Tocqueville 2010, 1.2.10, 636).

10. Because the human soul could never be completely satisfied with material goods, he predicted that there would be sporadic outbreaks of extreme spiritualism, including religious revivals (Tocqueville 2010, 2.2.12, 939–41). He nevertheless thought that such events and groups would remain the exception and never become the rule.

living under egalitarian conditions in a politically and, indeed, humanly salutary manner that Tocqueville recommends is to decentralize as many political processes and decisions as possible. Individuals who become active in politics quickly learn the need to join with others in order to achieve their own goals. Having learned both the techniques and advantages of organization in politics, Americans not only had applied them to promoting their economic interests but also had used them to support a variety of opinions about moral and intellectual questions. In other words, their decentralized political institutions had provided Americans with the experience that had given rise to general belief in the doctrine of "interest well understood," on which, Tocqueville suggested, the preservation of religious sentiments also depends.

Contrary to the impression he left in his analysis of democracy in America in volume 1, in his second volume Tocqueville showed that neither the individual self-restraint (or morality) nor the limitations on political experimentation (or "imagination") that preserved limited government and thereby individual freedom in the United States were primarily results of religious belief. On the contrary, he indicated, religious beliefs were and would continue to be held under democratic conditions primarily as a result of self-interested calculation. So, for example, the limitations on the American "imagination" in the arts reflected their special historical relation to England, as a result of which they did not feel a particular need to develop their own literature (Tocqueville 2010, 2.1.9, 763–74). American resistance to general theories advocating radical experimentation in politics resulted from the practical experience afforded by decentralized political institutions (2.1.4, 737–41). And finally, he admitted, the severe "mores" he had observed in American women resulted more from democratic social conditions, which made it hard for a man to convince a woman he loved her if he was not willing to marry her, and economic circumstances, which generally kept married men and women working in separate locations, women in the house and men in the fields or the marketplace, than they did from religious beliefs, strictly speaking (2.3.8, 918–25).[11]

In the 5 years that had intervened between the two volumes, Tocqueville finally explained, he had come to understand the threat to the preservation of individual liberty in democratic times somewhat differently. It was not so much that the majority would impose its will politically or intellectually on the minority, as he had originally feared. The danger was, rather, that the effects of ever more centralized political authority and economic organization would gradually erode the grounds of all individual initiative and inde-

11. See also the discussion of Tocqueville in Zuckert (1976, 43–48).

pendence. The obvious, though by no means easy, way of countering this danger was to institute and preserve as many decentralized institutions as possible.[12]

As a result of this new understanding, Tocqueville was able, moreover, to avoid the contradiction at the root of his analysis of democracy in America in volume 1. As he first presented it, the preservation of American political liberty in the form of limited government depended on the exercise of what he himself dubbed the "tyranny of the majority" in the realm of public opinion. Religion was his main example.[13] By linking religious belief almost exclusively with the individual's natural desire to prolong his own existence and only secondarily and indirectly with the rule of public opinion, in volume 2 Tocqueville no longer had to argue, as he had in volume 1, that religion paradoxically kept Americans free politically by shackling their minds and imaginations. In volume 2 he positively associated religion more closely with the freedom of thought and depth of soul he himself most wanted to preserve. Instead of putting a cap on the American imagination, Tocqueville had come to think that simple religious beliefs in addition to the experience Americans gained through church could help them not only maintain respect for the dignity of the individual soul or conscience but also learn how to marshal the support of others when they disagreed with the majority.

ALMOST 2 CENTURIES LATER

Life in the United States has changed greatly in the almost 200 years since Tocqueville published his classic study in 1835–40. As a result of the waves of immigration, white Anglo-Saxon Protestants no longer constitute a majority of the population. Most people now live in urban areas; both the economy and the government have become primarily national. There has, moreover, been a "revolution" in American "mores." The cohabitation of unmarried couples is now not merely tolerated but legally protected; the divorce rate seems to have stabilized at a fairly high rate, but the number of illegitimate

12. For a fuller elaboration of this argument see Zuckert (1983, 421–32).

13. In the section titled "Of the Power Exercised by the Majority in America over Thought" (Tocqueville 2010, 1.2.7), he states, "If America has not yet had great writers, we do not have to look elsewhere for the reasons: literary genius does not exist without freedom of the mind, and there is no freedom of the mind in America. The Inquisition was never able to prevent the circulation in Spain of books opposed to the religion of the greatest number. The dominion of the majority does better in the United States: it has removed even the thought of publishing such books. Unbelievers are found in America, but unbelief finds, so to speak, no organ there. . . . Here, the use of power is undoubtedly good. I am, consequently, speaking only about the power itself. This irresistible power is an unremitting fact, and its good usage is only an accident" (419–20).

births continues to climb. The religious beliefs of the majority no longer impose the same severity of morals Tocqueville observed in Jacksonian America.

In their book *American Grace: How Religion Divides and Unites Us*, Robert Putnam and David Campbell argue that in the past 50 years American religiosity has experienced a shock and two aftershocks: "The Sixties represented a perfect storm for American institutions of all sorts—political, social, sexual, and religious. In retrospect we can discern a mélange of contributing factors: the bulge in the youngest age cohorts as the boomers moved through adolescence and into college, the combination of unprecedented affluence and the rapid expansion of higher education, 'the Pill,' the abating of Cold War anxieties, Vatican II, the assassinations, the Vietnam War, Watergate, pot, and LSD, the civil rights movement, and later the environmental and gay rights movements" (Putnam and Campbell 2011, 91). Especially relevant for later developments was "the explosive emergence of the 'sex, drugs, and rock 'n' roll' youth counterculture." Attitudes toward premarital sex changed markedly, with the percentage of Americans believing it was not wrong doubling from 24% to 47% between 1969 and 1973, and then drifting upward through the 1970s to 62% in 1982. At the same time, public opinion polls showed that confidence in all institutions, religious as well as governmental, declined markedly. And liberal churches began to hemorrhage members.

The 1970s brought a reaction, however. Church attendance nationwide stabilized in the 1970s and 1980s and may even have risen slightly. But the churches many people attended changed. The mainline Protestant churches lost members, while the ranks of both evangelical Protestant denominations and the rapidly growing evangelical megachurches that disavowed denominations and termed themselves simply "Christian" or "community" increased.

However, by the early 1990s the evangelical boom was over and a second "aftershock" set in. Just as many Americans had been repelled by the lax morality of the 1960s, so by the 1990s many Americans had become increasingly unhappy about the growing public presence of conservative Christians. "As early as 1984, according to Gallup polling, most Americans opposed the idea of religious groups campaigning against specific candidates, although most agreed that religious leaders should speak out on the moral implications of public issues." But "symbols of the Religious Right, such as the Moral Majority and Jerry Falwell, were viewed unfavorably by most voters. . . . Young Americans came to view religion, according to one survey, as judgmental, homophobic, hypocritical, and too political" (Putnam and Campbell 2011, 120–21). And a second major change in American attitudes toward religion began to emerge. More and more respondents to polls began to characterize themselves as having no religious affiliation at all. "The incidence of 'nones' was about 5–7 percent in the pre-boomer generations who reached adulthood before 1960, doubled to about 10–15 percent among the boomers (who came of age in the 1960s, 1970s, and 1980s), and after 2000 doubled again to about 20–30 percent among the post-boomers (who came of age in the 1990s and 2000s)" (123).

The most recent Pew Research report on "America's Changing Religious Landscape" shows that these trends have persisted (Pew Research Center 2015a). The percentage of the American public identifying as "Christian" has fallen from 78.4% in 2007 to 70.6% in 2014, and the percentage of those declaring themselves to be "unaffiliated" has grown from 16.1% to 22.8%. Mainline Protestant denominations and Catholics suffered the largest losses (3.4% and 3.1%, respectively); the decrease in the percentage of respondents identifying as Evangelical dropped less than 1%. Although men, whites, and non-Southerners were a bit more likely to be "nones" than women, blacks, and Southerners, Putnam and Campbell observed that the "nones" were drawn almost exclusively from the center and left of the political spectrum. They thus concluded that "the rise of the nones might be some sort of backlash against religious conservatism" (Putnam and Campbell 2011, 127). The authors of the 2015 Pew report mentioned above suggest that the decreasing number of Americans identifying as Christian or with specific denominations may be related to an increase in intermarriages between a partner who identifies as Christian and one who does not. Since 2010, one in five religious intermarriages has been between a Christian and an unaffiliated partner, as opposed to a mere 5% of such marriages before 1960. And as the last two Pew studies show, the unaffiliated are young. (Whereas the median age for American adults is 46 and that of mainline Protestants is 52, the median age of the unaffiliated was 36 in 2014, down from 38 in 2007.)

The political significance of the rise of the "nones" at present is unclear. An observer might speculate that if and when the unaffiliated who marry Christians or members of other faiths have children, they may be tempted to join a church or synagogue, as many of the "baby boomers" did, "for the sake of the children." If so, the number of religiously unaffiliated Americans would drop. One could also see the drop in explicit religious affiliation to be a later extension of the tendency Americans have displayed over the past century to declare themselves "independents" rather than partisans and of the dramatic drop in popular trust in all institutions.[14] The rise of the "nones" may also affect the definition and electoral successes of the two major American

14. Lydia Saad (2015) reports, "Confidence in religion began faltering in the 1980s, while the sharpest decline occurred between *2001 and 2002* as the Roman Catholic Church grappled with a major sexual abuse scandal. Since then, periodic improvements have

political parties. In an article published in *USA Today* on June 17, 2015, Rick Hampson observed that the Democrats and Republicans have come to differ in important ways in their appeals to the religious beliefs of Americans in general, as well as to specific religious groups. "In 2012 Barack Obama got 70% of the religiously unaffiliated voters, compared with 26% for Mitt Romney. . . . Conversely, in recent general elections three in four evangelicals have gone Republican." Hampson concludes that the rising number of "nones" has not influenced American politics much yet, because many don't vote. (Although they constitute 23% of the population now, in 2008 and 2012 they account for only 12% of the electorate.) "Evangelicals, on the other hand, are big voters . . . . So they remain a potent force, as evidenced by a string of victories in 2014."[15] He thus emphasizes the difficulty currently facing Republican candidates who have to appeal to the religious right in the primaries and then try to attract a broader, more secular constituency in the general election. Tocqueville would argue that we ought to be more concerned about the destructive effects of religion becoming a partisan issue and mode of identification on religion, because he thought that attempts by religious officials and organizations to affect public policy directly would undermine faith in such officials and organizations in the long run.

Religious affiliation and identification are not the same as religious beliefs, however. The authors of the 2015 Pew Report observe that "the unaffiliated are generally less religiously observant than people who identify with a religion. But [they emphasize (literally in italics)] not all religious 'nones' are nonbelievers. In fact, many people who are unaffiliated with a religion believe in God, pray at least occasionally and think of themselves as spiritual people" (Pew Research Center 2015a). Although 22.8% of the Americans surveyed described themselves as "unaffiliated," only 3.1% described themselves as atheists and 4.0% as agnostics. The percentages of both atheists (from 1.6%) and agnostics (from 2.4%) have grown since the 2007 survey, but the 2014 results suggest that more than 90% of the Americans surveyed still believe in God ("or a universal spirit," as the Pew pollsters put it in their 2012

---

proved temporary, and it has continued to ratchet lower." From a high of 68% in 1975, her figures show, the proportion of Americans with "a great deal" or "quite a lot" of confidence in the church or organized religion fell in 2015 to 42%. The church and religion still rank among the more respected American institutions, however—fourth behind the military, small business, and the police, and just ahead of the medical system, at a time when fewer than one in four Americans have confidence in several others, including Congress and the media.

15. Hampson (2015) reports that as a member of a Methodist youth group in a Chicago suburb where Hillary Clinton grew up, she worked in the inner city and babysat for Mexican farm workers' kids, and she has since participated in a Washington Prayer group and sometimes carries a Bible.

survey). In 2012 74% of those surveyed also said that they believed in some form of life after death. But in the vast majority of cases, these beliefs were not strongly sectarian or dogmatic. A majority of only Mormons and Jehovah's Witnesses (which together compose approximately 2.4% of the adult population) maintained that their own religion was the one true faith leading to eternal life. And of the 84% of Americans then surveyed who described themselves as "affiliated" with a religious group or denomination, 44% reported that they had changed denominations within their lifetimes, and 54% said that they frequently attended a variety of different kinds of worship services (Pew Research Center 2015a).

The ever more generalized beliefs and religious practices of the American public correspond to predictions Tocqueville made about the ways in which religion would have to adapt and be adapted to democratic social conditions, if it were to survive. If "religions [are going] to be able. . .to persist in democratic centuries," he warned, they "must be more discreet than in other centuries in staying within the limits that are appropriate to them and must not try to go beyond them; for by wanting to extend their power beyond religious matters, they risk no longer being believed in any matter" (Tocqueville 2010, 746). Their continuing power and influence will depend "a great deal on the nature of the beliefs that they profess, on the external forms that they adopt, and on the obligations that they impose." With regard to the beliefs, he observed that "men similar and equal easily understand the notion of a single God, imposing on each one of them the same rules and granting them future happiness at the same cost" (747). But he warned that in democratic times, religions would need to minimize their forms and ceremonies, which "leave . . . men living during these times . . . cold" (750). Because men living at such times "attach only a secondary importance to the details of worship," religious officials should "distinguish very carefully between the principal opinions that constitute a belief and that form what theologians call the articles of faith, and the incidental notions that are linked to them" (751).[16] Nor should religious authorities seek great deeds of self-sacrifice from their flocks on behalf of the faith. Tocqueville thought that it was imperative to preserve belief in a few fundamental religious truths, precisely because human beings living in equal

16. Tocqueville explicitly recognized the importance of "forms" in maintaining beliefs, but he thought under democratic conditions that such forms should and would be minimal: "They fix the human mind in the contemplation of abstract truths, and . . . by helping the mind to grasp those truths firmly, make it embrace them with fervor. I do not imagine that it is possible to maintain a religion without external practices, but on the other hand I think that, during the centuries we are entering, it would be particularly dangerous to multiply them inordinately; that instead they must be restricted and that you should retain only those that are absolutely necessary for the perpetuation of the dogma itself" (2010, 750).

conditions tend to become isolated from one another and interested only in their own private affairs, and the souls of such human beings became excessively attached to material enjoyments. "The greatest advantage of religions," he saw, was "to inspire entirely opposite instincts. There is no religion that does not place the object of the desires of men above and beyond the good things of the earth, and that does not naturally elevate his soul toward realms very superior to those of the senses. Nor is there any religion that does not impose on each man some duties toward the human species or in common with it" (745). But Tocqueville nevertheless cautioned ministers and priests not to think that religion could diminish the love of riches characteristic of human beings living in democracies. Religions should seek only "to purify, to regulate and to limit the overly ardent and overly exclusive taste for well-being that men feel in times of equality" and to persuade men "to enrich themselves only by honest means" (751).

In *Democracy in America* Tocqueville consistently argued that people would retain their religious beliefs only if church and state were separated. But the relation he saw between explicitly religious organizations and politics was complicated even in Jacksonian America. In contrast to Europe in his time, he observed, in the United States religious officials often prayed to God not merely to support democracy at home but to spread its principles and institutions abroad. Religion generally thus appeared to be a source of support for the government and not a source of criticism or opposition. And the oaths of individuals not willing to swear on a Bible were not trusted. But, he maintained, the most important way public officials could positively foster and preserve such beliefs among their constituents was to act as if they held such beliefs themselves.

Public opinion polls show that Americans today continue to expect declarations of faith and religious affiliations from public officials. Two-thirds of the Americans polled in 2012 thought that it was important for a president to have strong religious beliefs.[17] In the past 5 years only one member of the US Congress declared that he did not believe in God or a universal spirit, and only one member of the 114th Congress declared that she was unaffiliated.[18]

17. There is some evidence that this expectation may be decreasing. Leonhardt and Parlapiano (2015) report that, as opposed to 18% in 1958, 54% of the Americans polled in 2012 said that they would vote for an atheist president (in comparison to 96% who would vote for an African American, 95% for a female, 94% for a Catholic, and 91% for a Jew).

18. The only congressman who declared that he did not believe in God or a universal spirit was Peter Stark of California, who served from 1973 to 2012; the only member of the 114th Congress who has declared herself unaffiliated is Representative Kyrsten Sinema, a Democrat from Arizona. In 2012 10 members of Congress refused to say whether they were affiliated or not; that number dropped to nine in 2014. See Pew Research Center (2015b).

Tocqueville understood that such public professions of religious faith might well be politically motivated. He did not think that religious faith would last under democratic circumstances unless it became a part of a public dogma concerning "interest well understood." Rather than constituting examples of politically motivated hypocrisy, he suggested, these professions of faith on the part of public officials could be understood as teaching by means of example what cannot be taught by precept.

Widespread American beliefs in a supreme deity and afterlife today do not appear to be a result of public inculcation or even the sort of informal social pressure Tocqueville found so tyrannous in Jacksonian America. Such beliefs have arguably been preserved by an even stricter separation of church and state than Tocqueville prescribed. Since World War II, the Supreme Court has drawn the line between church and state much more rigidly than it was drawn in the early nineteenth century, first by declaring publicly required professions of faith, in the form of the pledge of allegiance to the flag or as an oath of office, to be unconstitutional infringements of the freedom of religion protected by the First Amendment, and second by proscribing prayers and Bible reading in public schools as an unconstitutional "establishment."[19] In explaining their decisions, the justices repeatedly stated that they were trying to protect dissenters from exactly the kind of informal social pressure Tocqueville had described as the "tyranny of the majority," which, he had also observed, was exercised particularly with regard to religion.

As Putnam and Campbell (2011) discovered, moreover, American religious organizations still constitute some of the most important examples of the voluntary "moral" and "civil" associations Tocqueville thought were so important in effectively preserving freedom of speech and economic enterprise in the United States.[20] Like local institutions of government, churches serve as free schools in the techniques and importance of the art of organization. Martin Luther King's Southern Christian Leadership Conference trained the leaders of nonreligious civil rights organizations such as the Congress for

19. *West Virginia Board of Education v. Barnette*, 319 U.S. 624 (1943); *Torasco v. Watkins*, 367 U.S. 488 (1961); *Engel v. Vitale*, 370 U.S. 421 (1962); *Abington School District v. Schempp*, 374 U.S. 203 (1963). See Strout (1974, 205–313).

20. "There is nothing, in my opinion, that merits our attention more than the intellectual and moral associations of America . . . . The intellectual and moral associations are as necessary as the political and industrial ones to the American people, and perhaps more. In democratic countries, the science of association is the mother science; the progress of all the others depends on the progress of the former. Among the laws that govern human societies, there is one that seems more definitive and clearer than all the others. For men to remain civilized or to become so, the art of associating must become developed among them and be perfected in the same proportion as equality of conditions grows" (Tocqueville 2010, 902). See Strout (1974, 102–9).

Racial Equality (CORE) and the Student Nonviolent Coordinating Committee (SNCC) (see Lincoln 1985, 95–122); participation in these civil rights groups, in turn, taught future activists in the women's liberation movement the importance not only of consciousness raising but also of organization (see Evans 1979). Many of the leaders of the opposition to the Equal Rights Amendment, pro-life, and antiabortion movements also acquired their practical training and organizational skills through previous community service as volunteers, especially in connection with their churches. As Tocqueville observed, in a democracy it is difficult for an individual to articulate and defend an unpopular "minority" position; people are much more willing "to take a stand" if they can get others to line up with them. But unlike the regular religious denominations that have historically served as spawning grounds for the leadership and organization of intense, "single-issue" groups, these "causes" tend to have relatively brief organizational lives. In the 1980s Robert Bellah and his coauthors complained about the increasingly self-centered, "naval-gazing" character of the "new spirituality" (Bellah 1985, 219–49). However, as Putnam and Campbell (2011) report, the 2004 and 2006 General Social Surveys showed that frequent churchgoers are more generous than their non-churchgoing fellow citizens; they are more likely to contribute money and volunteer to help charities or needy people. In general, they found that religious Americans are more likely than nonreligious Americans to belong to community organizations and serve as officers in them and to take part in local civic and political life, by participating in local elections, going to town meetings, or joining demonstrations to further social and political reform.

When religious officials and organizations become active as such in American politics, however, there tends to be a negative reaction. Because Americans continue to judge things on the basis of their own practical experience, they do not want others—either public officials or religious leaders—to tell them what to think. Only 37% say that they become uncomfortable when politicians discuss their own religious beliefs. But two-thirds or more of the American public do not think that churches should endorse political candidates; two-thirds also think that liberals have gone too far in trying to keep religion out of public life. Understood to protect the freedom of individuals and communities to express their religious convictions, there was widespread support for the Religious Freedom of Religion Act when it was proposed and passed by the US Congress in 1993. In spring 2015, however, when the Indiana legislature passed a state version of the same law that was perceived to justify private businesses discriminating against gays and lesbians, there was such a national public outcry against the legislation that the governor and legislature immediately retracted the bill. As James Madison observed in *Federalist* 10, in a nation in which every religious group constitutes a minority, all can agree on the importance of no one's being subordinated to the dictates of another's faith. But Tocqueville would not have been surprised to learn that the Indiana legislators were reacting to threats of economic boycotts and business closures, if they did not repeal the law. He had argued that religious considerations alone would never outweigh the materialistic commercial interests of most Americans. Religion retains its hold on the minds and mores of Americans, if and when it is seen to be consonant with calculations of their self-interest, primarily but not solely economic.

In sum, the broad outlines of Tocqueville's analysis of the role of religion in America seem to hold true today. An overwhelming majority of Americans believe in a supreme deity and some form of immortality. And they expect public officials to articulate and act on such beliefs. They do not approve of religious leaders or institutions attempting to influence political decisions directly, however. To the extent to which religion has become associated in the public mind with the Republican Party and conservative politics, organized religious institutions are apt to suffer. (They have already suffered another decline in public confidence.)

Tocqueville observed that the most important effects of religion on American politics were indirect, on American mores (sentiments and opinions), more than direct, on the form of government and legislation. In the past century, sexual mores have changed; indeed, they seem to be becoming even more liberal, since younger Americans are more tolerant of homosexuality and same-sex marriage than their parents. The economic forces that once kept men and women separate now bring them together in the workplace. But although Americans overwhelmingly accept contraception (80%), premarital sex (64%), and divorce (64%), as well as a bare majority (52%) accepting having a baby out of wedlock, according to a 2010 poll, they still take marriage vows seriously. Only 8% think that it is acceptable for a married man or woman to have sex with someone other than his or her own spouse (United Press International 2009). Marriage is, after all, not simply a religious ceremony; it is a legal contract with economic consequences. And, as Tocqueville observed, practically minded Americans are concerned about both matters of law and economics.

Despite the Supreme Court, it is still probably true, as Tocqueville observed, that "in the United States . . . there are some who profess Christian dogmas because they believe them and others who do so because they are afraid to look as though they did not believe in them." But it is no longer true that "Christianity reigns without obstacles, by universal consent" (Tocqueville 2010, 292). Most Americans still appear to adhere to the most general tenets of scriptural religion. Today, however, not only literary authors and professed atheists but Buddhists and Baha'i also feel free to dissent. In the more restricted sense that Tocqueville presented in volume 2, however, religion in America still remains very much alive, if not well. A devout Christian, Jew, Muslim, or Hindu might well find the religious beliefs and practices of his American associates all too loosely or generally defined. Their faith does not prevent most Americans from seeking to acquire material goods. It may, indeed, even facilitate the process.[21] Nor do the religious beliefs of Americans prevent them from exhibiting rather loose personal morality—in public as well as in private. The professed religious beliefs and affiliations of American congressmen have not prevented some from engaging in scandalous financial and sexual shenanigans. To the faithful, American religion may generally appear to be all too secular. But from an essentially political, Tocquevillian perspective, the saving minimum is still in place. An increasingly sharp division between left and right extremes in American parties and politics is worrisome, but in the early twenty-first century American politics remain free and the outcomes of increasingly bitter partisan divides moderate. Religious and secular beliefs coalesce in the conviction that matters of individual conscience should be free from governmental control. There are still some things the vast majority of Americans do not think government should do, and these limits are still associated with the widespread popular American belief in the sanctity of the individual spirit or soul.

REFERENCES

Bellah, Robert N. 1975. *The Broken Covenant: American Civil Religion in Time of Trial.* Chicago: University of Chicago Press.

———. 1985. *Habits of the Heart.* New York: Harper & Row.

Evans, Sara. 1979. *Personal Politics.* New York: Knopf.

Galston, William. 1991. *Liberal Purposes: Goods, Virtues, and Diversity in the Liberty State.* Cambridge: Cambridge University Press.

Hampson, Rick. 2015. "Religion and Politics: Do the 'Nones' Have It?" *USA Today,* June 17. http://www.usatoday.com/story/news/politics/elections/2015/06/17/jeb-bush-evangelicals-christians-republicans-election/28863301/.

Lawler, Peter Augustine. 1992. *The Restless Mind: Alexis de Tocqueville on the Origins and Perpetuation of Human Liberty.* Savage, MD: Roman & Littlefield.

21. Murray (2012) argues that churchgoing among the white working class has declined, eroding the social capital that organized religion once provided. But the Pew Forum's Religious Landscape Survey, conducted between May 8 and August 13, 2007, shows that income varies greatly within and across American religious groups. A higher percentage of Hindus (43%), Jews (46%), and Mainline Protestants (barely, 21%) earn $100,000 or more a year than of the American population as a whole (18%), but a larger percentage of Evangelical Protestants (34%) and Historically Black Protestants (47%) earn less than $30,000 per year as compared to 31% of the American population as a whole.

Leonhardt, David, and Alicia Parlapiano. 2015. "A March toward Acceptance When Civil Rights Is the Topic." *New York Times*, June 30, A3.

Lincoln, Eric. 1985. *Race, Religion, and the Continuing American Dilemma*. New York: Hill & Wang.

Macedo, Stephen. 1990. *Liberal Virtues: Citizenship, Virtue, and Community in Liberal Constitutionalism*. Oxford: Clarendon.

Murray, Charles. 2012. *Coming Apart: The State of White America 1960–2010*. New York: Crown Forum.

Pew Research Center. 2015a. "America's Changing Religious Landscape." May 12. www.pewforum.org/2015/05/12.

———. 2015b. "Faith on the Hill: the Religious Composition of the 114th Congress." January 5. www.pewforum.org/2015/01/05.

Philpott, Daniel, Monica Toft, and Timothy Shaw. 2010. *God's Century*. New York: Simon & Schuster.

Putnam, Robert D., and David E. Campbell. 2011. *American Grace: How Religion Divides and Unites Us*. New York: Simon & Schuster.

Rahe, Paul. 2009. *Soft Despotism, Democracy's Drift: Montesquieu, Rousseau, Tocqueville and the Modern Prospect*. New Haven, CT: Yale University Press.

Rickey, Russell E., and Donald G. Jones. 1974. *American Civil Religion*. New York: Harper & Row.

Rousseau, Jean Jacques. 2012. *The Major Writings of Jean-Jacques Rousseau*. Trans. and ed. John T. Scott. Chicago: University of Chicago Press.

Saad, Lydia. 2015. "Confidence in Religion at New Low, but Not among Catholics." *Gallup Poll*, June 17. http://www.gallup.com/poll/183674/confidence-religion-new-low-not-among-catholics.aspx.

Strout, Cushing. 1974. *The New Heavens and New Earth: Political Religion in America*. New York: Harper & Row.

Tocqueville, Alexis de. 2010. *Democracy in America*. Ed. Eduardo Nolla. Trans. James T. Schleifer. Indianapolis: Liberty Fund.

United Press International. 2009. "U.S. Poll: Adultery Unacceptable to Most." June 25. http://www.upi.com/Top-News/2009/06/25/US-poll-Adultery-unacceptable-to-most/96431245965385/.

Zuckert, Catherine H. 1976. "American Women and Democratic Mores." *Feminist Studies* 3:43–48.

———. 1983. "Reagan and That Unnamed Frenchman (De Tocqueville)." *Review of Politics* 45:421–32.

Index

A

B

C

F

G

H

I

J

K

L

M

N

O

P

R

S

T

U

V

W

Z